620.004 K35c   F-V
KENNEDY
CAD : DRAWING, DESIGN, DATA
MANAGEMENT
                 29.95

WITHDRAWN

CAD

**DRAWING
DESIGN
DATA MANAGEMENT**

CAD DRAWING DESIGN DATA MANAGEMENT

E. LEE KENNEDY

WHITNEY LIBRARY OF DESIGN
an imprint of Watson-Guptill Publications, New York

To three great Kennedys
Sue, Smith, and Brook

First published in 1986 in New York by Whitney Library of Design
an imprint of Watson-Guptill Publications
a division of Billboard Publications, Inc.
1515 Broadway, New York, NY 10036

Library of Congress Cataloging-in-Publication Data

Kennedy, E. Lee.
    CAD : design, drawing, data management.

    Includes index.
    1. Computer-aided design.   2. Engineering—Data
processing.   I. Title.
TA174.K46   1986   620'.00425'0285   86-22388
ISBN 0-8230-7104-9

Manufactured in U.S.A.

First printing, 1986
1 2 3 4 5 6 7 8 9 / 91 90 89 88 87 86

All artwork is the author's own except where otherwise noted

Senior Editor: Julia Moore
Associate Editor: Victoria Craven-Cohn
Designer: Jay Anning
Production Manager: Hector Campbell
Set in 10-point Helvetica Light

Acknowledgments

As with most endeavors each of us pursues, the fruits of our work are seldom the product of one mind. *CAD* is no exception. Many people helped make the book possible. Some gave encouragement, others advice and support, while many contributed with examples of their work or products.

From the beginning, I wanted the book to be a generic primer on CAD for the design community and one that would dovetail with other books from the Whitney Library of Design, which I have admired since my early days in architecture school.

I have four very special people to thank at the Whitney Library of Design. Former executive editor Stephen Kliment, with whom I developed the concept; former editor Susan Davis, who taught me the value of critical review; senior editor Julia Moore, who showed me how important a good editor can be to the way a book turns out; and associate editor Victoria Craven-Cohn, who gave me complete and intelligent editorial supervision and production support.

I would also like to thank my friends and colleagues who contributed their advice, support, and artwork.

Finally, I would like to express a special note of thanks to several companies for their help and support, and for offering me the use of their computers and software to prepare many of the drawings for this book. Most of the line figures were drawn on a NEC HO3 computer owned by The Miller Organization using MiCAD Systems enhancements to AutoCAD® software. Most of my three-dimensional drawings and the color plates were created on an Apollo computer using Autotrol Technology Series 5000, Plan, and my color software. The early drawings were created on my Apple II+ using a combination of Appleworld (USA Software) and the CAD software I wrote for the Apple in 1981. The line drawings were plotted on Hewlett-Packard, CalComp, and Houston Instrument pen plotters using technical pens on vellum. The one- and two-point perspectives were plotted with ballpoint on Mead Mark 1 coated cover stock, an excellent quality and durable media for presentations, while the dot matrix screen "dumps" were generated on my Integral Data Systems printer. All of my screen photographs were taken with a 35mm Nikkormat using a 50mm F1.4 lens with closeup lens, no color correction, and Kodachrome daylight ASA 64 film. A dark plastic garbage bag taped to the CRT and covering the camera proved to be the easiest way to exclude reflections from the face of the CRT.

Contents

Part I

BASICS

To understand and appreciate CAD (Computer-Aided Design), you need to know something about computers—not a great deal, but something. In the first two chapters, you will learn the fundamentals of CAD. Chapter 1 deals with CAD system components in a very broad way. It is a chapter about whats, not hows or whys. Chapter 2 compares the differences between manual drawing and CAD drawing. This foundation leads you into Part II Drawing.

1

CAD Components

A computer consists of a device that manipulates data for you plus a means to enter variable data and a means to extract answers. Your pocket calculator is a simple computer. You enter numbers (**data**) in the calculator, and it **manipulates** the numbers and displays (**extracts**) the answer. **Alphanumeric computers** manipulate text and numbers only, whereas **graphics computer systems** are used for drawing. CAD graphics computers manipulate alphanumerics and graphics in a manner particularly well suited for applications in architecture, engineering, facilities management, and interior design.

COMPUTATIONAL POWER

Computers, like automobiles, are measured by their speed and power. Computational power is a combination of processing speed and memory capacity. Computational speed is achieved primarily with hardware (the stuff you can physically touch), such as the green boards inside the computer cabinet to which the electronic components are attached. The most visible and best-known piece of hardware is the tiny black rectangle called an **integrated circuit**, or **chip**.

Processing speed is determined, in part, by the bit size, a **bit** being the fundamental computational unit. Speed increases exponentially as bit size grows. Thus, a 32-bit computer processes information much more than four times faster than an 8-bit computer. Bit size has grown over the years, until 8-bit and 16-bit computers have been succeeded by 32-bit computers, the current standard. (There are even 64-bit computers that are used for some graphic displays.)

Numerical calculations affect processing time.

Integers are stored in a very efficient manner and consequently can be processed more quickly than real decimal numbers (which may be accurate to many decimal points). The accuracy of a CAD computer far exceeds construction accuracy. Memory size is important because it represents the space available to store data. Memory capacity is measured in bytes. One **byte**, consisting of eight bits, can represent one letter, number, punctuation mark, or special symbol. (See Chapter 13 for a discussion of computer logic.)

A computer contains three different memory areas, each equally important. One stores the fundamental instructions that the computer uses for housekeeping functions; it's called **read-only memory (ROM)**. The second memory area stores and processes data and instructions in a working memory area called **random-access memory (RAM)**, also called **core memory** or simply memory. It is here that your software program is executed.

Programs—from word-processing programs, spreadsheets, and database management systems to CAD programs—are called **software**. The software contains the instructions necessary to run your program. As you run software, you enter and use specific data relevant to the problem at hand. You **store**, or **save**, this data in a working file. You use software and files concurrently, and both are kept safe in a third, permanent memory area: an internal hard disk or an external disk drive, cartridges, or magnetic tape.

As you will soon discover, identical results can be achieved with computers using different methods. Some of the methods are elegantly simple, while others are as subtle as a sledgehammer. Hardware and software interact in a complex fashion, working in concert to achieve the desired results. Most tasks that can be performed on a large computer can be duplicated on a smaller model—perhaps not with the same speed, power, or simplicity, but performed nonetheless. So, while all computers will "get you there," the power and speed of the more sophisticated hardware and software will be as high as their price.

A FIRST LOOK AT COMPONENTS

The brain of a computer is called the **central processing unit (CPU)**. The CPU processes information by comparing one item with another (actually one number with another) and then performs this or that procedure according to the governing instructions of the program you are using.

A program always executes the same sequence of procedures, but it accepts different values for a given variable to produce different answers. In order to perform your instructions, a computer has a means of entering data (**input**) and of extracting and displaying data (**output**). It files the results in a **storage device**.

Computers are classified according to their computational power as **mainframes**, **minicomputers** (Figure 1.1), or **microcomputers** (Figures 1.2 and 1.3). But because of rapid changes in technology, these categories are not distinct: a standard feature of one category may be optional in another category today and standard tomorrow. Mainframes traditionally are installed in specially air-conditioned rooms and are too large and bulky to be moved easily; micros fit on desktops; and minis fall somewhere in between. Despite their small size, however, micros may encompass exceptional computational power.

1.1 *Minicomputer CAD system showing all components. (Courtesy of CalComp, a Sanders company)*

Computation: The Central Processing Unit

In a mainframe system, all the computations and memory functions are handled by the CPU, and display functions are managed by multiterminal graphics workstations. Data entered on one terminal is quickly available to any terminal in the system. Modest price and fast, task-specific software have made microcomputer CAD systems popular contenders in the competitive professional CAD market.

Standalone computers are self-contained computers linked in a communications network, appropriately called a local-area network (LAN). Figure 1.4 shows a typical local-area network connection, in which one terminal may be shut down without affecting the performance of the others.

1.2 *Microcomputer CAD system showing integrated components. (Courtesy of AutoCAD® by Autodesk, Inc., Sausalito, CA)*

1.3 *Microcomputer CAD system. (Courtesy of CalComp, a Sanders company)*

1.4 *A local-area network provides the means by which standalone computers can communicate with one another so that data on one terminal can be used by another. (Courtesy of Apollo Computers, Inc.)*

Computer Instructions: The Software Program

Although a computer is capable of performing any logical task, you must tell it what task to perform and how. These instructions constitute a computer program—the software. Because computers are consummately precise, programs must be correspondingly precise. Parenthetically, there are programmers and nonprogrammers—precise and "nonprecise" people, if you will—and little else between. But you do not have to be a precise person or a programmer to *use* a program or a CAD system, and you certainly should not feel intimidated by the mystique of programming. For the time being, you need only know that programming is a precise set of instructions and that the majority of programs fall into four categories: word processing (text manipulation), spreadsheets (number manipulation), database management (data manipulation), and graphics. You will learn more about programming as you progress through the book.

Data Entry: Input Devices and Methods

A computer program solves a given problem using different values that you enter for each variable, such as drawing scale. Data is entered using any of several **input devices** or methods: keyboard, graphic cursor, menu, or digitizer. Giving up the pencil to enter data with such devices as a stylus, mouse, or puck is easy for most people, and you don't have to be a crack typist to operate a CAD computer. Let's look at each means of input in detail.

Keyboard

The original computer input device was the **keyboard**. Because a computer interprets keyboard input exactly as you enter it, the keyboard is the most accurate of all input devices. In early computers, the keyboard served as both the input and the output device. Actually, it was a teletypewriter keyboard. Many keyboards still bear the word *bell* on the G key, a vestige of the time when a bell tone signaled the end of a teletypewriter message.

In many ways similar to the standard typewriter keyboard, it performs all the functions you expect of a typewriter. But five keys merit attention because the computer interprets each in a special manner: the numerals 1 and 0, the uppercase *O*, the lower case *l*, and the carriage return. In reading a typed page , you readily understand the context in which each of the four characters is used, but the computer accepts each keystroke literally; consequently, you must use each correctly. The carriage return will advance a line and return to the left margin, but its primary computer function is to signal the completion of an instruction to the CPU and order its execution. On some computers, this key is called the Enter key.

Three other special features may be included on a computer keyboard. First is a numerical keypad that simulates an adding machine. Like accountants who enter columns of numbers, computer users prefer the numeric keypad over the numbers on the top row of keys. Second, a heavily used keyboard feature on some CAD systems specifies **point entry**. Examples are Key

1, used to enter points; Key 2, to draw a line from the last point; Key 3, to draw a line from the last point in an alternative line texture (such as dashed); and Key 4, to drag and insert figures. Last, a **function keyboard** may be included to perform specific drawing, programming, or other actions that you may define. These keys are called **user-definable**.

Graphics cursors

While it is possible to draw on a computer using only the keyboard, it is generally quicker and more comfortable to use a method that functions like the computer's pencil. These include the stylus, puck, mouse, joystick, and thumb wheels. They control the location of the graphics **cursor**, an image you move anywhere on the CRT screen to indicate a point location. Typically, the cursor consists of two intersecting lines called **cross hairs**. To enter a point on a computer drawing, you center the cross hairs at the desired location and press a point entry key.

The **stylus**, or **pen**, shown in Figure 1.5 is the most familiar computer pencil. It is connected to the computer by a cord and activates a point on the screen when the pen is pressed against the magnetic surface of the **bit pad** (also called a **graphics tablet**). The computer reads the location of the point and displays it on the screen.

The operation of a **puck** is similar to that of the stylus. A mini keyboard atop its boxlike housing can be used to activate points and perform additional functions. A **mouse** and a puck have similar shapes, but with a mouse, the point location is calibrated by the movement of a ball in its base rather than by activating a point magnetically. The mouse can be used on any flat surface and does not require a magnetic bit pad. You should find both the puck and the mouse comfortable and easy to use.

Copied from arcade games, the **joystick** was one of the first CAD pencils. It responds quickly to hand action but inconsistently to drawing movements. **Thumb wheels**, though awkward to master and generally unpopular, provide positive horizontal and vertical movement. Because they are contained in a box that is seldom moved from its location on your desk, you can locate the thumb wheels without looking.

With CAD drawing, you use your drawing hand for drawing and typing, alternately grasping and releasing the graphics input device. For that reason, you will find that reaching for a mouse or a puck is faster and less fatiguing than reaching for a stylus. In most cases, you can grasp either one without looking away from the face of the CRT and with little hand reorientation.

Menus

You can also enter data by a third means, the **menu**. A computer menu resembles a restaurant menu: You select an option from a list of items, using the keyboard or graphics cursor to enter your choice. Menus take many forms: on-screen, attached to bit pads, or separate menu devices. Programs directed by menu input are said to be **menu-driven**, whereas programs activated solely by keyboard entry of commands are called **command-driven**. Most CAD programs employ menus as the primary means of input but also permit the user to enter commands on the keyboard.

A menu is ideal for entering known options and is particularly well suited for work with standardized, repetitive, or complex processes. If a menu cannot cover every variable, it will list common values and ask you to enter unlisted ones. Compare, for example, a program that asks you to enter a drawing name and the scale. The number of possible entries for a drawing name is limitless, whereas there are only about eight commonly used architectural scales. A menu cannot list all the possible

1.5 *The stylus was the first "pencil" used with a magnetic menu board. (Courtesy of Autotrol Technology Corporation)*

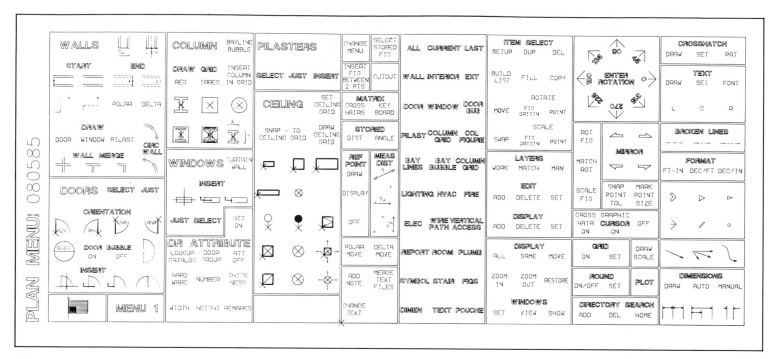

1.6 *A digitizer menu attaches to a magnetic bit pad.*

names of drawings, so you have to enter the drawing name from the keyboard; but you could select the scale from a menu.

When you select a graphics menu option, the program executes a segment of the software (a subroutine) or prompts you to enter additional menu items. Virtually all software programs run (are executed) with a menu similar to the ones in Figures 1.6 and 1.7.

CAD graphics menus used for architectural, engineering, and design work combine a matrix of small pictures and short command descriptions into a graphics display that resembles a checkerboard. Each square represents a graphics item from the figure library (see page 141) or an instruction (for example, to set the drawing scale). Graphics programs require menus that often list as many as 500 items. Ideally, all options available on a

menu are displayed concurrently for easy access. Figure 1.5 shows a typical preprinted menu attached to the face of a magnetic bit pad.

Menus can also be displayed on the CRT, but graphics menus are too large to display the entire menu on a CRT screen at one time. Consequently, the screen menu is subdivided into smaller segments for easy display, so that each segment occupies a small area of the screen next to your drawing. Screen menus, like the one in Figure 1.7, have become very popular. You select a menu option with the stylus, mouse, or puck by centering the cursor over the desired item and pressing the correct function key. You will find the combination of screen menu and puck to be the fastest and most comfortable of all the various input methods.

1.7 *An on-screen menu, this one from Personal Designer program, has a hierarchical stack of menus. When you select "arcs," for example, a subordinate menu will prompt you to enter different types of arcs. (Courtesy of Personal Systems Business Unit, Computervision)*

1.8 *Digitizers are large bit pads. (Courtesy of CalComp, a Sanders company)*

1.9 *Optical scanners do the work of digitizers, except automatically. (Courtesy of Skantek Corporation)*

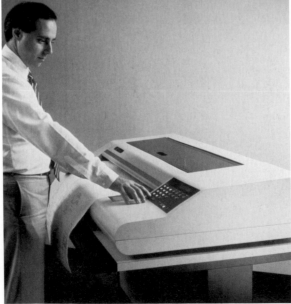

Digitizers and scanners

The last input devices are the digitizer (Figure 1.8) and the scanner (Figure 1.9). A **digitizer** is a large bit pad. You use it to trace a large drawing into the computer. It's an ideal method for tracing approximate graphics data, such as topographic contours, but tracing drawings on a digitizer is no more accurate than manual tracing. Consequently, the common belief that because computers are accurate, tracing with a digitizer corrects dimensional inaccuracies is false: The digitizer will not correct dimension errors. Although you can straighten and otherwise clean up lines as you trace (digitize), it is a slow, tiring process and should not be used for architectural and engineering drawings unless it is absolutely necessary.

A **scanner** is fundamentally an automatic digitizer that captures an image of the drawing in much the same way that a photocopy machine does. The image is automatically converted into a digital computer image, but scanners, like digitizers, do not correct dimension errors.

Data Retrieval: Output Devices

Ultimately, the value of a computer is measured by the results it produces. You will use a CRT to display your designs. You may print what used to be your yellow trace sketches using a dot-matrix or other hard-copy printer. The finished drawing may be printed on a hard-copy printer or by a pen or electrostatic plotter.

CRT

No one calls it a **cathode-ray tube** anymore, but the **CRT**—or **VDU (visual-display unit)**, as it is called in Europe—looks like a television set and also comes either in black-and-white or color. The vertical dimension of the screen is approximately 80% of the horizontal dimension, but the size of the screen is measured like a television screen: diagonally. Although they look alike, a television and a CRT monitor are quite different electronically.

Your technical interest in a CRT will probably be limited to the resolution of the CRT display. **Resolution** is a measure of the fineness of detail, which is determined by the number of pixels per inch across and down the screen. A **pixel**, short for *picture element*, is an individual screen dot. Resolution below 50 pixels per inch is too coarse for most CAD applications: Drawings tend to look as though the lines are constructed of blocks. Circles, for instance, look "stair-stepped," and space becomes so limited that it is difficult to show all the necessary information.

Figure 1.10 shows a screen with low resolution, about 35 pixels per inch. Most CRTs have resolution in the range of 60–70 pixels per inch and are quite suitable for most design applications. By the way, even though some graphic shapes may appear jagged or stair-stepped on the CRT, a plotter will draw the graphics as you intend them to look. Resolution above 70 pixels per inch is a luxury for CAD drafting, but it is a necessity for high-quality imaging and computer renderings. Color Plate 1 (page 97) shows a CRT with high-quality image resolution. This CRT is ideal for presentation-quality renderings and motion picture graphics.

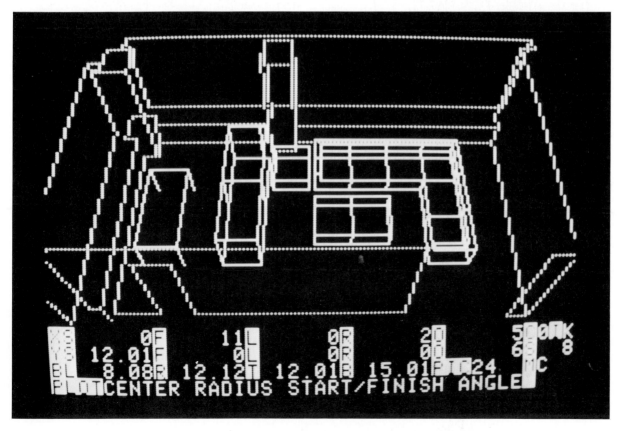

1.10 *Low-resolution CAD CRT display has a resolution of approximately 35 pixels per inch.*

1.11 *Dot matrix printer output of a graphics screen is fast and useful as a check print. You can recognize the dot matrix printer by the "stairstepping" in curved lines.*

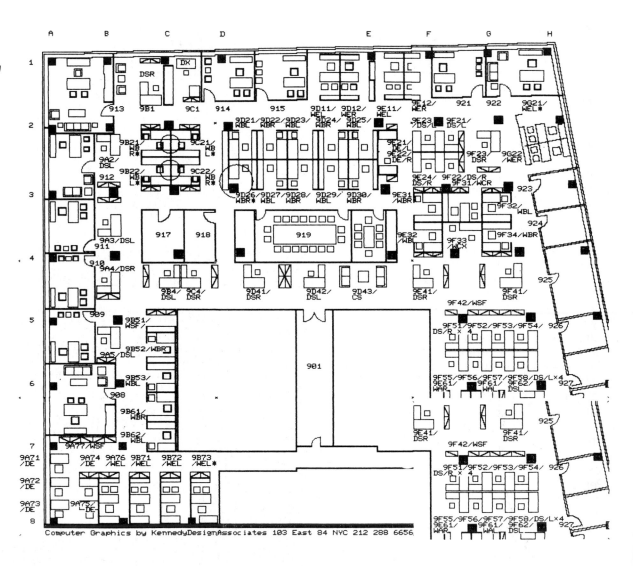

Plotters and printers

The one who really does the drafting is not a person but a **plotter**, which physically draws on paper or acetate film. High-quality pen plotters have been available for many years. A **line printer**, commonly a **matrix** (or **dot-matrix**) **printer**, prints dots on paper. These dots may be assembled to look like alphabetic characters or assembled as lines, circles, or other graphics. This dual capability makes the matrix printer ideally suited for printing sketches and such data as furniture inventories or door schedules. (Figure 1.11).

A quick graphic copy can be reproduced from the existing CRT image by recording, or dumping, the "lit" image pixels and the dark background pixels. The **dump print** (Figure 1.11) made of the temporary image takes the place of the print made from a pencil sketch on yellow sketch paper. Other printers, such as the **hard-copy printer** (Figure 1.12), produce an electrostatic acetate transparency or opaque white print, which are dumped from the screen.

Eventually, you will want to plot full-size architectural, engineering, or interior drawings, which can be achieved with either a pen or electrostatic plotter. This equipment is available in various sizes, the largest of which is capable of printing on drawing media up to 36 inches wide. Acetate film, vellum, bond, and coated stocks are typically used for plotting.

Pen plotters are of two types: flat-bed and roll-bed. **Flat-bed plotters** hold the paper stationary while the pen traverses the paper. Today, flat-bed plotters are usually used only to plot oversized drawings. They have been replaced by **roll-bed plotters**, which move the paper in one direction as the pen moves in the other direction. These plotters are compact and popular in design offices. A typical roll-bed plotter is shown in Figure 1.13, a sample plot in Figure 1.14.

1.12 *Hard-copy printer produces a replica of the screen image. (Courtesy of CalComp, a Sanders company)*

1.13 *Pen plotters are the backbone of any design office. This HP "E" plotter can accommodate any width of paper up to 36 inches wide and any practical length. (Courtesy of Hewlett-Packard Company)*

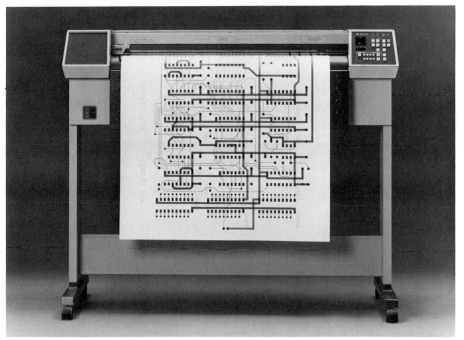

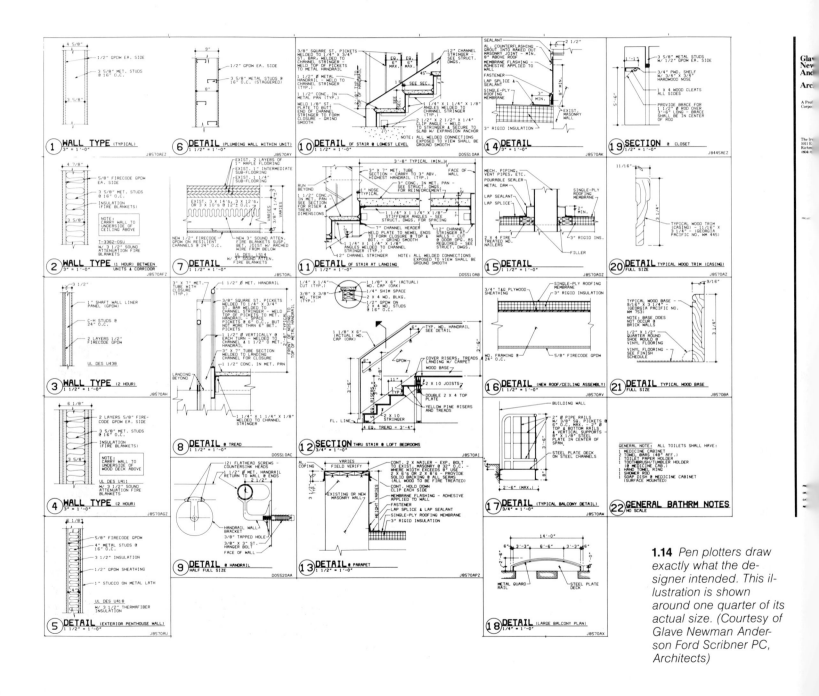

1.14 *Pen plotters draw exactly what the designer intended. This illustration is shown around one quarter of its actual size. (Courtesy of Glave Newman Anderson Ford Scribner PC, Architects)*

In manual drawing, you select the pencil weight or pen size before drawing. In CAD drawing, you select a pen number before drawing. When you plot, the line width or color is determined by the pen you place in the corresponding pen location of the plotter's pen carousel. Consequently, you can plot the same drawing with different colors or plot the drawing at different scales using different pen weights. Drawing with great accuracy, the pen plotter produces a finished copy that is exceptionally crisp. Pen plotters generally accommodate one to eight pens (Figure 1.15), allowing you to mix pen sizes and colors in your final drawing.

The **electrostatic plotter** (Figure 1.16) works like a photocopy machine, except that it reads the image electronically from the computer rather than by optically scanning an original drawing. These machines can be 20 times faster than pen plotters, and color models can produce a wide range of filled chromatic shapes. Volume production is necessary to justify the cost, but if you need to plot more than ten drawings a day, you should consider an electrostatic plotter. A sample of 400 dot per inch resolution electrostatic plots is shown in Figure 1.17.

Data Storage

As you draw, the computer converts the graphic image you see on the CRT into a sequential set of numbers (or digits—hence the name **digital computer**). Your drawings (or, rather, numbers) are stored in RAM, the computer's temporary memory, and each addition or correction you make to a drawing adds to or revises the numbers. As you work on a drawing, however, you need a way to hold on to the drawing data. You'll want to store a drawing and work on others. But watch out: When the power is turned off, either intentionally or accidentally, all data in RAM is lost.

That's why you save your drawings. **Saving** is

1.15 *Plotter pens come in three tip types: technical, felt, and ballpoint. (Courtesy of Hewlett-Packard Company)*

1.16 *Electrostatic plotters, while more expensive than pen plotters, are significantly faster. (Courtesy of Versatec, a Xerox company)*

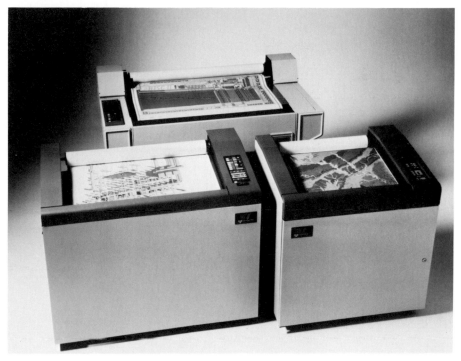

1.17 *Sample print from a high-resolution 400 dot per inch electrostatic plotter. This illustration is shown around one quarter of its actual size. (Courtesy of John Burgee Architects, with Philip Johnson)*

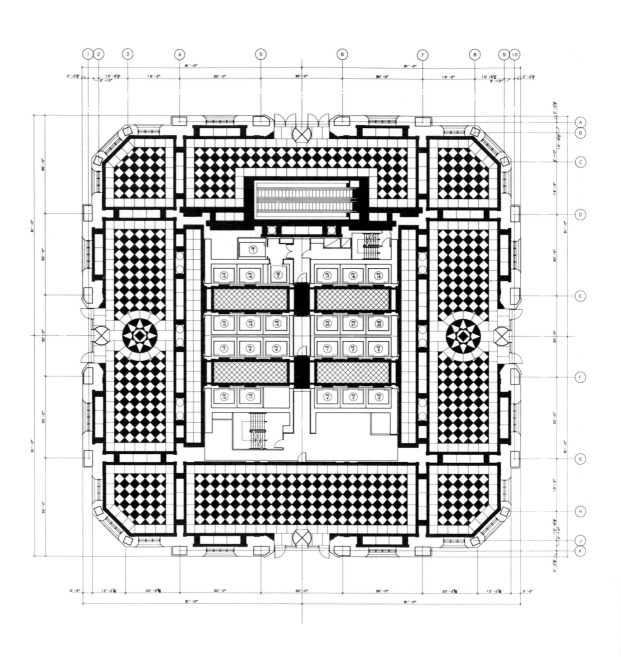

copying data in RAM onto a magnetic storage medium in a manner similar to recording on an audiocassette or a VCR tape. Saving is the most important task in operating a computer. If you learn nothing else, learn how to save your data.

Smaller programs are loaded from your disk into RAM for execution. Larger programs, and those using data files, are too large to fit in RAM and remain on the disk until needed. The programmer decides which segments of the software or data are loaded into RAM and when.

Most data is stored magnetically on one of four different, though similar, media: the familiar floppy disk or diskette; a magnetic tape; a tape cartridge; or a hard disk. Each is placed in a **disk drive**, a device that saves (**writes**) data to the disk or tape or retrieves data by **loading** (**reading**) the contents into RAM.

The best-known medium is the flexible vinyl 8-inch **disk** or its smaller counterparts, the 3½-inch or 5¼-inch **diskette**. These familiar **floppies** are the most convenient means of saving and loading data, although the capacity of each disk is small compared to other media. Capacity ranges from 143K (143 kilobytes, or 143,000 characters) for a 5¼-inch diskette to 1.2MB (1.2 megabytes, or 1,200,000 characters) for an 8-inch disk. The floppy drive has the distinctive door seen in Figure 1.18.

Magnetic tape was first used on early mainframe computers and continues to be used today, primarily for archiving large amounts of infrequently used data. Tape diameters range from 7 inches to 10½ inches, and contain between 300 and 3600 feet of ½-inch tape. A large tape stores the equivalent of 50–75 disks, depending on the computer system. Tape drives, like the one in Figure 1.19, are used to store large amounts of data and to make copies

for permanent storage and back-up.

High-density **tape cartridges** are certainly the most compact and convenient of all media, and they have begun to replace disks. The cartridge resembles a VHS videotape cartridge and holds 150–600 feet of ¼-inch tape. Since a 600-foot tape can store about 45MB, the cartridge can substitute for conventional magnetic tape as an archive medium.

The most convenient storage format is the **hard disk**, available either as a sealed **Winchester disk** or as a removable **platter**. As many as 12 platters can be stacked into a sandwich called a **disk pack**. Because data is compressed into a smaller space, hard disks store data more efficiently, but they require more care. To insure top performance, hard disks are generally inaccessible to all but service people. While hard disks may hold as much as 300MB of data, there are some very compact ones with 1MB capacity.

The advantages of a hard disk are memory capacity, shorter access time, and convenience. You can transfer the software and data from your floppies to the hard disk and organize the library for easy access. It's there when needed, and you avoid having to load floppies each time one is needed. CAD systems require a hard disk to accommodate the extensive software and large drawing files.

Now that you have finished Chapter 1, you should understand the basic concepts and physical components of a CAD system. In the next chapter, you'll learn how CAD drawing differs from manual drawing. After you have learned how to draw and manage CAD in Chapters 3 through 12, you can delve into the more advanced concepts of computers in Chapters 13 through 15.

1.18 *A floppy-disk drive is used to load software and to copy or archive drawings. (Courtesy of Autotrol Technology Corporation)*

1.19 *Tape drives do the same thing as floppy-disk drives, except faster and with greater memory capacity. A large tape may store the equivalent of thirty floppies. (Courtesy of Autotrol Technology Corporation)*

2

CAD: A Different Way to Draw

CAD is a different way to draw in some very exceptional ways. Manual drawing may be the easier way to enter drawing information initially, but you will soon discover that the ease of changing and correcting CAD drawings eclipses manually erasing and redrawing work. Besides being faster and more sophisticated, CAD has revolutionized the design process by integrating drawing functions with design analysis and by joining text data with graphics to create intelligent drawings.

DIFFERENCES BETWEEN MANUAL AND CAD DRAWING

As an architect, engineer, or designer, you communicate your ideas and designs with drawings. CAD is simply a different means to communicate your work. CAD drawing differs from manual drawing in two respects. First, the methods differ: CAD is a different way of doing the same thing—it's a difference in process. Second, CAD drawing differs fundamentally from manual drawing in that some aspects of CAD cannot be duplicated by manual drawing—it's a difference in content.

Methodological Differences

You draw a circle manually with a compass or a template. With CAD, you draw a circle with the graphics cursor, entering points to define the circle mathematically (the center and radius, for example). The computer calculates the size and displays the circle. While the methods differ, the product remains the same: A circle is drawn.

Means of data entry

When you draw manually, you pick up a pencil and draw. When you draw with CAD, you enter points and the computer draws for you. All CAD graphics are drawn with an **initial point** and an

end point. You begin a line with a point and end it with a second one, or you construct a circle with a center point and the radius or two points on the diameter of the circle. Some graphic shapes require you to enter more than two points: the ellipse and the polygon, for example.

You enter points by typing the coordinates on the keyboard or by moving the cursor to the desired location. Pressing a special function key on the keyboard or button on the mouse causes the line to be drawn from the initial point to the end point. You can then draw another line from the end point or enter a new initial point. In some cases, you push an alternative function key to draw a dashed line. This is the simplest form of graphics entry.

Dimensioning a drawing

Dimensioning tells you how long a distance is—or should be. Often, manual dimensioning is a process of putting down the number you know it should be. You would certainly not "scale" a drawing to ascertain the true length, because manual drawing is too inaccurate for construction. Manual dimensions can be rendered "accurate" by inserting a note of warning: "Contractor shall verify all dimensions and be responsible. . . ." Not so with CAD. In CAD, entering points accurately insures drawing precision, thereby allowing you to dimension automatically and correctly. From the beginning, what you see better be what you want, for it is surely what you'll get, irrespective of what appears to be correct. Figure 2.1 shows an early CAD sample of dimensioning. As in manual dimensioning, the "correct" dimensions were entered.

On a CAD terminal, you enter two or more points, and the computer calculates the

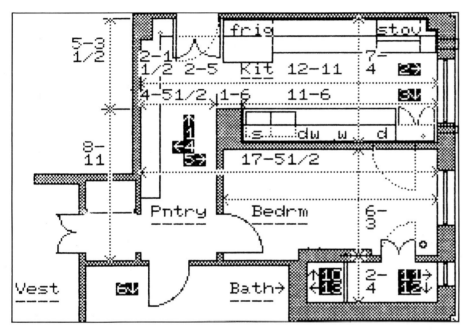

2.1 *Manual dimensioning is virtually extinct now but it was the only technique available when this drawing was created.*

dimension, rounds it off to a predefined minimum tolerance (say, ⅛ inch), and places the dimension (with decimal or fraction) on the drawing. Figure 2.2 shows an example of automatic dimensioning. Some CAD systems support (permit) **associative dimensioning**: When you move a wall, for example, the dimension is automatically changed.

Grid snap

If you have ever drawn a plan or detail on blue fade-out grid paper and maintained all the drawing points at grid intersections, then you've employed the manual version of **grid snap**. With CAD grid snap, you establish an imaginary drawing grid, for example, 2″ in the X direction,

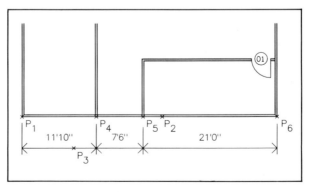

2.2 *Automatic dimensioning is an architect's dream. The points have been entered in sequence—point 1, point 2, etc.—which defines the direction and location of the string. Lengths are calculated, and automatically inserted with the dimensions.*

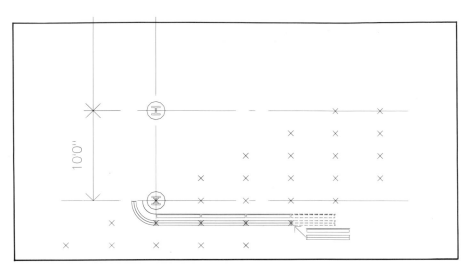

2.3 *Grid snap allows you to create an imaginary matrix and force an entry to the closest grid loca-* *tion, shown here 60 inches along the X axis and 30 inches along the Y axis.*

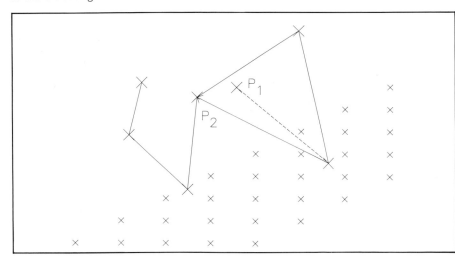

2.4 *Point snap, like grid snap, forces entry to a selected location; unlike grid snap, it forces entry to an element of a* *graphic entity. The end of the solid line was entered at point 1, but snapped to the line break at point 2.*

and 14′–7⅝″ in the Y direction, and any point you enter will be forced to this grid (relative to the Cartesian origin $X = 0$, $Y = 0$, $Z = 0$, or 0, 0, 0). Thus, X points can be drawn at 0, 2″, 4″, 6″, 1′ = 0″, −26′–2″, and the like—always on a 2″ module. Accordingly, Y points will be entered at 0, 14′–7⅝″, 29′–3¼″, and so on. If you're placing windows at 5′ − 0″ centers along a wall, set the round-off to 5′ − 0″ along the wall line. You need only approximate the location because the computer will **snap** to the correct location, inserting window figures along the way. Figure 2.3 shows a grid snap set at 5′ − 0″ along the X axis and 2′ − 6″ along the Y axis. The cursor figure is represented as a solid-line window section, showing the final location in dashed line. Further discussion of grid snap and figures is covered in Chapters 3 and 5.

Point snap

In manual drawing, you connect one line to another visually, but in CAD, the computer works for you. CAD **point snap** searches out a known point or location and snaps to that point. By placing the cursor as close as visually possible (having defined the search tolerance earlier), you let the computer work for you. This popular feature is shown in Figure 2.4.

Point snap is a great technique for insuring accuracy at any time, but particularly so when the drawing on the screen is too small to be viewed comfortably. In some CAD systems, you must snap to the end of a line, while others support snaps to any point, to the closest point, or to multiple locations along a line.

Fundamental Differences

There are a number of functions you can perform on CAD that you cannot perform manually. Three primary examples illustrate this fact. Manual drawing accuracy is based on visual accuracy, but CAD is based on the actual point and thus is very exact. Second, to change a drawing manually, you must erase and redraw, but with CAD, the computer automatically redraws corrections for you. And third, CAD gives you a tool to keep track of any item on the drawing. For example, you no longer need to count the doors yourself to create a door schedule; the computer employs intelligent graphics to inventory and sort them for you into a bill of materials. This feature alone makes CAD a design revolution.

Precision

With manual drawing, you draw first and dimension later. With CAD, you measure first and then the computer draws. The lengths of all distances are determined before the computer draws a line. When you dimension in CAD, the computer "reads" the distance and tells you the value. Because you can't fudge CAD lines, dimensions will always close. Manual drawing simply cannot compete with CAD precision. Tolerances in CAD may be defined tightly or loosely, depending on the level of accuracy required. You might elect to round dimensions to the nearest ⅛ inch, even though some CAD terminals are capable of 8- or 12-decimal-place accuracy (far greater accuracy than is required in most construction work). Or you might set steel to ±¼-inch tolerance, while a finish carpenter would have to work with closer tolerances.

Where computational precision is crucial—for instance, in determining a road profile involving accumulating values—the 12-place accuracy of a CAD terminal is necessary. Because of CAD's inherent precision, you must "think accuracy" from the beginning. Gone are the days when the dull 6B pencil on yellow trace deceives you into believing that the stair will fit. But if you enter points sloppily in CAD, you'll be wasting one of CAD's primary gifts: precision.

Editing

A prime example of what you can't do on the boards that you can do on the tube is **editing**.

On the boards, you erase and redraw. On CAD, you edit: You erase, alter, or copy, and the computer removes, changes, moves, or duplicates automatically. Computer editing is a quantum advance over working with pencil and paper. Because it is so important, Chapter 7 is devoted exclusively to editing.

Intelligence

Compare Figure 2.5, a selection of **entities**, with Figure 2.6, samples of **associative graphics**. The **intelligence** that belongs to an entity is established by the software, and it is generally limited to one generic description, such as line, circle, or crosshatch. **Associative intelligence**, on

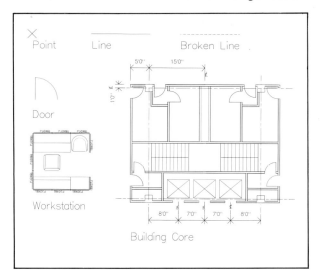

2.5 *An entity is simply an identifiable graphic element. Some editing procedures work on part of an entity; others require identification of the entire entity.*

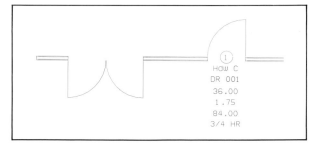

2.6 *Intelligent graphics make it possible to extract text data from a graphic entity. Here, one door is shown without its intelligence, while the second is shown with intelligence; each item is called a tag.*

the other hand, is defined by the user and may consist of any number of data fields, each of which may contain any type of data. The constituent parts of a door schedule are typical of associative graphics.

An **entity** is any element on a drawing defined by a beginning and an end, including a point, line, dimension line, dimension, letter, word, circle, facet of a polygon, or segment of a continuous line. Look at Figure 2.5 again: There is no manual counterpart. (See Chapter 5, where entities are covered in detail.)

Associativity is the joining of graphics with text data and the ability to store, keep track of, sort, and selectively inventory that data. When you point to a door on the drawing, the data "associated" with the door is read from the disk into a working area, where it can be sorted and inventoried. Data for a door could include width, height, and hardware group, for example. Using the same associative data, you can generate a door schedule or a hardware schedule, using different items of information sorted from the data.

Refer back to Figure 2.1, the manually dimensioned floor plan. This drawing is really nothing more than a map of lighted and darkened pixels representing a floor plan. You might call it a "dumb" drawing because it lacks the means to store and extract text data with the graphics. You cannot point to any element in that drawing—say, a wall—and have the software recognize the pixels as a "wall." Fortunately, very few nonintelligent CAD systems like this still exist. (Chapter 6 discusses associative graphics in detail.)

WHY CAD DRAWING CAN BE BETTER
The previous discussion of fundamental and methodological differences between CAD and manual drawing certainly suggests many reasons why CAD drawing can be better. The following discussion emphasizes CAD's advantages over manual drawing, not merely their differences.

One of the most welcome labor-saving features of CAD drawing is **dimensioning**. The computer will dimension for you—no more adding strings of eighths and sixteenths. You select the points, and the computer does the rest: measures, places the dimension line, rounds off the dimension as you direct, and displays it in a preselected architectural or engineering format. All CAD computers support metric and imperial dimensioning and can display distances in the scale of your choosing: inches, feet, feet and inches, millimeters, centimeters, meters, or parsecs—with or without decimals (accurate to as many places as you wish) or fractions (accurate to the denominator of your choosing).

When you select a set of parameters to display information in a particular manner, as in dimensioning, the process is called **formatting**. Consequently, you might format dimension text to be displayed "above and parallel to the line," as shown in Figure 2.2

Points can be entered accurately without your having to define the location precisely. Accuracy is achieved through several means: keyboard coordinate entry, graphic grid snap and point snap, and dimension tolerance. These techniques allow you to enter approximate locations near the correct points. The system then finds the correct location for you.

Editing an Entity
Once the graphics are created (data is entered), you can manipulate the lines, change the dimensions, move part of the drawing to another location, erase part of the drawing without disturbing surrounding parts, change the size of an element, rotate or mirror entities (architects need not enter the note "similar opposite hand" anymore), duplicate in other locations, or save a

segment of the drawing to be used elsewhere. You might even electronically move part of the drawing from one level—think of it as an acetate sheet used in overlay drafting—to another level. (See Figure 2.7 and the section on levels in Chapter 3.)

Entity editing, a feature indigenous to CAD, renders CAD fundamentally different from manual drawing. No erasing shield ever had that power. And it is all because the data is entered and remembered as an entity by the computer. For example, you might swap all the 18″ columns for 21″ columns, rotating the perimeter ones 90°. Or perhaps you want to add gypsum board enclosures only to those columns on an open floor, excluding those in the core. A **global edit** will change all the columns in the drawing, whereas a **local edit** will only affect selected columns.

The first step in editing is called **isolation**. You must separate (isolate) what you want to edit from the balance of the drawing. Following are six brief descriptions of entity editing.

Erasure

You can **erase** any entity partially or completely. Even though a line may intersect other lines, you can also selectively erase a line just by touching it, leaving the balance of your work in place. You can also save a copy of the line and place it in the electronic counterpart of drawing templates, your **figure library**, for later use.

Move

CAD enables you to move graphic elements around. Look at the door that was moved (**translated**) in Figure 2.7. First, the door is copied into a temporary memory area in RAM called a **buffer**. Next, replacing the cross-hair cursor with the door, move the door to the new location (called **figure dragging**), and when you have located the door correctly, insert it into your drawing.

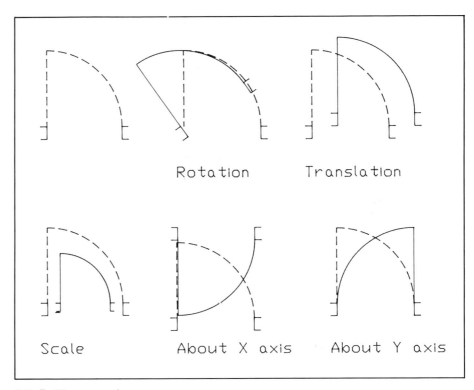

2.7 *Entities, once isolated (or selected), can be manipulated. Here, a door has been modified from its original state.*

2.8 *Stretching can be a powerful tool; or father some bizarre results.*

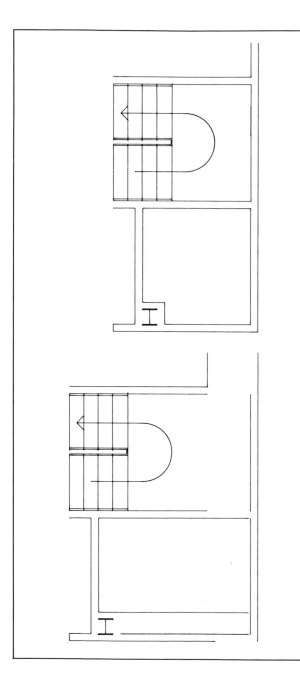

Change

With CAD, you can change the size of a figure, rotate it around its origin or any other point, or both. You can exchange a solid line for a dashed line (to represent demolition) or move the line to another level. If the figure is, for example, a door symbol, created with the text "3' – 0" painted metal," you could change the width to 2' – 6" and the finish to stained wood. In Figure 2.7, can you identify the changes in scale and rotation?

Stretch

Figure 2.8 shows a powerful CAD editing technique: **stretching**. Used carefully, you can extend or reduce the size of an entity along any axis. The figure also demonstrates an important lesson: Whereas the stretch worked perfectly for part of the drawing, another part failed to stretch correctly. There is one way to avoid the mistake and one way to fix it. First, learn to save your work periodically, particularly before editing and *especially* before using one of the more exotic CAD techniques. It is frequently easier to load a recent drawing again, even if you have to repeat some work, than it is to unscramble a mess. But if you have to fix a mistake like this, you'll find it faster, cleaner, and less frustrating to erase all stray graphics first and start fresh. If you try to patch or restretch this drawing back into the original location, you may find Murphy's law hard at work—and an even bigger mess on your hands.

Duplication

With CAD, you need draw a figure only once. After you save the figure, it becomes a permanent part of your figure library, the CAD equivalent of drawing templates. You can then insert the figure as needed, once or many times. You can also duplicate the figure in a two-dimensional matrix, or **array**, as is done with columns or light fixtures. (Chapter 5 discusses duplication and arrays in detail.)

Substitution

If you insert the wrong figure or change your mind, you can substitute a new figure. Figures have an origin point. You substitute one figure in the exact place of another by locating the origin of the figure to be replaced, deleting the original figure, and inserting the new figure at the same location. On some systems, the entire process is automatic (see Figure 2.9).

Uniformity and Consistency

Because CAD produces uniformly consistent graphics, standard drawing practices are possible. Lettering styles, heights, dimensioning standards, line and crosshatching consistency can be established and maintained. Figures used for doors, door bubbles, arrowheads, section cuts, dashed lines, and many others can be standardized and controlled by the project manager or the CAD system administrator. Professional-quality CAD systems let you create your own logos, lettering fonts, dimensioning standards, and crosshatch patterns.

Levels

CAD software lets you separate information electronically into multiple **levels**, also known as **layers**, the equivalent of acetate film layers used in overlay drafting. The difference between CAD and manual drawing lies in the flexibility with which you can move between levels. While working on a selected **active level**, you can simultaneously display any other desired levels and edit still another selection of levels. You may change any level at any time. Levels are often displayed in different colors to help distinguish them. You may also display a drawing to indicate which pens have been selected for plotting. (See Color Plate 2, page 98.)

Graphic Intelligence

Determining how "smart" your drawing is depends on how sophisticated the CAD

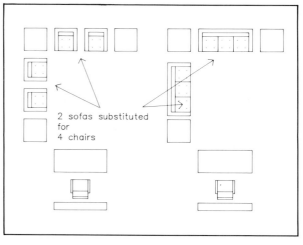

2.9 *Duplication and substitution are also powerful editing tools. The furniture on the left was duplicated as a group in one move. Then, the sofas were substituted.*

2 sofas substituted for 4 chairs

software and hardware are. Early drawings on my Apple computer had no intelligence. When I drew a line, the computer lit the pixels between the two ends of the line. In saving the drawing, the disk recorded each lighted and darkened pixel, some 53,760 of them, as a map (a **pixel dump** or **bit map**). Sophisticated CAD systems save considerably more information. When you draw a circle on a given level with a specific pen, this information and the two points describing the circle are saved. Although this increases the size of the drawing file, this data is essential for creating and maintaining an intelligent drawing.

Repeating Tasks

One of the most important and powerful tools is the computer **loop**. Loops repeat a specific task for a specific number of times. Drawing columns at grid intersections is an ideal application. Loops appear to run effortlessly and automatically, and they can be programmed to run in tandem (one after another) or as a **nested loop** (one loop placed within another). (In Part V, you will learn how computers perform loops.)

Drawing columns on a floor plan demonstrates how a nested loop works. The outer loop sets the first horizontal location. Then the inner loop places the first seven columns horizontally at 30-foot centers. When the inner loop finishes, the outer loop moves the starting point vertically 30 feet. The inner loop again places seven columns horizontally. The outer loop indexes vertically a third and last time, and the inner loop draws the final seven horizontal columns. The complete nested loop terminates when the outer loop finishes its last loop. (Look at the columns in Color Plate 2.)

Standard Tasks

Almost any task you wish the computer to perform can be activated automatically or semiautomatically. Being able to create or customize miniprograms gives you design flexibility to execute complex drawing procedures. Writing a program may seem overwhelming at first, but like drawing bending-moment diagrams, it gets easier with practice. Your system software documentation will provide details applicable to your computer. Macroprogramming varies with each computer and CAD system, but it is quite similar to fundamental programming, both of which are covered in Chapter 15.

Design Calculation Tasks

Design programs solve standard problems using different variables, or parameters. Sizing a stair is representative. You enter the occupancy type, the floor-to-floor dimensions, and the stair plan configuration, and the program generates several plan options, based on the optimum riser/tread ratio, minimum plan dimension, door clearance, or headroom clearance. (You'll find more about design applications in Chapter 8.)

CAD requires some additional thought and planning before you begin. You will determine dimensioning accuracy and drawing levels much earlier than with manual drawing. The discipline CAD imposes upon your design planning is extremely valuable, and it forces you to resolve major dimensions early in the design process.

WHEN DRAWING IS BETTER

Compared to you and me, CAD enters data more precisely, calculates more reliably, and draws more quickly. But you and I can create more imaginatively, analyze more flexibly, and think more decisively than any CAD program. There's no question that a computer performs selected tasks better than you or I, but design is a process that is rarely as precise, sequential, or logical as a computer. Design is loose and exploratory, often seemingly erratic, as it inches toward a design solution, tempered by the demands of the problem. While CAD draws better, you and I think better than the computer does. Advances in artificial intelligence will close this gap, but for now, we have the edge on the machine when it comes to thinking and deciding.

Besides, I *like* to draw. And so do most architects, engineers, and designers. It's an aid to thinking and a means of expression. Look at Figure 2.10: The drawing is both a record of the design process and a visualization of an idea, the design product. Look at the animated touch of the pencil. Best of all, it's portable and can be drawn anywhere. In the end, developing a concept requires only pencil, paper, and you.

When I'm designing, I want no interference—certainly no SYNTAX ERROR winking at me from the screen. Figure 2.11 shows a hand-drawn axonometric of offices drawn about as quickly as I can now create the same drawing on CAD. There are some drawing tasks that I readily surrender to the computer, namely, repetitive, complicated, and boring tasks. The ones I have fun doing, I'm not ready to turn over to CAD. But it probably won't be long until I find a more satisfying way to execute the fun drawings on a computer. In the meantime, Part II will teach you the fundamentals of drawing with CAD.

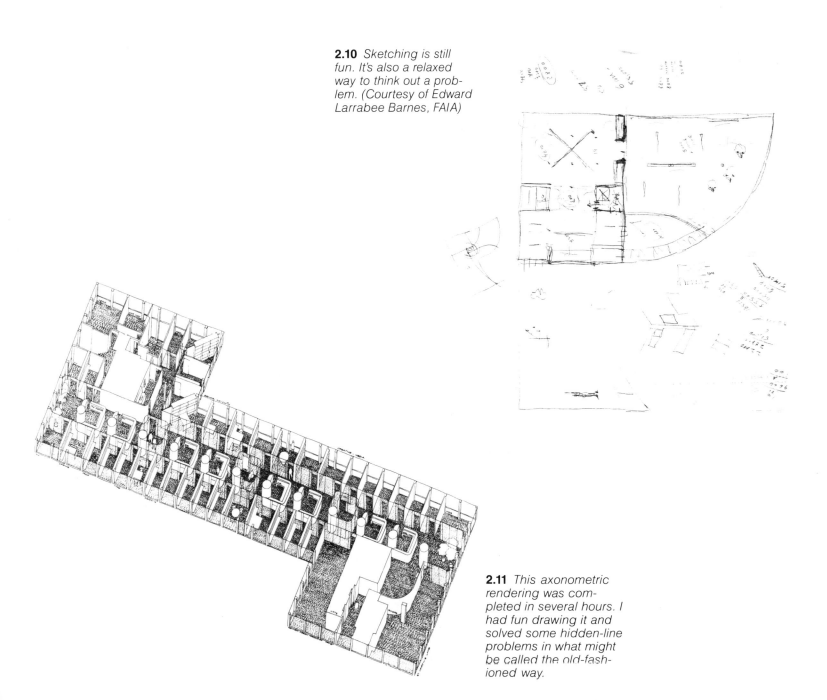

2.10 *Sketching is still fun. It's also a relaxed way to think out a problem. (Courtesy of Edward Larrabee Barnes, FAIA)*

2.11 *This axonometric rendering was completed in several hours. I had fun drawing it and solved some hidden-line problems in what might be called the old-fashioned way.*

Part II

DRAWING

CAD is primarily a drawing tool. In this part, you'll learn how to draw with *computer-aided drawing*. The drawing set-up is covered in Chapter 3: everything from cursors, coordinate geometry, levels, and display to initialization. In Chapter 4, you'll learn how to draw lines, geometric shapes, textures, text, and dimensions. Finally, in Chapter 5, you'll work with more sophisticated graphics—multiple lines, duplication, entities, figures, display control—and be introduced to editing and drawing management.

3

Computer Drawing Set-up

In manual drawing, you learn certain fundamentals of drafting: how to use a pencil and scale, the importance of keeping a sharp pencil point, how to draw a true straight line with a parallel bar, and how to letter and dimension. CAD drawing also requires understanding of a few basics. Your pencil is now a cursor working on a Cartesian coordinate grid, and your computer offers you more templates than you thought possible. You will be able to work on multiple levels, displaying or editing other single or multiple layers concurrently. Best of all, your terminal will keep track of everything for you.

CURSORS
The **cursor** replaces your pencil for entering **points**. The cursor consists of two intersecting lines, and you must imagine that the point of a pencil is at the intersection. To enter a point, move the cursor intersection to the desired location and press a **point key** to activate the point. Each CAD system uses a different point key entry method. Some, for example, use four specially designated function keys to enter a new point, draw a solid line, draw a dashed line, or insert a figure. Others use a single key and rely on the context of the command to determine whether the point entry is an initial, intermediate, or last point.

Cross Hairs
Figure 3.1 shows the traditional **cross-hair cursor**, which often extends the full width and height of the screen; others are smaller crosses (*x*'s) or alternative drawing axes, such as the isometric cursor. For most line work, the simple cross-hair cursor is preferred. The snap cursor (Figure 3.2) shows how close you must place the cursor in order to "grab" a point. The box in

the center shows the snap tolerance graphically. If you change the tolerance, the box grows (or shrinks) accordingly. Notice in this example that the tolerance is set differently for each axis. Because you need place the rectangle only around the working point, not precisely at the intersection, you can draw more quickly and accurately. When you press a graphics function key to activate a snap point, the computer responds by highlighting the new location or by forcing the cursor to move to the new location. A variation of the snap cursor splits into two cursors when the graphics function key is activated: The snap box jumps to the snap point, releasing the cross hair so that you can move it to a new location.

Figure Cursors
By replacing the cross hairs with any figure (a door, a line, a building core), you can move the figure around the drawing until you establish a new location. Each figure has an origin, or reference point, and when substituted for the cross-hair cursor, the cross-hair intersection becomes the figure origin. You can rotate the figure, change its scale, or offset the figure from its origin point. If the figure fits, press the figure function key and insert the figure into the drawing. You can also snap the figure origin to a known point or grid location. Look at Figure 3.3, in which the cursor is represented in dashed lines.

COORDINATE GEOMETRY AND ROTATION
If you thought you'd never have to face geometry after high school, welcome back to Cartesian coordinates. With CAD, you simply need them as a base location from which to measure. Look at Figure 3.4. Not all CAD

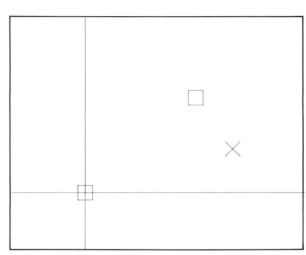

3.1 *(far left) The cross-hair cursor shows where the "pencil" is. The intersection marks the location where the next point can be entered. Move the cross hairs anywhere within the current screen view.*

3.2 *(left) The snap cursor displays a small box at the center that defines the limits of the point snap tolerance in both directions. Sometimes the snap location is temporarily identified by the box, while the cross is used to select the next point.*

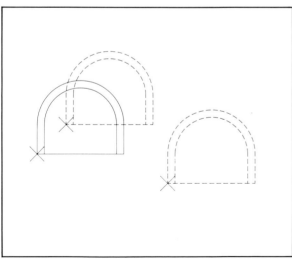

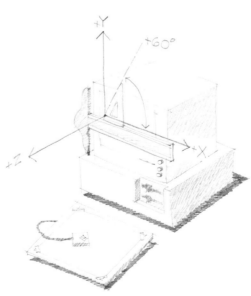

3.3 *(far left) The figure cursor replaces the cross hairs with any figure selected. Moving the cursor drags the figure, and allows it to be positioned before it is inserted onto the drawing.*

3.4 *(left) Cartesian coordinates are used to determine the location of a point: +X is to the right of the origin, +Y is up, and +Z is toward you from the CRT face (the X-Y plane). Angles are measured counterclockwise beginning with the +X axis ("east").*

computer systems use the same notations, but most recognize + X as *to the right of the origin* Cartesian notation, for your computer and the orientation, and rotation direction of angles for your computer. (Three-dimensional geometry and rotation are covered in Chapter 9.)

Measurement Units

Each CAD computer will compute lengths and angles based on some standard of measurement, rounding off to a specified number of decimal places. Your CAD computer will most likely define the base unit as 1 inch, 1 foot, or 1 meter, expressing other units as a ratio of the base unit. The computer then converts to any other units. For architectural work, you'll use the imperial (English) measurements of feet, inches, and fractions. The largest denominator (or smallest fraction) is determined by the user. For metric dimensioning, you should be able to mix meters with centimeters or millimeters, but consult your system manual before attempting to change units from imperial to metric or vice versa in the midst of a drawing.

In addition to defining linear units, you must determine whether angles will be measured in degrees, radians, or both. Since many calculations utilize radians instead of degrees, ascertain which convention your system recognizes.

Because computers routinely work with either whole numbers (integers) or decimal numbers with an accuracy up to 10^{-38} (that's 0.000000-00000000000000000000000000000001), calculations may not take place as you expect. You may need that accuracy for surveying, road alignment, or the design of a building with complex curvilinear geometry, but for most construction involving right angles and dimensions under several hundred feet, accuracy to that magnitude, or even to six decimal places, is unnecessary.

Care must be taken in rounding-off numbers.

You are used to rounding 0.51 or greater to 1.0, but you may find that integer calculations "round" all numbers to the lower number: The decimal portion is simply removed (truncated). Multiplying only the integers of 4.25×7.80 produces 28, while multiplying the same two real numbers and displaying the integer answer produces 33. Higher precision *can* be better, but only if it's truly needed. Higher precision also requires more decimal places, increases the number of digits in a number, increases memory requirements, and slows computation time. Therefore, establish the level of precision consistent with construction tolerances.

There seems to be no middle ground for calculating architectural dimensions. Either the precision level is too low (integers) or far too precise. In some CAD systems, you can avoid answers like 0.666666667 inch (⅔ inch) by having the computer format all fractions to a convenient form, perhaps two or four decimal places. In this case, 0.67 inch is close enough, while rounding to the nearest integer, 1 inch, is probably unacceptable.

You will want graphics calculations to be performed in the sequence that insures the greatest accuracy. The standard sequence of calculation is rotation first, followed by scaling and linear translation, and then rounding. For figure insertion, the sequence is scale, rotation, and translation. These guidelines hold true for most construction applications.

LEVELS

If you have worked with overlay drafting, then the concept of **levels (layers)** will be quite familiar. When similar information in any drawing discipline is drawn on specific sheets of acetate, the architect or engineer can mix and match sheets to create a composite drawing for reproduction. A background plan can be mixed, for example, with a partition plan, duct layout, or furniture plan in order to create three different drawings. With CAD, the same data can be electronically separated onto levels (or layers) and later mixed and matched in ways impossible, or quite difficult, to achieve manually.

The number of levels available generally depends on the sophistication of the hardware and software. It's better to have more levels, but too many can be bewildering. You need a minimum of 16 levels, although 64 is better, and 256 is optimal. With 256, you can assign ten levels to each of the 16 CSI/AIA construction sections (20 levels is better for Sections 15 and 16: Mechanical and Electrical) and have some left over for general drawing, project management, a scratch pad, and your favorite palette of rendering colors. (Color Plate 3, page 98, shows my proposed standard for level designations and color coding.)

Each level is discrete: Drawing or text data belongs to only one level. For example, one level may contain the column grid, another level the columns, and yet another the gypsum board enclosures. Look at Figure 3.5 as you read the following criteria that govern the use of levels.

Active Level
Think of the **active level** as the top sheet of acetate on a stack of overlays. It's the level on which you are currently working and entering data. You work on one active level at a time, but you can change the active level with a press of a key, which is much easier than removing and retaping a drawing.

Display Levels
You can look at one level or several or all levels simultaneously. You might want to display the column grid and the column enclosures but not the columns, or you might like to view partitions, furniture, and ceiling lights together. You might even like to display one set of levels, work on another active level, and edit still another.

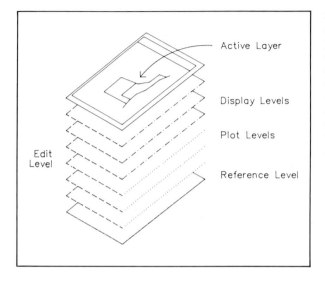

Active Layer

Display Levels

Plot Levels

Reference Level

Edit Level

3.5 *Layer (or level) selection determines how you use the data and drawings created on each discrete layer. You can work on one layer, display a selection of layers, edit a concurrent or different set of layers, while viewing a reference layer.*

Edit Levels
You can also select any one or several levels to be edited. For example, you can easily remove the crosshatching from a wall without removing the wall, if you created each on different levels. You can display both but edit only the crosshatch level. You erase (edit) the entire crosshatch area by enclosing the complete drawing within one large window that includes the wall, but the computer will only erase the data on the level selected for editing. Now, redisplay and verify your edit.

Ghost Level
On some systems, you can display a **ghost level** for reference purposes only. You cannot work or edit any information on a ghost level, but it's a handy tool if you need to refer to another drawing frequently.

Pen Levels
When you draw with different plotter-pen colors or widths, it is nice to know that you can display your work to distinguish segments drawn with various pens.

Moving to Another Level

If you elect to move information from one level to another, you can select the errant graphic entity and reassign it. If you have a color CRT, you'll see the entity change color, signaling a successful transfer.

DISPLAY

The CRT display is the only visual link with your drawings. Because the screen is smaller than most drawings and cannot display small data at a suitable resolution, you will want to **zoom** in to enlarge some areas in order to view details. Zooming translates along the Z axis. Once you've zoomed in, you can **pan** (translation along the X or Y axis) across or up and down the drawing to view adjacent areas. In addition to zooming and panning, you can manipulate the display in several ways.

Screen Scale

"Why isn't the screen at ⅛" scale?" At first, you may be tempted to put a scale to the CRT face, only to find that you can't scale the CRT. Bear in mind that the CRT display size has no relationship to the drawing scale or plotting scale. The CRT display can be any size you want it to be: You can display a drawing at ⅛" scale on a 13" monitor if you wish, but the same zoom instruction given to a 19" monitor will display the drawing at ³⁄₁₆" scale or thereabouts. It is more useful to be able to zoom as required. If you do not instruct the computer to the contrary, the CRT will display the drawing at the largest size that will fit the screen. This is called a default view. The word **default** is computer jargon denoting any predefined standard that will be activated in the absence of other instructions.

Window Selection

The basic detail view is the **window**, so called because of the rectangle defining the view. One very useful feature on some CAD systems is the ability to interrupt a command in progress in order to zoom into a larger view, continue the command, zoom out, and resume the command.

Dynamic Pan and Zoom

In a simple zoom, you select a window different from the current CRT display and redisplay the new image. CAD systems capable of **dynamic pan and zoom** perform display changes with the same animation of a motion picture camera. The process is complex and requires advanced hardware, but the results are spectacular. The most significant component is the **graphics processor**, hardware designed for the sole purpose of speeding redisplay. This is the ultimate in display control and is available on professional-quality systems. Figures 3.6 through 3.8 simulate the concept of zooming and panning.

Multiple Displays

Figure 3.9 shows a four-window display that you can use to show any combination of plans, elevations, details, or three-dimensional views. You can work on one of the views while using the others for reference.

Display Speed

Display times vary tremendously. Small drawings **redisplay (repaint)** more quickly than large ones. A large drawing, twice the size of a companion drawing, may require five times the redisplay time. Three-dimensional drawing generation, hidden-line removal, and surface shading require considerable calculation and therefore longer redisplay times. On the other hand, redisplay time shortens significantly when drawing intelligence is separated from graphics data. Any graphics processor speeds redisplay, and auxiliary graphics coprocessors (often a card full of chips that is inserted into your computer) have become an increasingly popular means of speeding up displays.

3.6 *Full view is often confusing to the new user, because he or she expects the full view to be displayed at true scale. CRTs are not for scaling. The dotted rectangle defines the window view shown in Figure 3.7.*

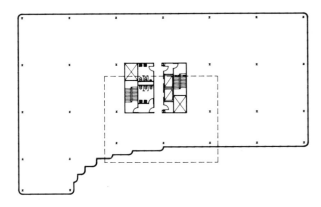

3.7 *A window view displays a close-up zoom view.*

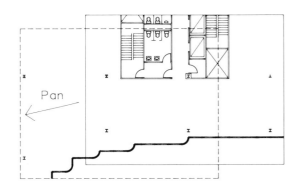

3.8 *Panning is a process that moves vertically or horizontally—here, a move to the left of the view in Figure 3.7.*

Pan

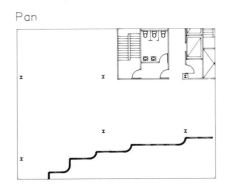

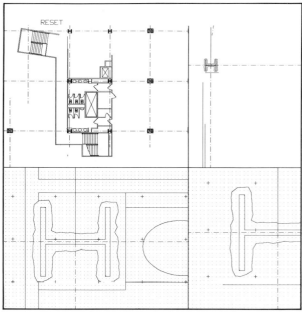

3.9 *Multiple windows offer the user either different viewing angles or overall-detail views of the same drawing, shown here as a "dumped" print. (Courtesy of Haines Lundberg Waehler, Architects, Engineers, and Planners)*

There's a popular misconception that display speed determines the primary worth of any CAD system. Display time is but one factor in evaluating performance. While no drawing should ever require more than three minutes to display, a skilled user working with rich software and a flexible CAD system can affect performance more significantly than redisplay times. In fact, the time spent designing, thinking, and making decisions—not repaint time—represents by far the greatest percentage of the time spent at the computer.

Color

Black-, green-, or orange-and-white CRT displays are considerably cheaper than full-color displays. Although the difference in cost between top-of-the-line color and black-and-white monitors may be more than the cost of some micro systems, you will never regret buying color. Aside from adding flash to your marketing presentations, color is a great aid in separating levels of discrete information, examining interference, or displaying multiple levels or pen assignments. With a color CRT, you can distinguish different information that would otherwise fuse into adjacent graphics. For architectural renderings and surface shading, color is a must. (Chapter 9 is devoted to three-dimensional drawing, color, and shading.)

INITIALIZATION

Whether drawing on paper or on a CRT, you must make several decisions before you start: paper size, units, computation precision, scale for various drawings, text and dimensioning standards, grid snap, level assignments, and the angular reference line. Your system manual will identify the parameters you must set. Your technical representative can help you set up these parameters initially, so that when you start up the computer (a process called **booting**), your software will be **initialized** with these preset parameters.

Default Values

With each subsequent boot, the software will be initialized with the same preset values, known as default values. Even though default values can be changed, your CAD software will initialize all the parameters listed in the preceding paragraph with default values.

If you're drawing doors, for example, you can change the default door width, and all subsequent doors will then be drawn at the new default value until you change it again.

Drawing Origin

When you draw manually, dimensions are usually referenced to a site benchmark location, often after the building is designed; and then only for the purpose of locating the building on the site. In CAD, every drawing has its own benchmark, or origin, a Cartesian 0, 0, 0 location from which all dimensions and points are referenced. Unless you instruct the computer otherwise, grids, grid snap, and angular references will commence at the origin. You may set a new temporary or permanent origin at any time in the drawing process.

Graphic Input Modifications

If you make no modifications to the graphics data, you will get exactly what you ask for: A 100-foot building will be drawn 100 feet long. You can scale an entry to $\frac{1}{8}'' = 1' - 0''$, rotate all door symbols by 135°, or offset all entries, say, $14'-6\frac{1}{2}''$ to the right ($+X$) and $3\frac{5}{8}''$ down ($-Y$). By modifying graphics input, you maintain a constant reference point and alter the manner in which graphics are entered. This technique can be particularly useful when working with complex geometrical shapes.

Modifications of scale, rotation, or translation may apply globally (to all graphics entries) or locally (to any single or several selected drawing entries). For example, when you set the scale of your drawing to $\frac{1}{8}'' = 1' - 0''$, you are instructing the computer to scale down, or reduce, all your entries to a scale of $\frac{1}{8}'' = 1' - 0''$

(1/96th full size). Consequently, when you instruct the CAD terminal to draw a line 96 feet long, it will actually enter a line 1 foot long in the database.

Typically, figures are drawn full size. Thus, a desk 60" × 30" is stored at that true size and scaled when the figure is entered. If you wanted to change the size of the desk to 72" × 36", you would reset the figure scale before inserting the figure. The change in size should be reflected in the graphics cursor. On some CAD systems, you can rescale the desk as 72/60 × 36/30, which saves having to make the conversion.

Graphics rotation works the same way as scale, but it applies to rotation around the Z axis. Professional systems include rotation about the X and Y axes as well. Global rotation lets you

enter data in X/Y coordinates, but it places the graphics skewed and saves having to make all the calculations (see Figure 3.10).

Translation simply offsets any entry by the amount specified in the X, Y, or Z offset. Acquaint yourself with the scaling, rotation, and translation conventions of your CAD system, because conventions vary.

Dimensioning Grids
One feature most CAD users like is never having to look for the scale a friend borrowed. You initialize the scale you want and display it on the screen. If you like, you can create a cursor that has a built-in scale, but chances are you'll never use it, because the following techniques are easier and faster.

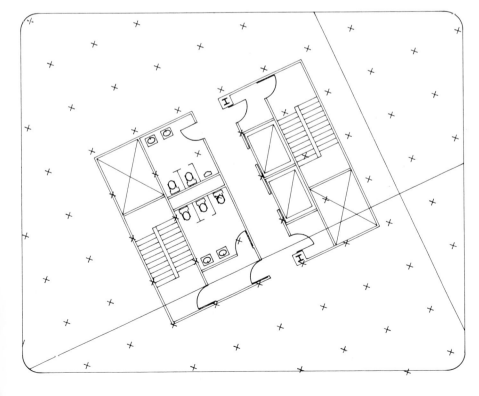

3.10 *Global rotation of the entire drawing relative to the CRT makes drawing on an angle easy.*

Grid displays

You can display two different grids: a **perimeter grid** (along the bottom and side of the CRT), which resembles a scale (Figure 3.11), or the **matrix grid**, which is a field of dots (Figure 3.12). Perimeter grids display quickly and are quite versatile when used in conjunction with cross hairs. Matrix grids cover the CRT screen and are extremely helpful, but they repaint more slowly.

3.11 *A perimeter grid displays any scale selected, along two edges of the CRT. Here, the X scale matches the Y scale, with small reference ticks set at 12 inches and large ticks every five feet. When the view size changes, the perimeter scale changes accordingly.*

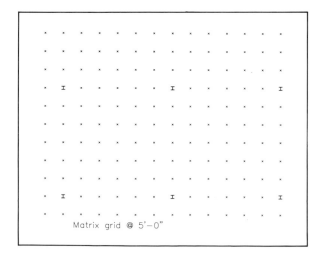

Major Grid @ 5'–0"
minor grid @ 12"

3.12 *A matrix grid displays the scale in a pattern over the face of the CRT.*

Matrix grid @ 5'–0"

You'll find that each grid has its own uses.

Changing the grid is easy. You can change it at any time without modifying the drawing scale. Try to define a grid for your current work that is small enough to be meaningful but large enough not to clutter the screen. This is particularly important when you use a matrix grid. Even though each grid is displayed over the drawing, the grid does not become a permanent part of the drawing.

When you zoom in or out, the grid changes size to reflect the correct scale and drawing origin. You may specify different scales for each of the X, Y, and Z axes. Civil engineers often take advantage of this feature, increasing the vertical scale in cross-section drawings to accentuate small vertical changes, like those found in drainage and road profiles. Unlike manual drawing, where distances are measured using the scale, the on-screen grid is used only for reference.

Matrix grids may be rotated and offset from the origin, and because of the ease in defining and displaying matrix grids, you will find them a useful design tool for verifying the location of any pattern. For example, points on a matrix grid might represent ceiling tile intersections, a fast technique for locating all ceiling grid intersections. (No more late hours spent drawing grids on reams of yellow tracing paper!)

Try setting your X grid at 30' – 0" and the Y grid at 28' – 8" while drawing the column grids. Then set the grid at 1-foot intervals as you lay out a plan. Finally, set the detailing grid at 1/16 inch. Study Figure 3.11 again. The grid is divided into 5-foot increments and further subdivided into 1-foot increments. This grid is good for drawing plans and elevations.

Grid snap tolerance

Since the eye is capable of subdividing the distance between two tick marks into four approximately equal segments, you can now refine your dimensioning from 1 foot in the example above to approximately 3 inches—but not precisely 3 inches. You were introduced to grid snap in Chapter 2. Refer to Figure 2.3, showing the grid snap tolerance set at $X = 60''$ and $Y = 30''$. Entering a point within a point halfway between the grid location "rounds" your entry to the closest point. In Figure 2.3, the point snaps to an imaginary grid, the location of the last mullion. Continuing the example above, the grid display is initialized to 1 foot for secondary ticks and 5 feet for primary ones. Setting the grid snap tolerance to 3 inches forces any new point entry to the 3-inch module. Try to set grid snap to the smallest dimensioned unit with which you are currently working, but make sure it's large enough to be seen without excessive zooms or redisplays.

Point Snap Tolerance

Sometimes called object or entity snap, **point snap** can search for the closest point or the first point it encounters within the snap tolerance window. I like to set this value at one half the minimum dimension of that with which I'm currently working, which for a 4-inch wall, is a point snap tolerance of 2 inches. Refer back to Figure 2.4, where the end point of the new line was entered near a known point. The entered point snapped to a known location, the closest point, or the intersection point of two already constructed lines. Try not to confuse **grid snap** with **point snap**. You should also determine whether grid snap and point snap interact or work independently on your computer. If they interact, point snap tolerance may only work if the tolerance is equal to or greater than the grid snap tolerance.

Snap Locations

So far, you've seen how to snap to the end of a line—actually to the **end point** of an entity. Both Figures 2.4 and 3.13 show examples of end-

point snap, namely to the end of a line. You may find that there are more end points than you guessed. A circle, for example, may have in addition to an invisible center, many end points as it is actually a multisided polygon. You may want to snap to a location other than the end point: perhaps the closest point, the midpoint, a perpendicular point, or a tangent point. An example of this snap is shown in Figure 3.13. But more about that in the next chapter.

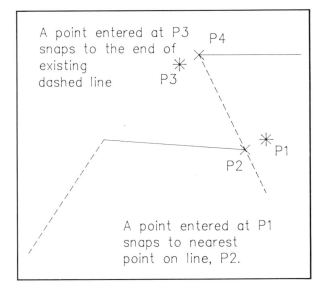

A point entered at P3 snaps to the end of existing dashed line

P4

P3

P1

P2

A point entered at P1 snaps to nearest point on line, P2.

3.13 *Point snap determines whether the entered point will snap to the end point of an entity or to the closest segment of the entity. Point 1 entered snapped to the closest segment, point 2.*

Beginning to Draw

The first three chapters have given you a solid grounding in the fundamentals of CAD. Now you're ready to draw. You'll begin with the basic entry—the point—and then learn to enter points with different input devices and entry methods. You'll progress to lines, finishing with complex graphics.

POINTS

When you draw a line manually, you draw almost unconsciously, simply setting the pencil where you want to start, rolling it along a straightedge, and stopping when things look right. Dimensioning is not a prerequisite of drawing— you draw first and dimension later. CAD drawing reverses the process: You enter starting and ending points at specifically known or dimensioned locations and do so quite consciously. The line or other graphics follow.

Entry, Working, and Reference Points

An **entry point** is any point you enter onto the CRT. Each time you enter a point, it becomes both the **initial point** for a subsequent companion point and the **ending** (or last) **point** of the companion previous point. Look at Figure 4.1. Point P1 is the initial point for the line connected to the subsequent ending point, P2. Point P2 then becomes the initial point for a subsequent point, P3, and so on.

A **working point** is any point that the CAD system actually uses. When grid snap or point snap modes are inactive, entry and working points coincide. If, however, either snap is active, the computer will establish a new working point, based on grid- or point-snap criteria. In Figure 4.1, working points P1–P10 match entry points, whereas the entry point P11 snaps to P4, the revised working point for P11.

A **reference point** is one whose coordinates

are remembered by the system for future use. In the example above, once point P2 became an initial point for the next line segment, point P1 became a reference point called the **last-point input**. Your CAD system may be capable of remembering more than one previous point.

Drawing Points

There are two ways to enter points. X and Y— and sometimes Z—coordinates may be typed on the keyboard, or the point may be located graphically with the cursor. Points may be displayed as dots, crosses (you define how large), or not at all, and they may or may not become a permanent part of the drawing. If the points are displayed temporarily, they will vanish when you redisplay the drawing.

Keyboard entry

Study Figure 4.2 for a minute so that you understand the coordinates represented by the points at 2,2; 3,4; −2,6; and so forth. You will recognize the coordinate format as $+X2, +Y2$. These pairs are called **absolute points**, that is, points entered in units measured from the origin, $+X$ to the right, $+Y$ up.

Alternatively, you might wish to enter a new point at a location relative to the last point rather than to the origin. Figure 4.3 shows a sample in which, starting at point P1 ($+X2, +Y2$), point P2 was located at $r+X3, r+Y4$, a **relative point**, measured from the last point. Other points in Figure 4.3 were similarly located.

Figure 4.4 shows another form of relative point entry: **polar point** entry. The starting location remains 2,2, but rather than moving incrementally along Cartesian coordinates ten units in both the $+X$ and $+Y$ directions, you move 14.14214 units at an angle of 45°, reaching the final point at 12,12.

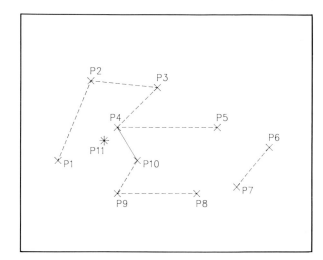

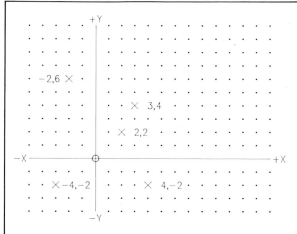

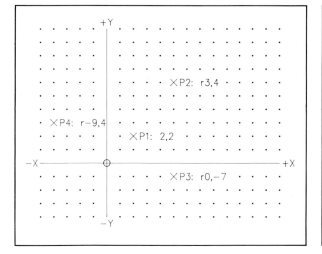

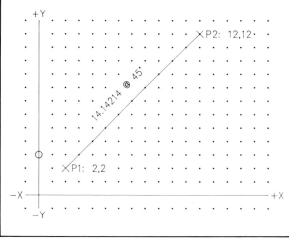

4.1 (far left) Point entry commences at point 1 and continues through point 5. Graphically, use a pen, puck, or mouse to enter points, pressing the point entry function key or keys.

4.2 (left) Absolute points are entries made at fixed locations from the origin. Note the locations of each pair of points, annotated in the form X, Y. Each tick represents one inch.

4.3 (far left) Relative points add or subtract a value from the last-entered point. The first entry is point 1, an absolute entry. Subsequent points are entered using a relative point notation.

4.4 (left) Polar-point entry works well when you know the length of a line and its direction. Here, a polar entry is entered from point 1 (2,2) of 14.14214 inches at 45° to generate a final location at 12,12.

Cursor entry

Graphic points are entered by centering the cursor (or the figure origin) at the desired location and activating a point function key. Graphic point entry is sensitive to grid snap and point snap tolerances. Points entered with the cursor migrate to the correct working point location, whereas points entered on the keyboard are unaffected by snap tolerances.

Rubberbanding, a useful feature on many CAD systems, allows you to preview what a line, rectangle, or circle will look like before you draw it. With it, a temporary figure is displayed using the first point of entry as a reference. As you move the cursor, a line or figure flickers between the entry point and the cursor origin to let you preview its final shape. When you enter the final point, the preview figure is replaced by a permanent figure.

Three-Dimensional Points

Since three-dimensional capability is not mandatory for drafting, many architectural drawing programs are not capable of generating (supporting) three-dimensional images and therefore do not accept Z coordinates. Changes in the Z coordinate do not become visible until the image is rotated. The point $+Z0$ is taken to mean "elevation 0." You might, for example, set the Z elevation to $+Z8'-0''$ and draw a ceiling in its normal location. If you rotate your image, you'll find the ceiling $8'-0''$ above the floor, and you'll be on the way to drawing an interior perspective—but more about that in Chapter 9.

Offset Point Entry

You might want every point entered to be located at a predetermined distance from the entry point, called **offset point** entry. You establish the offset for each axis. Thus, setting the offset at $X+6$, $Y+0$, $Z-2$ adjusts each entry point by these values. For example, a point entered at $+X5$, $+Y7$, $+Z5$ establishes the working point as $+X11$, $+Y7$, $+Z3$.

LINES

Points and lines go together. While the point remains the basic CAD entry, the line is the fundamental graphics element. All graphics constructed on the screen consist of lines and line elements, including circles and text. On some CAD systems, point entry is interpreted differently, depending on which function key is selected: You may set a new point, draw a line or a broken line, or insert a figure. Point function keys are located on the keyboard and may be duplicated on a puck or a mouse. Other systems treat a point, line, or figure like any other graphics command.

Regardless, line texture indicates the line as solid or one of several that is intermittently discontinuous. Figure 4.1 shows different line segments concluding with point P11 snapping to the previous point, P4.

Solid Lines

A solid, continuous line is only one pixel wide no matter how magnified the drawing appears and is called a **standard**, or **default**, **line**. Several additional solid lines are shown in Figure 4.5.

Broken Lines

Intermittently discontinuous lines—**broken lines**—are, in effect, a series of short, solid lines. You will discover that drawing broken lines takes significantly longer than drawing solid lines if each line segment must be drawn separately. Several samples are shown in Figure 4.6. You can set the size of major and minor dashes as well as the space between them. For example, you can draw a dashed line consisting of a ½-inch dash separated by a ¼-inch gap. But how do you draw a line if it fails to terminate with a dash? How is the broken line resolved? By default, broken lines start with a complete dash and continue without change until reaching the end point, truncating the last segment, if necessary.

To improve the visual appearance of a line, each end dash can be proportionately

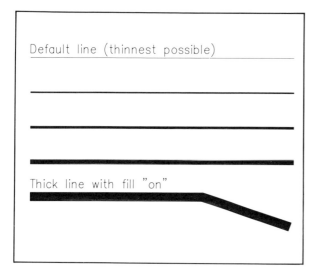

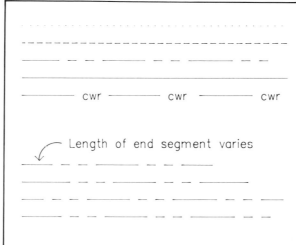

4.5 *(far left) Solid lines. Line width can be controlled in three ways: draw them thicker, draw several single lines close to one another, or select a wider pen at plot time.*

4.6 *(left) Broken lines include dashed, phantom, and centerlines.*

shortened to accommodate the balance of preset dashes and spaces. Be careful, though. Some systems modify dash and gap lengths throughout the line as the overall line length varies. The variations in segment lengths produce inconsistent line quality. Many architects overcome this shortcoming by creating a broken-line figure with fixed line-length segments, copying the line to the drawing, and editing the unwanted length. (Figures and duplication are covered in Chapter 5.)

Construction Lines
Like reference points, a **construction line** is entered for reference or layout purposes only. In some CAD systems, you draw construction lines exactly as you would manually, tracing heavier lines to outline permanent work. But for the most part, the computer draws temporary construction lines to aid layout. When you finish, the construction lines are removed automatically.

Multiple Lines
A real time saver is the double-line command, which draws multiple parallel lines (with or

without a centerline) as you enter a single construction line. By varying the line texture from solid to dashed, dotted, centerline, and so on, this command can display different wall or HVAC duct conditions. The command will miter a corner after you've entered the subsequent line segment, so the command will always appear to be one step behind. To be really useful, the means must exist to remove excess lines at overlapping intersections. Because your construction line may not coincide with the center of the double line, this command can be frustrating, but once you've mastered it, you'll appreciate its power and the time it saves. Sample double lines and walls are shown in Figure 4.7.

Interpolated Lines
A line, curved or straight, that is derived from entered points but that differs from the entered line is said to be an **interpolated line**.

Figure 4.8 shows one sample, the **fillet line**, connected at each intersection by tangent radii. Fillets are commonly used in the design of mechanical piece parts (**computer-aided manufacturing**, or **CAM**) and can be effectively

4.7 *Multiple-line entry allows you to draw any line shape with parallel lines and, in some cases, allows you to mix line "texture" from solid to broken. Note how the corners automatically miter, and how wall intersections are resolved, sometimes called "justification."*

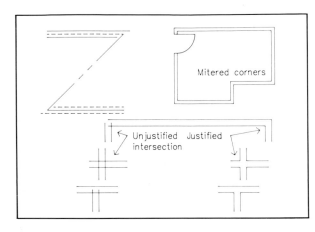

4.8 *Fillet lines are simply lines with rounded corners. It's a great tool when you're drawing curb lines. Note how the radius and line texture can vary.*

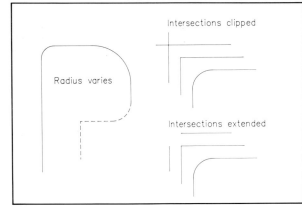

4.9 *A smooth curve, or spline, is generated as the computer reads several previous points and builds a multiple curve through each of the points. Ideal for drawing topographic contours.*

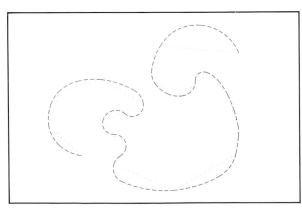

used in site work, especially in drawing curb lines and other curve-to-tangent line geometry.

Smooth curves (also called **spline curves**), shown in Figure 4.9, are curved lines automatically generated during successive point entry. The curve passes through each entry point and changes the degree of curvature as the eccentricity is modified.

Line Quality

Drawing lines of varying width and weight (degrees of darkness) has long been a technique used by architects and designers to distinguish elements within a drawing: to suggest depth, to identify hidden or distant lines, or to improve the graphic quality of the drawing—all of which make a drawing "read better." As with manual drawing, you must direct the computer to draw the line quality you want.

You can increase the width of the line on the CRT display, on the pen plot, or on a combination of both. Displaying wider lines on the CRT lends richness to the drawing but often slows redisplay. This can be rectified by displaying all lines as standard lines while plotting with different pen widths. But using multiple pens can be a nuisance. One good solution is to draw several parallel lines close together, thereby gaining the best of both worlds: a wide line display using one pen.

You should find Figure 4.10 helpful in deciding which pen or line width you want to use on a drawing. As a point of reference, a plotter ballpoint pen is about 0.012 inch (0.3 mm) in diameter, or approximately the same size as an 00 technical pen, both of which draw a line about 1-inch wide at ⅛-inch scale (±0.01 inch).

Line Intersections

As you have seen, one of the most powerful features of CAD is the ability to snap to known points of graphic entities, usually interpreted as points on a line (curves often consist of straight line segments). The computer's ability to snap to

PEN SIZES
note: Ballpoint is .012" or .3 mm thick

4.10 *Pen and line widths can be varied to add richness to CRT displays and drawings. This chart shows several popular technical pen sizes and a range of open- and solid-line font sizes.*

	mm	fab	mar	koh
.005	.13	4X0	5X0	6X0
.007	.18	000	4X0	4X0
.010	.25	00	000	000
.012	.30		00	00
.014	.35	0	0	0
.016	.40	1		
.020	.50	2	2	1
.024	.60			2
.028	.70	2.5	2.5	2.5
.039	1.00	4	3.5	3.5
.047	1.20	5	4	4
.055	1.40		5	6
.063	1.60		6	
.079	2.00			7

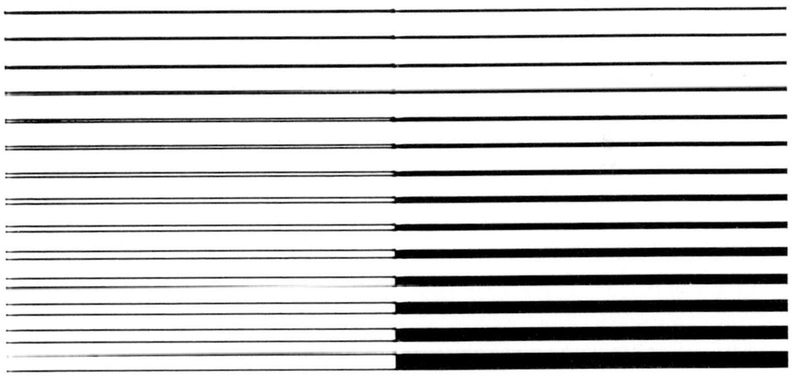

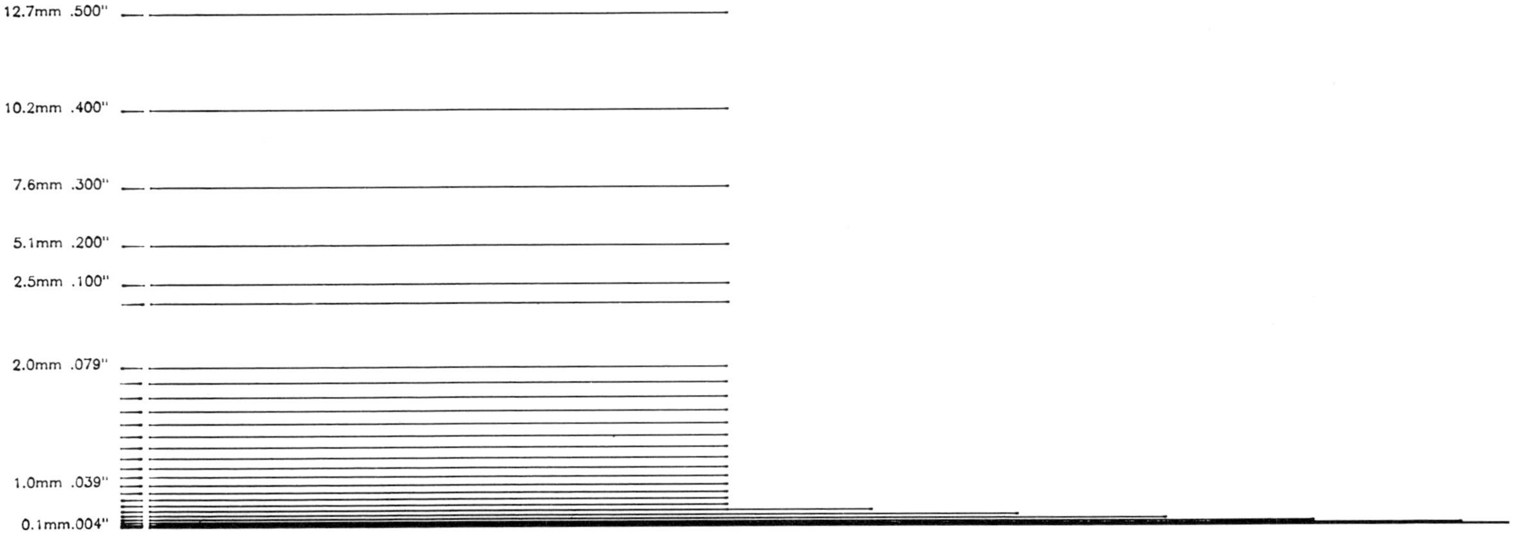

12.7mm .500"

10.2mm .400"

7.6mm .300"

5.1mm .200"

2.5mm .100"

2.0mm .079"

1.0mm .039"

0.1mm .004"

LINE SPACING
Increasing increments of .004" = .1 mm

4.11 *Line intersections are sometimes identifiable as entities, in which case light fixtures can be snapped to a ceiling grid.*

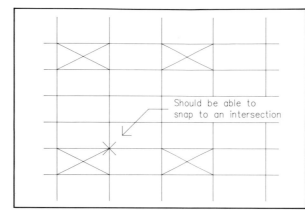

4.12 *Line leaders designate the end of a line. Here are some samples of single, multiple, and curved leaders, including one double-barreled line leader.*

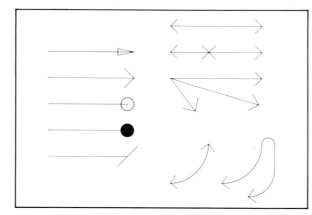

4.13 *Rectangles (and rectangular lines) are classicly efficient graphic shapes: Two points define four corners. Drawing a rectangle at any other angle requires the polygon command, or global grid rotation.*

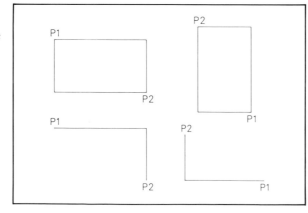

multiple locations is more desirable. For example, if the computer snaps to end points only and not to junctions of intersecting lines, as in a ceiling grid, the locating of light fixtures is hampered because the intersection point is the best location to snap a light fixture (see Figure 4.11).

Line Leaders
A **line leader** (or **line terminator**) is the arrow or dot at the end of any line used to point to or identify the contents of a reference note or to close a dimension line. Look at Figure 4.12. The leader may be created as a separate graphic figure, and like text, dimensions, and reference marks (the north arrow or section cuts), it may be separately scaled on the drawing because its size is determined by readability, rather than matching the scale of the drawing.

GEOMETRIC FIGURES
The next step up in graphic complexity from lines is **figures**. Figures are simply small drawings, the CAD equivalent of templates. They are also known as cells, blocks, symbols, or objects, among others. If you remember geometry from high school, you'll find it easier to construct rectangles, triangles, circles and ellipses, and polygons. But with or without the mastery of geometry, you'll no longer have to piece together ellipses from circle segments.

Rectangles and half-rectangles are the easiest polygons to draw because you need only determine the two opposite corners; the other two corners are "constructed" by intermixing *X*- and *Y*-point information of the entered points. Look at Figure 4.13. You enter points P1 and P2. The computer constructs point P3 using the *X* coordinate of point P1 and the *Y* coordinate of point P2, and it constructs point 4 using the *X* coordinate of P2 and the *Y* coordinate of P1. This concept applies, however, only to rectangles parallel to the X (and thus Y) axis.

Rotated rectangles can be constructed by rotating the grid (using the polygon command) or in the conventional manner, saved, and reinserted as a figure on an angle. Systems differ in their methods.

Interestingly, few systems include subroutines that specifically draw triangles. On the other hand, trigonometric functions are widely used in calculating point locations. Maybe it's too difficult to write a good fundamental software subroutine (otherwise called an **algorithm**) that defines a triangle. In the end, most triangles are improvised from rectangles (right triangles) or polygons (equilateral) or are merely constructed line by line (see Figure 4.14).

Circles are commonly constructed using three classic methods: center point plus radius; two ends of a diameter; or three points on the circumference. Arcs are constructed from three circumference points or the center point and two radial points (one must be on the circumference), and a hemisphere is constructed from two opposite points of a diameter. Ellipses use the same algorithms as circles, but they require additional axial definitions of eccentricity and rotation angle. **Eccentricity** is defined as angular rotation about either the X or Y axis, while **rotation** (or **inclination**) is defined as angular rotation about the Z axis. Best of all, gone are the days of fudging ellipses to fit your drawing. Figure 4.15 shows a mix of circle and ellipse construction.

If you study Figures 4.15 and 4.16, you will recognize that polygonal construction is essentially the same as circle and ellipse construction. All polygons are constructed as though contained within a circumscribing circle or ellipse and are defined in the same manner. Your only additional instruction is to indicate the number of sides and determine the location of one vertex.

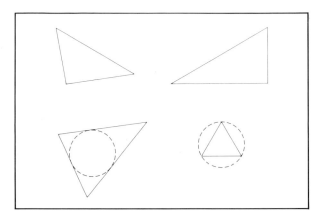

4.14 *Triangles are constructed using several different methods.*

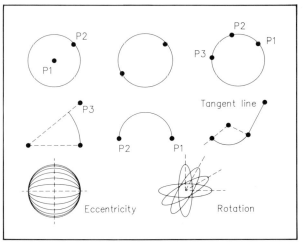

4.15 *Circles, circular arcs, and ellipses are simple to construct. Ellipses require two additional parameters: eccentricity and rotation.*

P2
P1
P2
P1
P3
P3
Tangent line
P2
P1
Eccentricity
Rotation

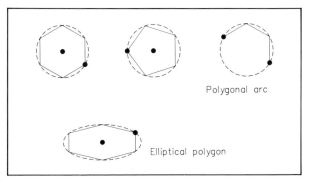

4.16 *Polygons and polygonal arcs are easy to draw on a computer. Polygons, ellipses, elliptical polygons, and circles are constructed in a similar manner.*

Polygonal arc

Elliptical polygon

4.17 *Linear match is the means whereby the computer is asked to align one point on the screen with another point. Here, points are snapped, and lines are drawn to a variety of conditions.*

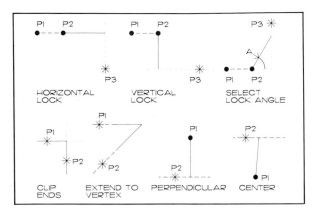

4.18 *Circular match parallels linear match in concept but involves curves.*

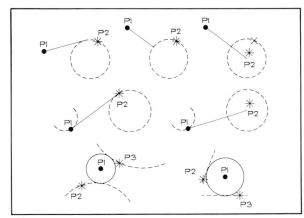

4.19 *Crosshatching and shading are enjoyable computer functions. In each, once a boundary is defined, the computer completes the task.*

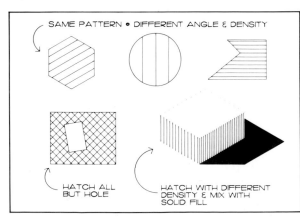

GRAPHIC ALIGNMENT

Drawings are often annotated "Align with face of wall." When a match is attempted manually, considerable calculation may be required and a lot of graphic shoehorning may be necessary. When the note is insufficient or not within accuracy requirements, a better method is needed.

This is another occasion when the computer shines: You enter the limits, and the computer finds the correct point. Data is quickly calculated, and figures are inserted accurately and quickly—there's no fudging. Study Figure 4.17, which describes several types of linear alignments. In a similar fashion, study Figure 4.18, which describes several circular alignments, many of which involve tangent lines.

TEXTURES

Textures include crosshatch patterns and solid shading, an effective technique for representing surfaces, textures, or material designations. Methods of texturing vary somewhat. Some systems require that you trace the outline to be textured. Others allow you to point (place the cursor) at any location within the boundary, and the computer will look for the boundary and automatically texture to the edge, filling the entire area. You can place textures on any layer with the same color or different colors. The software for drawing textures is well defined. CAD texturing is considerably faster than its manual counterpart, yet you will find that redisplay and pen-plotting time slows appreciably if crosshatching is extensive.

Crosshatch Patterns

Look at Figure 4.19. Although effective, manual **crosshatching** is difficult to erase completely, and heavy crosshatching stretches the drawing medium, distorting a print. Crosshatching with CAD is easy to create and edit (place the crosshatching on a separate layer to facilitate future editing). You can readily change pattern size and rotation. For example, two adjacent wythes of brick, one common and one finish brick, can be crosshatched with the same pattern: After you finish the common brick crosshatch, scale the finish brick pattern down about 40% and rotate the pattern 180°. On most CAD systems, the location of the pattern origin can vary.

Crosshatching can also be used to draw patterns, particularly ceiling grids or floor tiles. You can, for example, lay out each ceramic tile on a mural wall with absolute accuracy. Or you can use crosshatch patterns on surfaces in perspective drawings. Rotating the plan tightens the pattern, increasing the sense of depth. But for the most part, you will use crosshatching to indicate construction materials in the same way as you do with manual drawing.

On systems with low CRT resolution, pixel dot patterns may be substituted for crosshatch patterns, and while the pattern may not match a recognized architectural standard, you can overcome this with a key diagram. When the color-filled area is displayed on a black-and-white monitor or printed on a matrix printer, distinctive patterns are created from the color representations.

As the sophistication of the system increases, so does the flexibility to create, add, and modify patterns. One final note about crosshatch patterns: They are usually created using a nested loop. The actual pattern is relatively small, but it fits the irregular or larger shape by repeating until it fills the boundary.

Solid Shading
Whereas crosshatching is transparent and varies in pattern size, shading, is solid, opaque, and fills the entire area regardless of scale. You can see through crosshatching, but not through shading. Because solid shading conceals that which is behind, shading techniques can be used to overlay background planes, effectively removing hidden lines (more about this in Chapter 9). Since solid shading requires extensive plotter pen movement, you should allow extra plotting time to reproduce solid filled areas. On the other hand, electrostatic plotters display solid shading quickly and effectively.

To shade a spandrel, for example, you can either create the section directly or, using the outline of a previously drawn spandrel, trace a new boundary to shade the surface. Figure 4.19 also shows samples of solid shading. (Shading techniques are covered in Chapter 9.)

TEXT
In the context of graphics, **text** has many facets. Think of text as any annotated comments that you enter on the drawing, including drawing and sheet titles and dimensions. Text lies at the heart of intelligent drawings, a concept introduced in Chapter 2 and developed in detail in Chapter 6. Standard notes can also be created using the CAD word processor utility (software) and then inserted on multiple drawings or on different jobs by merging the notes onto your drawing.

I learned how to letter in architecture school, using the one acceptable style of lettering. With lettering template, chisel point, and pencil at hand, I lettered to whatever height was required, squeezing or stretching words as necessary. It was my hallmark, my signature, and one measure of the excellence of my draftsmanship.

Fonts
Most architects and designers find CAD lettering **fonts** (a graphic description of an alphabet) an unsatisfactory alternative to manual lettering—and understandably so. What designers are shown by eager CAD vendors is reminiscent of elementary mechanical lettering—almost laughably poor for professional-quality drawings. But once you

Clarendon
Helvetica Bold
Futura 1234567
Mirrored
Upside down

This text is Rong
This text isn't Wrong

AIA
RIBA

"Ragged right" text:

INSERT STAINLESS STEEL
ANCHORS @ 4'-0" O.C.
& FILL WITH NON-SHRINKING
GROUT

Justified text:

INSERT STAINLESS STEEL
ANCHORS @ 4' - 0" O.C.
& FILL WITH NON-SHRINKING
GROUT

*Text merged from word
processor or text editor:*

1. The General Contractor
shall ensure that all work
is completed in accordance
with the AIA GENERAL
CONDITIONS, latest revision.

4.20 *Text entry of notes eliminates the corn on your third finger. Here are several examples of direct graphic input plus notes created in the host computer text editor and merged onto the drawing.*

discover the control you have over font design and the computer's capacity to reproduce any press-on letter, you will be overwhelmed by the power at your fingertips.

CAD systems are capable of generating and manipulating fonts with varying degrees of typographic sophistication. Here is an overview of the features you would find in a high-quality CAD computer.

Figure 4.20 contains facsimiles of Clarendon, Helvetica, and Futura fonts. For computer applications, a font consists of approximately 96 displayable characters. Lettering may be all uppercase, all lowercase, or mixed (like the text in this book). The basic font may be compressed horizontally (condensed) or widened (expanded). The width of each line in the character is called a stroke (like the stroke of a pen), and the width of the stroke is indicated as light, medium, or bold (for example, Helvetica light). Italics are letters slanted to the right of vertical.

Spacing
Fonts that fit all characters into equal horizontal spaces are called fixed-space fonts and can be easily recognized because the *i* or *m* fits into the same space. Many typewriters and most CRT text displays incorporate fixed spacing. Columnar schedules generated on computers should be created with fixed spacing to protect vertical column alignment. On the other hand, text that adjusts the horizontal space to accommodate the variable width of each character is called proportional spacing, which is eminently more readable. Better books and executive typewriters feature proportional spacing. Proportional spacing is certainly more handsome than fixed spacing, but you will find that editing proportional text on drawings should be limited to special situations, as few CAD systems can substitute a *w* in place of an *i* with

the same ease that can be achieved with typesetting.

In general, font size is measured from the top of capital letters to the bottom of letters with descenders, in units called points. There are 72 points per inch. Descenders are the parts of some characters—g, y, and q, for example—that descend below the baseline. Since descenders require additional vertical space, some CRT displays and less-expensive line printers display the lowercase character's descender resting on the baseline, so g becomes g. I find this a nuisance; you may find the legibility unacceptable.

Linespacing, Letterspacing, and Justification

The space between successive baselines—called **linespacing** or pitch—may also vary, producing a range of spacing from nearly nothing to lots of white space, in which very fine adjustments are possible. Horizontal space between characters is called **letterspacing**.

Text may be aligned at the margin(s). Typically, a typewriter aligns at the left margin, called left justification. Right justification aligns at the right margin. But if both margins are justified, the margins are simply called justified.

Font Creation

One final note on text entry. You will have the option of accepting many default standards, those defined by the software. When you begin using any CAD system, it's best to accept the default values. Creating your own font is often complex and tedious work. I suggest that you work with the default text fonts until you gain experience and confidence; then you can try your hand at creating a font.

MEASUREMENTS

With manual drawing, you measure length with a scale. Alternatively, you might calculate a length, an angle, or an area using geometry or trigonometry. Once a drawing is complete, you dimension to match what the drawings should measure, perhaps verifying your calculated dimensions with those you established earlier.

You're one-up in CAD drawing. If you entered the graphics data correctly, finding any measurement is all but foolproof: Data items are necessarily entered accurately. You need only snap to the correct locations and the system does the rest. Look at Figure 4.21. If you snap to the first line (or, in some cases, to both ends), the system will calculate the length and angle of the line and the X and Y coordinate distances.

4.21 *Measurement of distances can be achieved on any computer system easily and efficiently.*

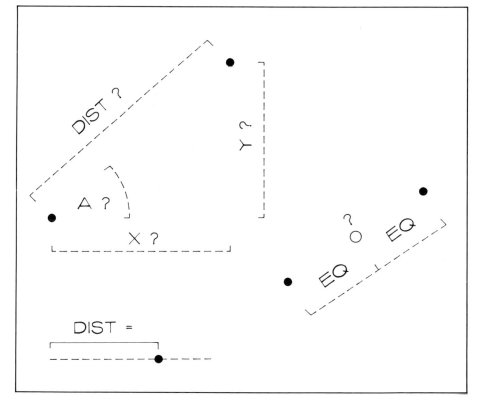

DIMENSIONS

The topics of dimensioning and accuracy have been covered in earlier chapters, but primarily in order to explain the relationship between drawing, accuracy, and units of measurement. Now we will take a look at how dimensions are placed on CAD drawings.

Dimensioning is as flexible as text annotation. You may accept the default standards or tailor most dimensioning formats to meet your specific needs. Look at Figure 4.22 for samples. The two common methods of dimensioning are linear for straight lines and radial for curves and angles. Dimension lines can be entered without dimension text; with dimension text automatically calculated and inserted; or with any dimension text you select.

Comments like "field verify" or "align with face of wall" can also be entered, but you'll never have to enter "n.t.s" (not to scale) again. If you draw with grid snap set to a convenient construction tolerance (partitions set to ¼ or ½ inch), the dimensions should total and close correctly. In this way, your work will always fall on a dimensional increment that prevents added dimensions from being rounded up or down incorrectly.

Dimensions may be measured successively, referenced from a baseline, or accumulated. Successive dimensions measure separate sections, creating a string of individual dimensions. A long string of successive dimensions is generally contained within an overall dimension. Referenced dimensions are

4.22 *Dimensioning may be automatic or manual or permit annotation. Cumulative dimensioning can also be helpful. Here are examples of the many options available.*

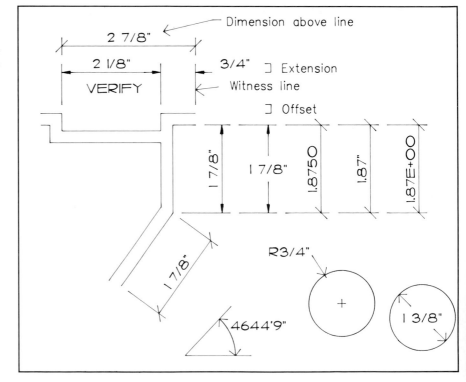

multiple dimensions, all measured from the same base point and shown on parallel dimension lines. Accumulated dimensions display increasing totals along a common dimension line, commencing at a benchmark location. Each total is indicated next to each arrowhead pointing away from the benchmark.

Dimensioning text may be placed above the dimension line, through the line, or below the line, and it may run parallel to the dimension line or parallel to the X axis. Typically, you can display feet and inch marks, although you may be able to modify this display. Fractions are shown horizontally (1/2), but some systems allow you to display them vertically ($\frac{1}{2}$). Text used in dimensions is set by the text command. Arrowheads need not look like the ones in your great-grandfather's drafting book. While similar ones are found on most CAD systems, you can generally design your own or use slashes or dots. You may also determine the size and offset of the extension lines and leader dimension lines.

Look again at Figure 2.2 for an example of how dimensioning works. Point P1 determines the starting location, while point P2 establishes the dimensioning direction—in this case, to the right and parallel with the X axis. Point P3 locates the dimension line, and point P4 determines the length of the first dimension. Successive points establish subsequent dimensions. The test of advanced dimensioning software is how the system displays a dimension when the text is longer than the dimension line: A dimension of 1' – 11¾", for example, will most likely be too long to fit between the extension lines on a ⅛-inch scale drawing, and you will be asked where you would like it placed.

5

Gaining Confidence

In Chapter 4, you learned the principles for drawing points, lines, figures, textures, and adding text—the foundations of drawing. You learned how to create on CAD what you already knew how to do manually. Now you're ready to expand your drawing skills by taking advantage of some computer graphics features: graphic control, figures, duplication, and entities.

DISPLAY CONTROL

You won't always want to view all the data on all levels of a drawing all the time. Although you may be working on the selected active work level, information that is not relevant clutters the drawing and slows redisplay. Therefore, you should limit what you see. You may view by levels or substitute faster-displaying (and consequently more-simplistic) graphics for more-complex graphics. You may highlight selected entities or be assisted by temporary reference graphics. For whatever reason, you will grow to appreciate the following features, all of which are designed to make your job easier and more productive by letting you control what you see on the screen.

Graphics Construction

Any permanent parts of your drawing, such as walls, doors, dimensions, notes, and schedules are called graphics construction. You may limit display without removing the graphics construction.

Level display

The most common means of controlling display is by limiting the number of currently displayed levels. For example, you display levels showing partitions, ceiling, HVAC, lighting, and structural plans in order to verify interference among parts above the ceiling while excluding furniture, dimensions, or power. Or you can compare ceiling fixture locations with furniture and power/telephone information. You can dimension partitions, or verify existing partition dimensions, far more easily by omitting the display of all levels except partitions, grids, core, and exterior walls. You can also speed redisplay by omitting text. Either exclude the text level or display text in the system's fast-font or line format.

As an alternative, some CAD systems allow you to load a drawing without displaying it. This handy technique reduces display time when you work on a large, complex drawing. You load the drawing, limit the viewing levels, and display only the desired ones. A similar technique works well with presentations: While you're viewing one drawing, you load a second one. When you're ready to view the waiting drawing, you *redisplay* the screen, thereby replacing the old image with the new one—it's a technique that makes redisplay appear faster than normal.

Suppressed definitions

Most display characteristics take immediate effect when defined (as do most other commands). Some display characteristics, however, can be defined but suppressed and selectively activated as required. For example, you can define a text font as 36-point Helvetica light. The drawing remembers that you want this font, but until activated, the screen displays text in the abbreviated and fast-displaying default font. Other parameters also require definition and activation: grids, grid snaps, color definitions, line-width control (double lines), filled wide lines (double lines filled with solid color), and filled polygons (polygon outlines filled with solid color). Because system capabilities vary, you should consult your user's manual to determine the characteristics of your CAD terminal.

Activation

When you define a display characteristic you can subsequently activate it individually or collectively. For example, you can define color 1 as red, assign red to level 5 now and level 7 later, or assign it to levels 8, 9, and 10. Or you might elect to activate the filled polygon display and neutralize (temporarily deactivate) grid snap and line width.

Temporary Graphics

Look at Figure 5.1. None of the graphics is a permanent part of the drawing. In fact, most will disappear when you redisplay the drawing. The most obvious is the cursor. Other examples include scale reference grids, construction points or lines, rubberbands (temporary lines or figures that stretch as you move the cursor), and temporary windows placed around graphics identified for zoom, edits, or bills of materials. You can display or mask temporary graphics to improve clarity or hasten redisplay.

Highlights

When you select an item on the drawing for editing or bill-of-material creation, you will want the computer to acknowledge your request. Highlighting is the computer's way of responding to you graphically. Each graphics segment will be augmented by a brighter, wider, or dashed line that duplicates the original image and confirms your intent. You will be returned to the original display when your current task is completed.

Identification with Colors

When you become comfortable with CAD, you'll discover the added value of using a color CRT to distinguish elements in a drawing. No longer only for show, color enables you to see separate elements without having to clear the screen.

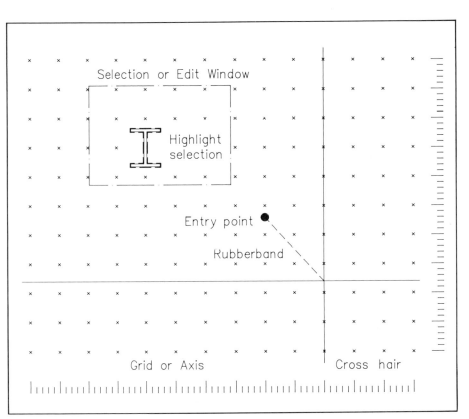

Look at Color Plate 2 (page 98). Any color can be assigned to any level. Consequently, more information can be superimposed and still be distinguished. You may find that some systems allow you to designate more than one color to a specific level.

Remember to think of a level as being like an overlay drafting sheet: Each CAD level contains a specific part of the composite drawing. Many CAD systems function quite effectively with only 16 levels. However, as the number of levels increases to 64, 256, and more, so does the

5.1 *Temporary graphics include grids, reference marks, cursors, rubberbands, highlights, and selection fences. These graphics display for assistance and reference only, and are not a permanent part of the drawing. Some may not reappear when the drawing is redisplayed.*

flexibility available to the designer. CAD systems that support 200 or more levels are capable of maintaining ten levels for each of the standard 16 construction sections designated by the Construction Specifications Institute (CSI) and widely adopted by the construction industry. For example, levels 80–89 are reserved for Section 8, Doors and Windows. If you look again at Color Plate 2, you'll see the CSI designations for 250 levels. At least one system is known to support 62,500 levels, far more than necessary.

In addition to separating information by level, you can designate information by pen. The number of pens you use is limited to the number of pens allowed by the plotter, typically eight, sometimes 16. Pen designation is most commonly used to plot information in a different color. Yet by specifying different pens for different lines, you can draw all lines on the CRT at the same default line width and still plot at different line thicknesses.

You can also either assign different pens to groupings of information on the same level or designate one pen for common information on different levels. Then you can display elements based on pens, rather than by levels. For example, all architectural information on levels 30 (CSI Section 3, Masonry), 80 (CSI Section 8, Doors and Windows), and 90 (CSI Section 9, Finishes) can be drawn with pen 1; structural information can be drawn with pen 2; mechanical, with pen 3, electrical, with pen 4; and so on.

Scratch Pad

If you want to sketch or create another drawing or figure, you have a built-in "roll of yellow tracing paper." Of course, you can save your current drawing, clear the screen, sketch, and then save the new drawing. But that's unnecessary. Simply move the display to the side and sketch. Save all the drawing or copy the segment you need. Alternatively, you can draw right over the existing finished drawing (you can do this, of course, by sketching on another level). I use levels 220–229 for sketching—they're my scratch-pad levels. When I've finished the drawing, I select the same level for editing and copy the sketch into my file. This eliminates loading and reloading the current drawing. And it's refreshing to sketch on a finished drawing, knowing that I can completely erase any doodles.

Drawing Status

While these CAD features give you considerable flexibility, so many choices may seem overwhelming at first. If you're experienced at drafting, you'll instinctively know when to use an F or 3H pencil to achieve the desired results on any medium. You confirm your pencil or pen selection by the "feel" and color of the line. You can also quickly see that you're on the correct level of acetate. With CAD, the dynamic status line keeps you abreast of where you are, giving you a running update of critical information.
Look-up status provides you with a reference library from which to find a multitude of other, less frequently needed status information.

Dynamic status

A very handy feature on many CAD systems is the continuously updated drawing status, which displays such information as drawing name, scale, last and current X, Y, Z coordinates, current active level, display and edit levels, grid and point snap criteria, and, perhaps, text, dimension, or crosshatch parameters. In a dynamic status display (see Figure 5.2), information is automatically revised as it changes. To preserve the largest possible area for drawing, you will find the dynamic status displayed along one of the boundaries, abbreviated to maximize content in the smallest possible space. One CAD system employs a unique means to identify the current active level: All other levels are displayed as dotted lines.

Look-up status

There's a host of information about your drawing stored in the computer. In addition to the items listed above, you can find everything from today's date and time to the name of the currently active figure, color definitions, dashed-line textures, and other parameters. When you initialize (see Chapter 3), values are stored as program **variables**. A variable called figure scale may contain the value 1/48 (the equivalent of $\frac{1}{4}'' = 1' - 0''$), or the variable active level may contain the phrase (string) "Interior Walls." (Variables and strings are covered in Chapter 13.)

You can retrieve these values with look-up status commands. The command to review the current font height might be, for example, ?FONTHT. As you become more experienced, you will come to appreciate the value of the look-up status commands.

COMMAND INTERRUPT CONTROL

It is not always possible to execute a complete command before entering the next command. You may start to draw a rectangle and discover that you need to **interrupt** the command in order to zoom out to see the other point, change the grid or point snap, or turn on another level before completing the rectangle. While your request is perfectly reasonable, not all software gives you this valuable flexibility. If you can't interrupt in this way, you'll have to plan better or erase the segment and start over.

FIGURES

A **figure** is any predrawn graphic that can be repeatedly drawn by inserting a copy of it anywhere on the drawing. You draw a figure once, and the computer draws it from then on. A figure can be as simple as a duplex outlet or as complex as a complete drawing. (By the way, don't confuse the use of the word *figure* in this context with figure illustrations in this book, as in "See Figure 5.3.")

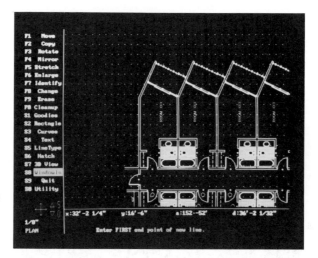

5.2 *Dynamic status display provides the user with up-to-date information on various drawing elements. Here you see the current cursor position displayed as an X and Y coordinate. Other status information can include drawing name, scale, layers in use, grid and snap tolerances. (Courtesy of Microtecture Corporation)*

Figure Creation

Nearly every CAD system includes a **figure library** of some sort. You should be able to create and modify figures with ease, adding to your figure library when needed. Gone is the time when you had to create a bit map (a map of lit and unlit pixels) or a **shape table** (a binary log of line vectors) in order to build your library. To create a figure, draw any graphics or text on the screen and save the drawing in your library. You can also create a figure by copying a portion of a drawing. If you create a figure on a specific level, that level information becomes a part of the figure, and the figure will be inserted on the same level as created. Most CAD systems allow you to defer level assignment by creating the figure on a neutral level (sometimes called level 0). The figure then assumes the level of the currently active level when it is inserted.

Every figure, like your drawing, has a reference point, its origin. You determine this origin when you create the figure and subsequently use the figure origin as the entry point during figure insertion.

You should be able to create figures at any scale and use them at any scale. If you cannot,

5.3 *A figure library contains standard drawings and symbols. Think of the library as the drawing templates. (Courtesy of T & W Systems, Inc., Huntington Beach, CA)*

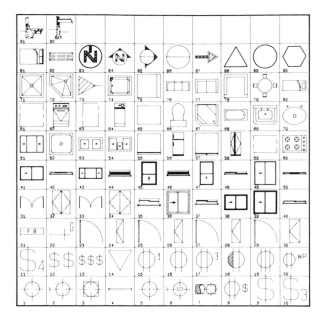

5.4 *Scaling each axis with different dimensions can be a powerful tool.*

you will need to create duplicate figures of the same shape at different sizes to be able to draw at different scales. Most figures used as symbols in a drawing are best created at full size and automatically scaled when inserted. Doors, on the other hand, can be created at a full scale size of 1″. When you insert the door, you dimension the width, for example, as 30 inches. First, the computer increases the size by 30, then divides the result by the drawing scale and places the door on the drawing at the correct size and scale. Other figures that have constant drafting sizes, such as section bubbles or north arrows, should not be scaled before insertion.

Some CAD systems designate a specific area in memory or in your drawing file for figures. If so, you may be limited in the number of figures you can have at any given time. If the figure library is integrated into the main drawing file, the library is unnecessary. As a matter of personal choice, I maintain a library of figures. You should develop a system that works best for you. See Figure 5.3 for a sample.

Modification

Naturally, it is useful to be able to duplicate figures in new locations, but figure insertion becomes a truly powerful tool when combined with the ability to modify scale, rotation angle, translation offset distances, and the hand of the drawing. You will recognize some old friends in Figure 2.7. You can draw any figure at any scale, increasing or decreasing scale by any fractional or decimal factor. Review the door example in Figure 2.7. You can also scale each axis. I had a lot of fun with the architectural man shown in Figure 5.4. He was originally featured as drawn on the left, but he seemed not quite right for renderings. I wanted him to be thinner and taller. He simultaneously grew in one direction and shrank in the other with the aid of differential scaling. The process is easy: You enter different scales for each axis (sometimes without intermediate calculations). Thus, my man lost about 40 pounds when scaled 140/180 in the X direction, and he grew 6 inches in the Y direction when scaled at 72/66. You apply the same technique to rescale a 72″ × 36″ desk to 60″ × 30″ or to change a workstation panel width from 30 inches to 36 inches (scale one direction 36/30 and the thickness remains 1/1).

You can rotate a figure by any angle, often about any axis. Multiple rotations may occur relative to the current rotation, just as with relative-point entry. Thus, you can rotate the door, say, 112° or 227° 36′ 43″ or Z − 45°, X − 35.27°, the isometric rotation (Figure 9.7).

You can offset (translate) the figure origin from the entry point in any combination of X, Y, or Z axes. For example, you might translate a door 60 inches along the X axis and 30 inches along the Y axis. When you insert the door, the center will translate to a new location (Figure 2.7).

I've yet to see the notation "Similar opposite hand" on a CAD drawing. First, draw one half of the figure and save a copy. Then select an axis about which to **mirror** an "opposite hand" image, or select a point about which to mirror "upside down and backwards." Reversing text in the figure is not always predictable. Your system may reverse the image without reversing the text, but more likely the text will either be reversed with the graphics or offset from its correct position. A sample of mirroring is also shown in Figure 2.7.

As with any major or unfamiliar edit, save your current work before proceeding. If you make a mistake or get something other than what you thought you should, you can reload your current drawing and try again. If you fail to save the drawing before attempting a major edit . . . well, you'll remember the next time.

Dragging and Insertion

You now know how to create and modify your favorite figure. Now place it into your drawing. First, select the active work level for figures created without level designation; then, select the figure you want to insert. You can insert the figure with or without previewing. If you forego preview, the figure will be inserted using the default rotation, scale, and translation. When you need to see (**preview**) how well the figure will fit, replace the cross-hair cursor with the **figure cursor**. As you move the cursor control, the figure **drags** across the screen until you align the **figure origin** with the proposed location. The display of the figure in the cursor may be abbreviated, but it is nonetheless a true replica of the figure.

You now modify the scale, rotation, translation, or hand. As you modify the figure, the figure cursor will update. Dragging lets you confirm the correctness of your figure before you insert it into the drawing. When you are satisfied that the figure is correct, insert it into the drawing using the figure insert key. As with other point function keys, you can snap the figure to a preset grid or to a given point on the drawing.

Centerline insertion

Drawing on CAD is electronic drafting, but getting CAD to calculate answers or to help you make decisions is CAD design. You determine what you want, and the computer determines how. If you decide to center a figure between two points, the computer will calculate the correct location (the **centerline**) and insert the figure (see Figure 5.5).

Multiple Insertions

You can insert as many figures as you wish by dragging them into new locations and inserting them. If, however, you want to insert several figures in a row (five workstations, for example) or in a pattern (columns or lights on a floor), there is an easier way. With CAD, you should never have to do the same thing twice. Determine how many items you want, and the

5.5 *Centerline insertion of drawing entities is inherent to most figure libraries, since most figures are created with centerline origins. Here the fixture is snapped midway between two points.*

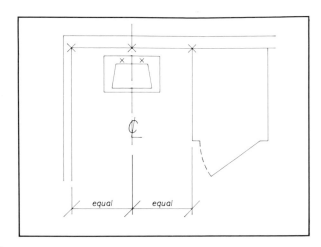

5.6 *Multiple insertions of the same figure equally spaced saves time.*

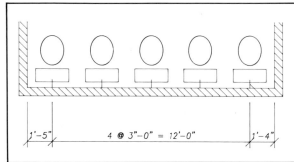

5.7 *Matrix insertion of drawing elements is performed easily and efficiently by any computer. Insert column 1 first, then instruct the computer to insert a matrix in two directions.*

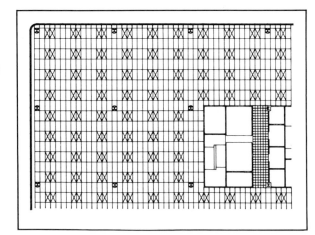

computer will draw the same figure repeatedly. As you gain skill, you will discover how powerful these commands are. You'll recognize the commands under the names *matrix*, *array*, or *multiple insert*. As with centerline insertion, the computer can divide the distance between two points into any number of equal spaces, and insert multiple figures (see Figure 5.6).

Loops

Computer loops repeat instructions. You duplicate a figure in multiple locations with a computer loop. A loop that inserts five waterclosets in a straight line, as in Figure 5.6, is a simple loop, whereas one that inserts, for example, three rows of columns, each containing six columns, is an example of a nested loop. The inner loop draws six columns and is contained (nested) within an outer loop that draws three rows: The outer loop simply repeats the inner loop three times. Figure 5.7 shows an example of looping in matrix insertion. (Loops are described in detail in Chapter 15.)

Circumnesting

Whereas nesting describes one activity being executed within another, **circumnesting** describes the successive building of one activity outside another. You begin with a small segment, duplicate and reinsert the small segment, and successively build a larger segment. As you repeat the process, the original small segment grows larger in increasing steps. For example, draw an office, as in Figure 5.8. Duplicate several until you have four or five offices (Figure 5.9). Copy the composite figure into the figure library and insert the copy (Figure 5.10). Mirror and reinsert the composite figure, containing all the offices along the bottom wall (Figure 5.11). Alternatively, rescale the figure ($X = 1$, $Y = -1$; or rotate X 180°), and drag the figure into place. Insert the figure. I'll come back in a moment to trim the ends of the walls.

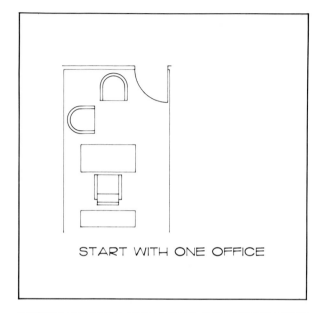

START WITH ONE OFFICE

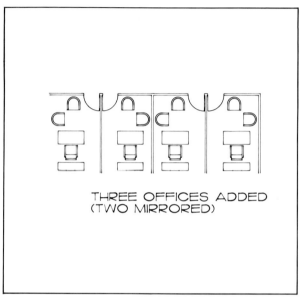

THREE OFFICES ADDED
(TWO MIRRORED)

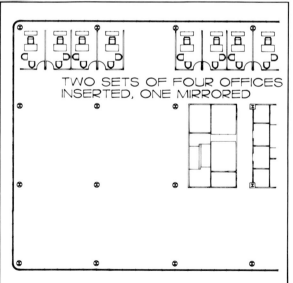

TWO SETS OF FOUR OFFICES
INSERTED, ONE MIRRORED

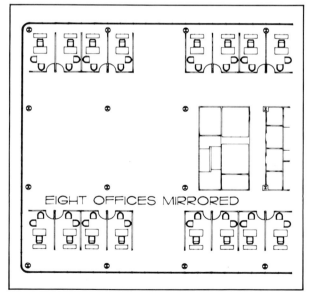

EIGHT OFFICES MIRRORED

5.8 *(far left) Circumnesting is a technique whereby one graphic entity duplicates into two, then duplicates again into four, then eight, and so on. Here's the start: one office with furniture.*

5.9 *(left) Circumnesting continues. Here one is mirrored then doubled.*

5.10 *(far left) Circumnesting moves on. Here the offices are inserted into the floor plan.*

5.11 *(left) Circumnesting progresses.*

5.12 *Almost-the-same duplication. Duplicate first then make minor modifications.*

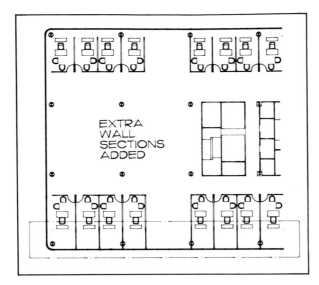

EXTRA
WALL
SECTIONS
ADDED

5.13 *Clean up the drawing.*

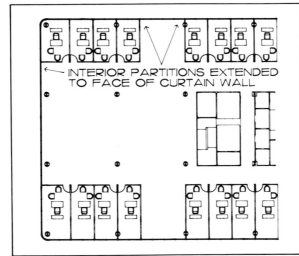

← INTERIOR PARTITIONS EXTENDED
TO FACE OF CURTAIN WALL

Subsets

With another technique called **subsets**, you draw and save independent but complete segments of a drawing: grid, dimensions, columns, partitions. When you are ready to plot, assemble all the subset components into a composite drawing. This popular technique allows you to work on smaller drawing segments, which load and display more quickly.

Almost the Same

What do you do when the intended duplicate is almost, but not exactly, the same? In many cases, proceed as though the two are the same, modifying the dissimilar portion. The trick, of course, is to modify minor portions, not major ones. Figures 5.12 and 5.13 demonstrate a typical situation. The vertical walls were stretched by placing a rough boundary, called a window, around one end to mark the section to be changed, snapping a cursor point at the end of the wall, and entering a new working point 30 inches in the direction to be stretched. The same technique can be used to reduce the length of all walls. The wall overlapped spandrels, convectors, dimensions, and column grids, all on levels other than the level containing the walls. By isolating the wall level for editing and surrounding all the wall segments to be shortened with a fence, the walls were simultaneously stretched by snapping onto one wall end and, in this instance, entering a relative point, $R + Y30$, on the keyboard. This edit is pure magic.

ENTITIES

By any name, an entity is a discrete and definable graphics item, usually a **graphics primitive**, such as a point, line, circle, polygon, text, or crosshatching. When you enter the command to draw a circle, the computer remembers not only the center and radius but the very fact that you're drawing a circle and not a rectangle or other entity. (The computer also remembers other fundamental information about the entity, such as the level on which the circle appears.) You can also insert a figure into a drawing that consists of many graphic items. And under some circumstances, a figure can be treated as a single entity even though it is a composite of many graphic entities. (Review Figure 2.5.)

Entity Selection
The principal value of an entity is its identifiability. Once you select any entity, you can change it, making entity selection one of the most powerful tools in CAD. You can select a graphics primitive, all entities within a window, or the last graphics entered. You continue the selection, adding and removing entities until the selection list is complete. Entities added will be highlighted, and entities removed will be "unhighlighted." Naturally, you can limit selection to specific levels.

You select a line, for example, by placing a point on or near the line, by pointing to its origin, or by enclosing one or several items in a window. In this manner, you select all or part of the items on the drawing, some of which might not even be visible.

You might select all walls on level 95, all dashed lines on levels 2 and 7, or the entire contents of the building core that includes walls, dashed lines, doors, and room finishes. Figure 5.14 shows some examples.

Manipulation
Once the entities are selected, you can edit the graphics and data with a variety of methods. Figures 2.7 and 2.9 will remind you of some of the manipulations possible. You can change, duplicate, or delete entities, and you can modify scale, rotation angle, and origin translation, mirror, change levels, and substitute figures. These modifications parallel those possible with

figures. (The balance are discussed in detail in Chapter 7.) In addition, you can extract intelligent data from the selected entities and sort, total, and display the data in some useful form. More about that will follow in the next chapter.

You learned earlier that you can identify and change graphics based on the level where the drawing data resides. Now you've discovered that you can select and change graphics based on the type of entity. In the next chapter, you'll learn how to identify and change graphics by the text associated with the graphics: intelligent drawings. Mastery of each means of selection and manipulation equips you with added drawing and editing tools.

5.14 *Entities may be isolated (or selected) for editing by isolating the graphic entity origin, selecting a random element, or by wrapping a fence around the entity. The ability to perform any or all of these will depend on the hardware or the database system.*

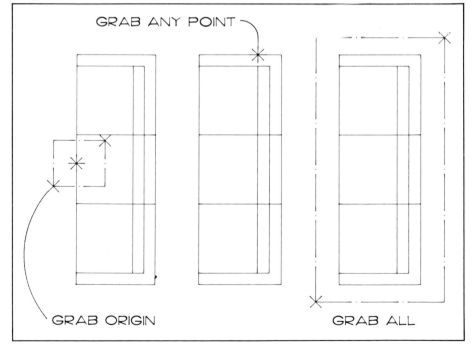

GRAB ANY POINT

GRAB ORIGIN

GRAB ALL

Part III

ADVANCED DRAWING

There is more to CAD than drawing. Chapter 6 introduces you to *computer-aided data management*, that is, intelligent graphics. You'll learn how to attach text or inventory information to graphics and manipulate the architectural database. Editing, which follows in Chapter 7, is in many ways thc most important chapter in the book. In Chapter 8, you'll discover *computer-aided design* and why the challenge of more software remains. Finally, in Chapter 9, three-dimensional drawing is covered in detail, from the mechanics to color rendering.

Intelligent Drawing: Associativity

You've learned that a line, a circle, or any picture with graphics elements can be represented by lighting the appropriate pixels. When you save the image, you record the state of each pixel on the CRT screen as "on" or "off" in what is called a pixel (or bit) map. There is no data stored with the pixel map, only a graphic representation. Consequently, no means of identifying any qualities about the graphics data exists. Graphics of this sort are called dumb (or unintelligent). Dumb graphics are typical of early CAD systems and paint-and-draw software found on many personal computers.

You've also learned that more-advanced computer graphics systems display a circle, for example, not by lighting pixels but by interpreting a graphic point as a circle, whose size is further defined by additional points representing the center, radius, diameter, or points on the circumference. As the drawing displays, the computer encounters the first point and translates the accompanying data (that is, circle) into a graphic image of the defined circle, drawing what you expect to see. When data items like a circle (or line or text) are integrated into any graphic element, the drawing becomes intelligent. How does the computer know to display a circle and not a rectangle? When you first create a circle, your instruction "draw a circle" is stored with the graphic point, and herein lies the core of **intelligent graphics**: interlocking graphics with text.

In Chapter 5, you were introduced to the precursor of intelligent graphics: entities. The text need not be limited to one item nor restricted in its content, as with entities. Any text may be used. For example, a line and quarter circle can be the graphic representation of a

door. Adding the door dimensions, frame, door material, and hardware specifications renders the figure quantitatively intelligent. This is called associativity because text is said to be associated with a graphics figure. An entity, for example, circle, is assigned one element of text by the computer. An associative figure is assigned as many fields of text as the user needs (see the door schedule above).

A CAD system without intelligent graphics is little more than an electronic pencil: computer-aided drawing. But CAD with intelligent graphics quantifies what you draw, making it a truly significant tool for the architect. In this chapter, you'll learn how to create intelligent graphics and build a graphics database. You can then extract and collate the data inventory into a suitable format. This is computer-aided data management. You'll discover, for example, how to create a door library, how to insert doors of correct size and swing with all the revised specifications, and how to generate a standard door schedule or a special schedule of only locksets and latchsets.

ASSOCIATIVITY AND THE GRAPHICS DATABASE

Since intelligent drawings contain graphics and text, you need to understand the foundation of the text behind the graphics: the computer database.

What Is a Database?

A **database** is a file of data arranged in a specific format. The precise organization makes it possible for you to rearrange the data. You can best understand one by examining the most universal example: the telephone directory, whose database contains the names, addresses, and phone numbers of all telephone subscribers. Standard white pages are developed from the complete subscriber list, organized and sorted alphabetically by last name. Yellow pages list selected business subscribers only and sort them first by business type, then by last name. Each uses the same database, selecting and sorting appropriate records that are then organized into each familiar directory.

Each subscriber in the database file comprises a complete **record**, which in turn consists of smaller units called **fields**. A field contains only one unit of data—in our example, the name, address, or phone number.

What Is a Graphics Database?
A **graphics database** combines a graphic figure with a database record. Together, they constitute an associative figure or group. When the figure is inserted into a drawing, both the graphics and the text with the figure become a part of the drawing. As you add associative figures—intelligent graphics—to your drawing, you also build a graphics database.

For example, the door library may contain many different door figures with different door sizes, hand, frame, and hardware combinations, but the graphics database for the project will contain only those doors you insert into a drawing. The door schedule is derived only from the doors in your drawing.

A graphics database is unique in two respects: It combines graphics and text to build the database; and it can be manipulated using a combination of graphic and text-editing techniques. And all databases, graphics included, have three processes in common. First, you create the database; then, you change or modify any of the data, as necessary; and finally, you extract the needed data.

CREATING A GRAPHICS DATABASE
The first step is to determine what data or information you want. Next, you design the components of the database so that you can extract the data you want easily from all the data you have. The telephone directory example demonstrates the principle: An alphabetical list of all the subscribers requires a field containing the last name so that the computer can sort alphabetically. In order to separate residential from business subscribers, an additional field is needed that identifies each.

You may want a furniture schedule that lists every piece in standard architectural format; or you may want a consolidated schedule of all furniture or a schedule by type and finish, or a schedule of locksets sorted by manufacturer and finish. To create a furniture database, you will need several figures and roughly 15 text fields to describe the attributes of each piece completely.

Text Components
Think of a file cabinet as a database devoted to the information about your furniture for a specific project. Think of each file folder as a record containing all the necessary information about every individual piece. Within each record, consider each element of data about every furniture item (such as quantity, type, size, and finish) to be a field. In the same way words join together to build sentences, fields join to build records. And just as sentences combine to build a complete story, records combine to construct a complete file (see Figure 6.1).

6.1 *Data fields and records form the basis for database manipulation. In this printout, each numbered line represents a discrete, complete record, which in turn consists of fields separated by a comma.*

```
 1.   DE7236,  WD,  OAK,  ,  ,  1111,  2500.00,  SAUDERS FURN,  MARSHALL,  100
 2.   DSL6072,  MET,  BEIG,  ,  ,  2221,  1250.00,  GILMORE FURN,  DIANN,  102
 3.   CE,  WD,  OAK,  LEA,  BRN,  3331,  1500.00,  GOSSETT CO,  MARSHALL,  100
 4.   DSR6072,  MET,  BEIG,  ,  ,  2222,  1250.00,  GILMORE FURN,  LINDA,  105
 5.   DSR6072,  MET,  BEIG,  ,  ,  2222,  1250.00,  GILMORE FURN,  GUINEVERE,  107
 6.   CP,  MET,  CH,  FAB,  SIENA,  4441,  400.00,  DUNCAN CHAIR,  DIANN,  102
 7.   CP,  MET,  CH,  FAB,  SIENA,  4441,  400.00,  DUNCAN CHAIR,  LINDA,  105
 8.   CP,  MET,  CH,  FAB,  SIENA,  4441,  400.00,  DUNCAN CHAIR,  GUINEVERE,107
 9.   SFL362128,  MET,  BEIG,  ,  ,  5551,  350.00,  REPASS CO,  DIANN,  102
10.   SC7218,  WD,  OAK,  ,  ,  1112,  1100.00,  SAUDERS FURN,  MARSHALL,  100
```

Fields

The field is the most basic, the smallest element of database information. A field can vary in length, but it can contain only one unit of information, which consists of either characters of text, called a **character string** (or **string**, for short), or numbers on which arithmetic calculations can be performed. Any number of fields can be used to complete the description of the item.

The sample furniture database consists of ten fields. Quantity is represented by a **numeric field**. Furniture type, finish, and room number should be **string fields** so that you can mix alphabetic and numeric designations like *A, 2, and A2.*

Records

A complete set of fields constitutes a record, a full description of any one piece: quantity, type, description, and size. For each piece added to the drawing, a new record is created.

You'll keep track of a database by organizing all the record fields in a specified order. You then enter data into each field in the same way as you fill out a standardized form or an address book: The furniture type, for example, will always be entered in the same field in the same location in each record.

Files

When you finish entering all the information (in fields) about each piece of furniture (in a record)

for a specific project, you will have a complete file. You've finished the design work, having entered records for each piece. Of course, you can add more furniture or change fields in any record at any time. Later, you can build a new file for another project using the same unique template.

Typically, all records are stored in a single computer file—the easiest file type to use and manage. As a database grows in size, the computer takes longer and longer to process data. Three elements may grow: the length of a field, the number of fields in a record, and/or the number of records in the file. There are no hard-and-fast rules to determine when processing time becomes excessive. Experience will guide you, although standard architectural door and finish schedules seldom exceed the limits. When many fields are used to form a complete description, some fields are infrequently used, but all must still be repeatedly processed, adding to the processing burden.

One way to reduce processing time is to reduce the contents of the file. Some efficiency can be achieved by subdividing a lengthy field into several shorter fields. But if you can't reduce the number of fields or records, you can subdivide a file into multiple files, selectively rejoining them as needed. For example, the furniture file contains one record for each item, each of which contains the fields described earlier. A companion finish file could contain additional fields for other finishes, catalog and fabric numbers.

The field containing the description is common to both files. It's called a **key field**. When the contents of one key field match those of a key field in another file, the two files can be **merged**. Only the furniture file is used to create a furniture schedule. But when creating a purchase schedule, the two files are merged to match furniture with fabrics.

Graphics Components

You've learned how text is organized into a database and how to create a figure. You can combine them to create a sample intelligent door, a figure with associative data. First, tell the computer that you are going to draw an intelligent figure; then, designate the graphic origin of the figure, as you learned how to do in Chapter 5. With the same CAD systems you may be able to assign a special associative name or number to the associative graphics. Next, draw the door and swing, and enter the text defining the door (for instance, type A, size, etc.) until all the door attributes are entered. Each item of text becomes a field (also called a **tag**), which may be entered large, small, or invisible, as you desire. After entering all the data in fields, tell the computer that you are finished adding text. The intelligent figure is complete, so save it.

Entering Intelligent Data

You create an intelligent figure only once, and you can insert the intelligent figure, like any other figure, as often as you like. If needed, you'll be prompted to enter any needed text.

Select an intelligent figure from your figure library, activate the figure cursor, and drag the figure into place. You may be aware that a figure contains text (and thus intelligence), but then you may not: The associative text may have been preset or may not display. All figure modifications apply: You can rotate, scale, or translate the intelligent figure upon insertion.

Typically, you enter door data as each figure is inserted into the drawing. You may be prompted to "Enter type of door: (A) flush, (B) folding, (C) glass . . . etc." If you answer A, the computer may store the word *flush* or the letter A in the field designated *door type*. Each succeeding field is answered in turn.

Predefined data

If you are working with figures that contain specific data that won't change, all of the intelligence can be predefined when the figure is created. When you insert the intelligent figure into your drawing, the associative data is automatically added to the drawing. Your job is made easier because you need to remember only one item of information.

Variable data

On the other hand, you can work with generic figures that prompt you to enter specific information. You may want to draw the same figure, substituting different values in the same fields. For example, you might substitute *wood* for *metal* in the field for door materials. A prompt will ask you to select W or M before storing the data with the figure in the drawing. There will be times when you want the ease of entering predefined data and other times when you want the flexibility of entering different data for a similar figure. Door insertion lends itself to a much appreciated auxiliary feature. When prompted to enter the width, the computer scales the door figure to the correct size and records the width in the proper field. In this way, only one door figure, rather than many, needs to be stored in the figure library.

In some applications, such as space planning, you can enter text independently from graphics. Fundamental forecasting reports are completely alphanumeric, and the data can be entered by anyone reasonably skilled with a keyboard, sometimes on a nongraphics terminal, which saves the graphics terminal for graphics. The alphanumeric data is later merged with affinity, stack, and block graphics.

CHANGING INTELLIGENT GRAPHICS

The heart of a database system is not the creation of the original entry but the ability to change the data after it has been entered. You can change (edit) the graphics in a figure or the text data associated with the figure. You can change a single-leaf door to a double-leaf door, revising the graphics but not the associative data. Or you can change the field description from an unrated door to a ¾-hour fire door, revising the associative data but not the door figure.

Selection

You must first decide which doors you want to change. You select the doors graphically by enclosing the part you want within a graphic window, or you select the doors by entering text that matches the contents of any field. In many instances, you can build a comprehensive selection list by adding and subtracting graphics. The CRT highlights the selected graphics, either by superimposing a secondary, duplicate image or by changing the color of the selected graphics. Deleting from the selection list removes the highlighting. Here's a sampling of methods used to identify intelligent graphics.

Graphic selection

The most direct way to build a selection list is by selecting visible graphics information. You could easily identify all the doors. The computer selects those records found within a window that belong to a specific file. Perhaps you've identified all the doors (the file) on the west side of the fifth floor (only those records), omitting other intelligent graphics, including furniture, power outlets, light fixtures, walls, and the like.

Intelligent graphics may be individually or collectively selected. To select one associative figure graphically, center the cross hairs on or near the graphics (some CAD systems let you search any point, while others require that you select the origin). In a global graphic selection, you can enclose as many associative figures as you want within one or several temporary selection windows. Every item you enclose is selected. Some CAD systems allow you to select the entire visible display, others the entire current drawing, regardless of the portion displayed. You can build a selection list by adding or deleting intelligent graphics as required.

Text selection

You can also select intelligent graphics by the information contained in any specific single or multiple field(s). You can identify doors in general or, for example, all type A1 doors, $3'-0'' \times 7'-0'' \times 1\frac{3}{4}''$. Thus, your selection can range from very general to very discrete. Being able to match the contents of any field to any text string increases the power of selection dramatically.

Text fields

Since each field of text stores specific text data and the sequence is fixed, you select text by the contents of a specific field. If field 3, for example, contains the manufacturer's name, you can identify all the door records containing the name ABC Company by matching the contents of field 3 of all records with that name. That is how the computer finds all the ABC Company records saved with each figure. It's a repetitive, but precise, procedure called **processing**— accurately performed by a computer, but boring and subject to error for humans.

Wild-card search

When you want to select *ABC* and *AFC* or *ABC*, *Anderson*, and *Archive*, you can either search for each of them individually or search for all of them using a **wild-card search**, which designates which characters are the same and which are different. A single wild-card character can substitute for one or more characters. In addition, multiple wild cards can be used.

The name *wild-card search* comes from card games that permit a card to substitute for any card you wish, as in "jokers are wild." Wild-card characters are usually those that are infrequently used in text, such as % (normally, spelled out), or are uncommon combinations, such as *$**. (There are ways to use wild-card characters literally, if you must.)

In a single-character search, you substitute one wild card for one character. Thus, to select *ABC*, *AFC*, and *ANC*, you can search for *A%C*. Your search will find any combination starting with *A*, ending with *C*, and containing any single character in between. *AAC*, *ABC*, *ADC*, *A7C*, and *A.C* would be found, but *ACB* would not. In another example, the combination "=7" finds any numeric field equal to 7. With multiple substitution, that is, where a wild card can substitute for one or more characters—the entry *A*C* will find *ABC*, *AFC*, and *American C*. The entry *A*C** will find, in addition to those combinations, *American Confectionary* and *AmerkanC onfectneeery*. This wild card performs the most global search of all.

Another powerful wild card searches for a multiple range of possibilities. The wild card *<A–D>+* will find any word beginning with the capital letters *A*, *B*, *C*, or *D*, while *<!A–D>+* will find any word beginning with a letter other than *A*, *B*, *C*, or *D*. A wild card like *>K or <Q* will find matches after *K* or before *Q*, such as *Manhattan*.

Numeric searches are fundamentally different from string searches: A numeric search looks for a value which is less than, equal or unequal to, or more than the number to be matched. Consequently, *>199* finds all values larger than 199 in a numeric wild-card search; *<>199*, all values unequal to 199; and *=>199*, all values equal to or larger than 199.

Using a search-and-replace wild card, the command */3/b* replaces all *3*s with *b*'s, and */$/ CAD* inserts the word *CAD* at the beginning of each line of a file. Wild-card searches like this are used for global file editing by advanced programmers and demonstrate the flexibility of search-and-replace wild cards. With a little practice, wild cards can be extremely powerful and helpful.

Editing

Graphics editing is covered in detail in Chapter 7, but let's look at some ways you can edit intelligent graphics. Just as graphics are changed using the graphics editor, text displayed in graphics can be changed using text editing within the graphics editor. Because intelligent drawings combine both graphics and text, either of which may not be visible, changing intelligent graphics requires safeguards to prevent an inadvertent change or deletion of one and not the other. Typically, a separate set of commands, different from both graphics and text-editing commands, are used to change intelligent graphics.

Changing graphics

Intelligent graphics are treated like graphics entities. Once you've selected an intelligent figure, you can change, edit, modify the entire intelligent figure, erase it (**delete**, in computerese), duplicate the same intelligent graphics in other locations, or copy any one or several intelligent graphics into a new graphics file in your figure library. You might copy all the furniture from one office into a composite file or substitute a right-hand door for a left-hand reverse-bevel door.

You can change the line texture or the level on which the figure resides. And of course, you can rotate, rescale, or translate the intelligent graphics. The real benefit comes from the ease of selection. Take care, however, that you don't remove the graphic image but unwittingly retain the intelligence.

Changing text

Changing text means changing the contents of a text field. You can change a passage lockset to a storeroom lockset simply by substituting one string of text (*storeroom*) for another (*passage*), or you can delete text altogether. (Actually, you change the text to a field with nothing in it, called a **null field**.)

EXTRACTING RESULTS YOU CAN USE

The objective of creating a graphics database is to extract tabulated results of the data you've entered. By now, the power of a graphics database—its flexibility and its usefulness in creating a bill of materials of any drawing element—should be apparent. This section explains how to organize, collate, and manipulate the data you have created and edited into a workable bill of materials.

When you have finished selecting associative graphics, the computer will extract all the associated data from those specific intelligent figures and place the data in a newly created temporary working file. Only the data from the selected graphics will be included. In this state, the data is simply a sequential list of each record.

Organizing Data

The first step is to organize the raw data into a suitable form. In the previous example of the telephone directory, the subscriber names were reorganized before the yellow pages were created. Alphabetizing, for example, rearranges data in "ascending" order. Understanding how sorting works will help you to develop and organize your own bills of materials. Look at Figure 6.2. Don't be deceived by its simplicity. You rearrange the fields as needed, discarding unneeded ones, and total the columns. In this furniture schedule, for example, the price is retained but repositioned to follow the manufacturer in the last field (the last report column).

Sorting

Sorting rearranges data. As you create a floor plan, you add furniture, draw walls and windows, then back to furniture and walls, and so on. As you work, records are added,

6.2 *Select and arrange fields in the desired format. Here, the data in Figure 6.1 has been sorted into a new format.*

```
 3.   CE, WD, 3331, OAK, LEA, BRN, GOSSETT CO. 1500.00
 6.   CP, 4441, MET, CH, FAB, SIENA, DUNCAN CHAIR, 400.00
 7.   CP, 4441, MET, CH, FAB, SIENA, DUNCAN CHAIR, 400.00
 8.   CP, 4441, MET, CH, FAB, SIENA, DUNCAN CHAIR, 400.00
 1.   DE7236, 1111, WD, OAK, , ,SAUDERS FURN, 2500.00
 2.   DSL6072, 2221, MET, BEIG, , ,GILMORE FURN, 1250.00
 4.   DSR6072, 2222, MET, BEIG, , ,GILMORE FURN, 1250.00
 5.   DSR6072, 2222, MET, BEIG, , ,GILMORE FURN, 1250.00
10.   SC7218, 1112, WD, OAK, , ,SAUDERS FURN, 1100.00
 9.   SFL362128, 5551, MET, BEIG, , ,REPASS CO, 350.00
```

changed, and deleted, without regard for any order. Sorting rearranges records into a new order according to the contents of a specific field. When you sort by furniture type, for example, all the chairs are grouped together, all the desks together, and so on. When you sort fields according to finish, then the walnut and metal furniture are grouped separately. And yes, you can nest sorts. For example, you can sort finishes within door type: glass doors subdivided into aluminum, steel, or wood, for example.

You can sort a door schedule by arranging the list by door numbers in ascending order (and then verifying omitted or duplicated numbers). Or you can sort by hardware manufacturer or by door size. Each sort can be varied to suit your particular needs. Some CAD systems allow you to renumber numeric fields, a great tool for closing gaps, eliminating duplicates, and shoehorning in additions.

Fields are sorted in ascending or descending order. Sorting in ascending order is an obvious process with numbers, but it is less obvious with letters and other characters. Computers remember each keyboard entry as a number, not as a letter or other character. When you enter the letter *A*, for example, the computer actually remembers the number 65, rather than *A*. When you ask the computer to print the letter *A*, it translates the stored number 65 back into the letter *A*. The computer has been programmed so that a specific number is assigned to every usable keypress or keypress combination.

Fortunately, nearly everyone uses the standard set of numbers set forth in the American Standard Code for Information Interchange, or **ASCII** (pronounced *ask-ee*), for short. Each upper- and lower-case letter, each number, symbol, punctuation mark, and control key (special function key) is assigned a number ranging from 1 to 128. For example, the ASCII

code for the character *2* is 50, as opposed to the arithmetic value of 2, while the codes for the letters *A* and *a* are 65 and 97, respectively. You cannot substitute a lower case *l* (ASCII code 108) for the number *1* (ASCII code 49), nor the letter *O* (ASCII code 79) for the number *0* (ASCII code 48), because the computer interprets each differently, even though they are similar visually.

The following examples sort doors in ascending order, first by door number, then by type, and finally by manufacturer. The first sample sorts by the lowest number, 001. The balance is not considered:

Number	Type	Manufacturer
001	A	XYZ
002	C	ABC
003	B	ABC

The next sample nests. The numbers 004 match, but *A* precedes *B* in the second field (the first nest). In the last sort, *A* precedes *a*, because capitals come first (the second nest).

004	A	ABC
004	B	ABC
004	B	abc

Finally, numbers precede the alphabet (*004* precedes *A04*):

004	b	z01
A04	A	AAA

Counting and arithmetic operations

A database should tell you both *what* it contains and *how many*. You can summarize multiple identical records into one line, summing the total quantity of items (Figure 6.3). In turn, you can obtain a grand total of all records (Figure 6.4). But the most powerful arithmetic feature is the ability to calculate a number from two existing fields and place the answer in a new field. Price extensions are typical: 3 posture

6.3 *Summarizing records condensed the working file by combining records with like fields.*

```
1.   1.  CE,  WD,  3331,  OAK,  LEA,  BRN,  GOSSETT CO,  1500.00
2.   3.  CP,  4441,  MET,  CH,  FAB,  SIENA,  DUNCAN CHAIR,  400.00
3.   1,  DE7236,  1111,  WD,  OAK,  ,  ,SAUDERS FURN,  2500.00
4.   1,  DSL6072,  2221,  MET,  BEIG,  ,  ,GILMORE FURN,  1250.00
5.   2,  DSR6072,  2222,  MET,  BEIG,  ,  ,GILMORE FURN,  1250.00
6.   1,  SC7218,  1112,  WD,  OAK,  ,  ,SAUDERS FURN,  1100.00
7.   1,  SFL362128,  5551,  MET,  BEIG,  ,  ,REPASS CO,  350.00
```

6.4 *Field totals can be obtained from any common field across all records. Here is the total of all quantities.*

```
1.   1.  CE,  WD,  3331,  OAK,  LEA,  BRN,  GOSSETT CO,  1500.00,  1500.00
2.   3.  CP,  4441,  MET,  CH,  FAB,  SIENA,  DUNCAN CHAIR,  400.00,  1200.00
3.   1,  DE7236,  1111,  WD,  OAK,  ,  ,SAUDERS FURN,  2500.00,  2500.00
4.   1,  DSL6072,  2221,  MET,  BEIG,  ,  ,GILMORE FURN,  1250.00,  1250.00
5.   2,  DSR6072,  2222,  MET,  BEIG,  ,  ,GILMORE FURN,  1250.00,  2500.00
6.   1,  SC7218,  1112,  WD,  OAK,  ,  ,SAUDERS FURN,  1100.00,  1100.00
7.   1,  SFL362128,  5551,  MET,  BEIG,  ,  ,REPASS CO,  350.00,  350.00
    10.  TOTAL,  10400.00
```

chairs @ $400 = $1200. Look again at Figure 6.4. You'll find your computer capable of calculating any business mathematics problem or a beam deflection with ease.

Merging

File merging joins the contents of two files to create a new file. You can append one file to the end of another, called **concatenation**, or side by side, called **lamination**. The entire contents of each successive line of one file is laminated to the end of each correspondingly numbered line of the second file. But laminating files of different lengths can produce unwanted results.

Field merging, however, is selective. Records of two partner files are merged by matching the contents of a field common to each file, called a key field. When a match occurs, the contents of each record are combined into a new record, producing a new file. For the architect or designer, this selective field merging is useful in generating typical schedules. Figure 6.5 shows two **partner files** prior to merging, and Figure 6.6

shows the new file after merging. Notice that the file lengths differ.

For example, let's assume that the door schedule information resides in a file consisting of 27 doors, each containing the hardware group in a specific field. Assume 8 doors in hardware group A, 9 in group B, and 10 in group C. A separate original hardware file contains one listing for each of the three hardware groups, along with information about such related items as locksets, hinges, and closers.

The hardware group (found in the records of both files) is the key field, the field used for matching. To generate a hardware schedule, a window is drawn around the selected doors, and the computer merges the door file and the hardware file by matching each hardware group key field: The door number and hardware group from the door file join with the corresponding hardware group details in the hardware file. Each of the 27 doors is matched with corresponding hardware: Eight doors will be matched with hardware group A details.

```
1.    1, CE, WD, 3331, OAK, LEA, BRN, GOSSETT CO, 1500.00
2.    3, CP, 4441, MET, CH, FAB, SIENA, DUNCAN CHAIR, 400.00
3.    1, DE7236, 1111, WD, OAK, , ,SAUDERS FURN, 2500.00
4.    1, DSL6072, 2221, MET, BEIG, , ,GILMORE FURN, 1250.00
5.    2, DSR6072, 2222, MET, BEIG, , ,GILMORE FURN, 1250.00
6.    1, SC7218, 1112, WD, OAK, , ,SAUDERS FURN, 1100.00
7.    1, SFL362128, 5551, MET, BEIG, , ,REPASS CO, 350.00

1.    DUNCAN CHAIR, 4441, POSTURE CHAIR, SWIVEL, CAT # A0000
2.    GILMORE FURN, 2221, DESK LEFT 42" RETURN 26" HIGH, CAT # B0000
3.    GILMORE FURN, 2222, DESK RIGH 42" RETURN 30" HIGH, CAT # B0001
4.    GOSSETT CO, 3331, EXEC CHAIR, SWIVEL TILT, CAT # C0000
5.    GOSSETT CO, 3332, LOUNGE CHAIR, GLIDES, CAT # C0001
6.    REPASS CO, 5551, 36" LATERAL FILE, 2 DRAWER, CAT # D0000
7.    SAUNDERS FURN, 1111, EXEC DESK, 2 PEDISTAL, CAT # E0000
8.    SAUNDERS FURN, 1112, 72" EXEC CREDENZA, CENTER DRS, CAT # E0001
```

6.5 *Partner files are used when you want to merge two files. Both files must contain a common field in order to merge the two records.*

6.6 *The completed merge.*

```
1.    1, CE, 3331, EXEC CHAIR, WD, OAK, LEA, BRN, GOSSETT CO, CAT # C0000
2.    3, CP, 4441, POSTURE CHAIR, MET, CH, DUNCAN CHAIR, CAT # A0000
3.    1, DE7236, 1111, EXEC DESK, WD, OAK, , ,SAUDERS FURN, CAT # E0000
4.    1, DSL6072, 2221, DESK LEFT 42" RETURN, MET, BEIG, , ,GILMORE FURN, CAT #B0000
5.    2, DSR6072, 2222, DESK RIGHT 42" RETURN, MET, BEIG, , ,GILMORE FURN, CAT #B0001
6.    1, SC7218, 1112, 72" EXEC CREDENZA, WD, OAK, , ,SAUDERS FURN, CAT #E0001
7.    1, SFL362128, 5551, 36" LATERAL FILE, MET, BEIG, , ,REPASS CO, CAT # D0000
```

Seeing the Results

All that remains is to arrange the data in a format that can be printed or integrated into your drawing. All the data still resides in a temporary file, in which each line represents a record containing the selected fields. Each column in the report constitutes a similar field.

Preparing a report

Your user's manual will show you how to preview the data in the **report editor**. First, decide how you want to arrange the report. For example, place the door type in the first column and the door number in the second. Once you've settled on the column order (field order), you can perform mathematical calculations on the contents of any column—for example, adding the number of doors (27, in this case). When the report prints, the total will appear at the bottom. Under some circumstances, you can summarize similar records, automatically tabulating the total and placing the quantity in a new column (field) of the report. An example is the hardware schedule summary: 8 in hardware group A, 9 in group B, and 10 in group C. Next, determine the column width and display justification: aligned right or left or centered. Text is usually justified left; numbers, right. Care should be taken when mixing integers with decimals in the same column to insure that the decimal point aligns vertically; otherwise, the column becomes difficult to read.

Printing a report on a line printer

Line printers sold in the United States are configured to print ten characters per inch—85 characters on standard 8½-inch-wide paper and 132 characters on "wide" (14⅞-inch) paper—and six lines per inch vertically. Printers vary considerably in printout capability, but those that generate 16.8 characters per inch allow you to compress a 132-character report onto a 8½-inch-wide sheet, thereby allowing you to interleaf your wide computer printout directly with specifications.

Chances are, your software will have some standard report layouts when you first generate any of these schedules. In time, however, you will want to modify the standard reports or create new ones. Before you embark on any major reports, verify that all the column widths of your reports will accommodate the respective field lengths of the data you enter. It is very disconcerting to discover that the catalog number you entered in a field is too long to fit. Worst of all, the computer may simply truncate the right end of the field, display the contents shortened, and not even beep at you.

Each sheet of a report consists of a head, body, and sometimes a foot. The head contains the title and column heads; the body contains the sorted data; and the foot contains footnotes or other supporting information. The head and foot are duplicated on each page of the report. Figure 6.7 shows a formatted report ready for printing. Also, you can print the drawing on a line printer or on your drawing—ideal for door and finish schedules.

Sample reports

Look at Figures 6.8–6.10. Each sample shows a report generated with typical graphics databases, printed on different output devices. Computers fundamentally calculate numbers or process data. Scientists calculate numerical equations. Design professionals and business people process data. Database management, whether graphic or nongraphic, is the backbone of data processing. While the concepts are not hard to comprehend nor the results difficult to appreciate, imaginative understanding is essential in order to achieve advanced skills with CAD. For those of you are who experienced architects, engineers, designers, or planners—but not experienced in computers—this chapter has introduced you to new conceptual material: the computer database.

Let's now turn to editing—perhaps, along with intelligent drawing—the richest tool of CAD.

6.7 *A formatted report is easier to read. Field separators have been omitted, column widths assigned, and fields justified left, center, or right to improve readability.*

6.8 (opposite page) *This door schedule is automatically created by enclosing the selected doors within a fence. (Courtesy of Microtecture Corporation)*

```
FURNITURE REPORT
----------------

ITEM  QUANTITY  GENERIC   NUMBER  DESCRIPTION    FRAME  FIN  INSET  FIN  MANUFACTURER   CATALOG
----  --------  -------   ------  -----------    -----  ---  -----  ---  ------------   -------

  1.        1   CE          3331  EXEC CHAIR     WD     OAK  LEA    BRN  GOSSETT CO     C0000
  2.        3   CP          4441  POSTURE CHAIR  MET    CH                DUNCAN CHAIR   A0000
  3.        1   DE7236      1111  EXEC DESK      WD     OAK               SAUDERS FURN   E0000
  4.        1   DSL6072     2221  DESK LEFT 42"  MET    BEI               GILMORE FURN   B0000
  5.        2   DSR6072     2222  DESK RIGHT 42  MET    BEI               GILMORE FURN   B0001
  6.        1   SC7218      1112  72" EXEC CRED  WD     OAK               SAUDERS FURN   E0001
  7.        1   SFL362128   5551  36" LATERAL F  MET    BEIG              REPASS CO      D0000
        --------
       10   TOTAL
```

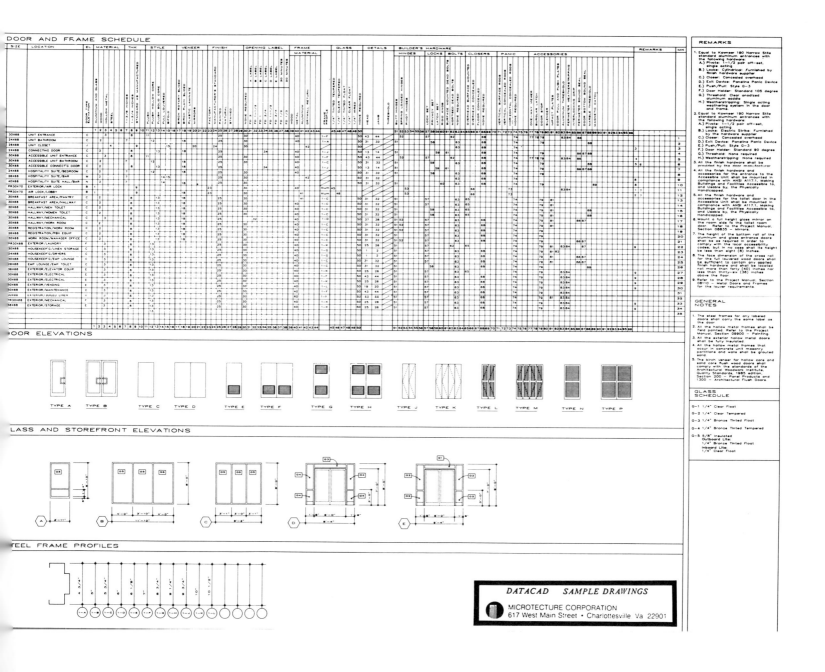

DOOR AND FRAME SCHEDULE

DOOR ELEVATIONS

GLASS AND STOREFRONT ELEVATIONS

STEEL FRAME PROFILES

DATACAD   SAMPLE DRAWINGS

MICROTECTURE CORPORATION
617 West Main Street • Charlottesville Va 22901

6.9 *Workstation standards with component inventories are ideal applications for the CAD workstation. This figure shows a sample layout of the workstation with the components inventoried at the bottom. The user can change the manufacturer, finishes, and costs simply by merging different files. (Courtesy of Glave Newman Anderson Ford Scribner PC, Architects)*

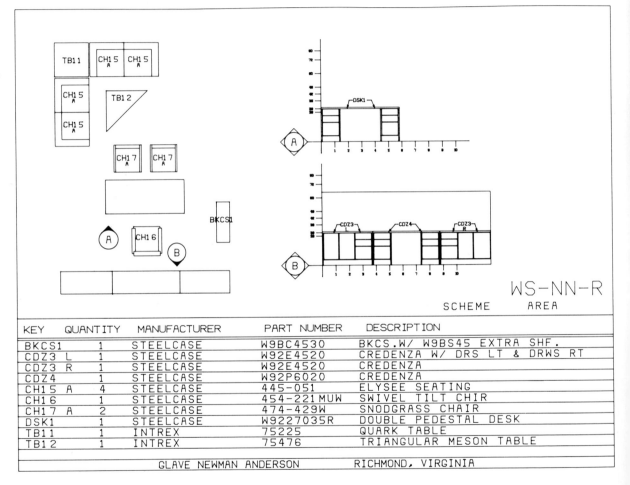

KEY	QUANTITY	MANUFACTURER	PART NUMBER	DESCRIPTION
BKCS1	1	STEELCASE	W9BC4530	BKCS.W/ W9BS45 EXTRA SHF.
CDZ3 L	1	STEELCASE	W92E4520	CREDENZA W/ DRS LT & DRWS RT
CDZ3 R	1	STEELCASE	W92E4520	CREDENZA
CDZ4	1	STEELCASE	W92P6020	CREDENZA
CH15 A	4	STEELCASE	445-051	ELYSEE SEATING
CH16	1	STEELCASE	454-221 MUW	SWIVEL TILT CHIR
CH17 A	2	STEELCASE	474-429W	SNODGRASS CHAIR
DSK1	1	STEELCASE	W9227035R	DOUBLE PEDESTAL DESK
TB11	1	INTREX	75225	QUARK TABLE
TB12	1	INTREX	75476	TRIANGULAR MESON TABLE

GLAVE NEWMAN ANDERSON   RICHMOND, VIRGINIA

```
Resource Dynamics Inc                                    Page # 4
RD1/PC:  FORECAST - Main Forecast Report with All Details   Jul 25 1986
               For OID's matching:  CHRM-BANK-*


Project:  worl



            DID:  CHRM-BANK-CPTL-PORT-
Organization Name:  portfolio


Comment:
```

Resource Type: Personnel				Resource Counts						Space Requirements					
Code	Title	Std	SF	Per 1	Per 2	Per 3	Per 4	Per 5	Per 6	Per 1	Per 2	Per 3	Per 4	Per 5	Per 6
PT	Partner	A	300	2.0	2.0	2.5	3.1	3.1	4.2	600	600	750	938	938	1266
SVP	Sr Vice President	C	200	2.0	2.0	2.5	3.1	3.1	4.2	400	400	500	625	625	844
VP	Vice President	D	150	2.0	2.0	2.5	3.1	3.1	4.2	300	300	375	469	469	633
ASST	Assistant	G	40	10.0	10.0	12.5	15.6	15.6	21.1	400	400	500	625	625	844
Personnel Totals				16.0	16.0	20.0	25.0	25.0	33.7	1700	1700	2125	2656	2656	3586

Resource Type: Equipment				Resource Counts						Space Requirements					
Code	Title	Std	SF	Per 1	Per 2	Per 3	Per 4	Per 5	Per 6	Per 1	Per 2	Per 3	Per 4	Per 5	Per 6
CCL	Coat Closet		15	2.0	2.0	2.5	3.1	3.1	4.2	30	30	38	47	47	63
LF5	Lateral File 5drw		18	2.0	2.0	2.5	3.1	3.1	4.2	36	36	45	56	56	76
LF2	Lateral File 2dwr		18	10.0	10.0	12.5	15.6	15.6	21.1	180	180	225	281	281	380
CP	Copy Machine		50	2.0	2.0	2.5	3.1	3.1	4.2	100	100	125	156	156	211
Equipment Totals										346	346	432	541	541	730

Resource Type: Support Space				Resource Counts						Space Requirements					
Code	Title	Std	SF	Per 1	Per 2	Per 3	Per 4	Per 5	Per 6	Per 1	Per 2	Per 3	Per 4	Per 5	Per 6
CF6	Conference Room 6		150	2.0	2.0	2.5	3.1	3.1	4.2	300	300	375	470	470	633
CF5	Conference Room 5		300	1.0	1.0	1.3	1.6	1.6	2.1	300	300	375	469	469	633
Support Space Totals										600	600	750	938	938	1266

| Totals | | | | | | | | | | 2646 | 2646 | 3307 | 4135 | 4135 | 5582 |

```
INTER-ORGANIZATIONAL CIRCULATION:   15%          397   397   496   620   620   837
INTRA-ORGANIZATIONAL CIRCULATION:   10%          265   265   331   414   414   558
-----------------------------------------------------------------------------------
Totals for CHRM-BANK-CPTL-PORT-        16.0 16.0 20.0 25.0 25.0 33.7  3308 3308 4134 5169 5169 6977
```

6.10 *Space programming is a natural CAD partner. Here is a sample forecast report detailing staff growth, space standards, and space requirements over the projected time periods. (Courtesy of Resource Dynamics, Inc.)*

7

Graphics Editing

Editing skills are more important than drawing skills. Anyone can learn how to draw on a CAD system, but skilled editing separates the expert from the novice.

We all change our minds, sometimes to accommodate the client, sometimes to improve the design, sometimes to correct a mistake, but often to refine our judgment. Each step of the decision process creates new options, clarifies directions, and sharpens goals. Since design is a process, design changes may be viewed not so much as revisions but as developments and refinements leading to a final decision.

As you gain skill in editing, you can simulate options by creating and saving alternative schemes. Then you load the scheme again, edit it, and save the revision. But how do you accommodate change, profitability and control the schedule? All work involves some change, which can normally be absorbed, but major changes can be catastrophic. CAD is the best available tool to manage changes.

I've grown so accustomed to CAD editing that I tend to forget just how powerful this feature really is. Skilled use of it can save your profit, time, and clients. Because editing is so easy, though, it's all too tempting to change documents indiscriminately. Be careful: Editing should not be abused.

EDITING IS MORE THAN ERASING
Don't confuse editing with erasing. Erasing removes data, but editing lets you copy, duplicate, move, and substitute drawing and text data in addition to erasing what you've drawn. With CAD editing, you temporarily remove the selected data, verify your decision, and then delete or revise. It's a process you can't easily duplicate manually.

Erasing removes data completely, although you *may* be able to recover it if you have a change of heart. **Changing** modifies the original graphics, most often the scale, line texture, or angular orientation. You can move part of a drawing to another location (translation), stretch, shrink, or move data from one level to another.

Duplicating lifts a copy of all or part of the original graphics and places the copy in a new location. The copy can be temporarily stored in the computer buffer memory or permanently saved on your disk. Sometimes you can change the data en route.

Substituting replaces the current graphics with new graphics without going through intermediate steps. For example, you might replace a bifold door with sliding doors simply by identifying the bifold and entering the file name of the sliding door.

The first law of editing: *Save before changing.* If in doubt, save. If the phone interrupts you, save. If thunderstorms are predicted, save. Forget where you are? Save. Before you attempt any major revisions, save your drawing. Did you forget the file name? Save a copy under a temporary name, like TEMPDRAWING or TEMP ABC.SEP1. If the drawing is important, *save* a duplicate copy.

We all make mistakes, and the worst time to make one is when you're editing. You can end up with a far greater mess than you had in the first place. So if you save beforehand and then make a massive error, you can load your saved copy and try again.

This chapter covers editing of general graphics and graphics text. Detailed requirements for editing figures and entities were discussed in Chapter 5, and special requirements for editing intelligent and/or associative drawings were covered in Chapter 6. Some duplication occurs in this chapter, but this only reinforces the importance of editing.

Text data consists of text files and software generally not used by CAD designers. CAD systems that supply text editors in the operating system or graphics are useful in editing large text or database files. Advanced users will find this capability extremely useful when working with intelligent graphics and merging large segments of text into drawings.

DETERMINING EDIT CRITERIA
You *can* edit an entire drawing in one fell swoop, but more often than not, you will want to edit only part of a drawing. Often the part you want to edit is intermixed with others. In order to edit specific parts, you need a method of distinguishing parts. The CAD software provides two methods: editing by levels and boundaries and editing by entity selection.

Any graphics can be edited by isolating the level on which the graphics reside and surrounding the item within an **edit boundary**. The edit boundary can be a point, but it is usually a rectangular window.

On the other hand, entities and intelligent graphics are isolated by selecting only those that meet your criteria, an entity type, or by the contents of a tag (data field). All graphics can be edited using level and boundary criteria, but not all graphics can be selected for entity or intelligent graphics editing.

Entity and intelligent editing tools are often more comprehensive than general editing tools. To take advantage of this increased capability, you copy a segment of general graphics into a figure library and then reinsert the figure and edit it as an entity.

Global and Specific Selection
A global edit covers a large area and includes broad editing criteria. Specific edits are discrete, making it possible to edit one line at a time.

Level Selection
Graphics are placed on levels to facilitate the organization and editing of data. For example, you can remove a door located on level 81, displayed in red, but keep the wall on level 92, in magenta. If you select only level 81 to be edited, you can easily remove the door without affecting the wall, even though your edit window might have included part of the wall.

In some systems, you can edit only those levels that are currently displayed, whereas in others, you can edit a different set of levels than those displayed. Multiple levels can be selected for editing; and in some cases, all but selected levels, a useful refinement of level selection.

Edit Boundaries
The edit boundary establishes a reference point for a specific edit. The boundary criteria will determine whether you edit inside the boundary, outside it, or partially both. The following are boundary criteria you can establish.

Inside and outside boundary edits
The most common edit removes the contents within the boundary of the window, as shown in Figure 7.1. If you reverse the procedure, everything outside the window will be edited—a **complementary edit**. Think carefully before you execute a complementary edit, because this command, infrequently used, reverses your normal instincts (see Figure 7.2). Did you save first?

7.1 *Editing inside a boundary is how most people think of editing.*

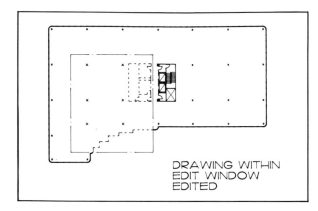

DRAWING WITHIN
EDIT WINDOW
EDITED

7.2 *Editing outside a boundary (sometimes called a complementary edit) is a powerful alternative when used cautiously.*

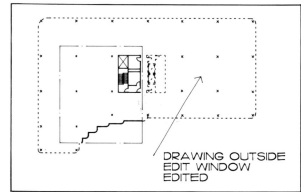

DRAWING OUTSIDE
EDIT WINDOW
EDITED

7.3 *Irregular edit boundary definition adds editing flexibility.*

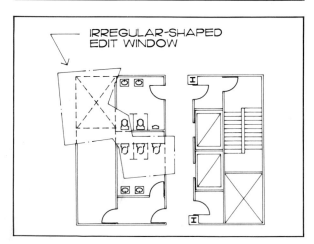

IRREGULAR-SHAPED
EDIT WINDOW

Regular and irregular boundaries

The most common edit window is an orthogonal rectangle. If the geometry of the area is oddly shaped or predominantly angular, some systems let you define an irregular boundary to accommodate your needs (Figure 7.3).

But if you don't use this technique frequently, you may find that editing with multiple rectangles is easier, since you won't have to learn another command. There's a good object lesson here. Often, a particular CAD drawing task can be achieved using different, though similar, commands, and you'll find it easier and faster to use several commands you know rather than a more sophisticated command you don't know.

Another technique works well when you must edit a long, angular area. Rotate the entire drawing, or the drawing grid, and then edit using standard orthogonal windows. When you have finished, rotate the drawing back to its original orientation.

ERASURE: REMOVING DATA

Because the erasing options are varied, let's look more closely at the most elementary form of editing: erasure.

The most basic of all erasures clears all data from the screen regardless of any other commands or action. It is also the most final. Commands like this are usually followed by the prompt "Are you sure? (Y,N)." You must answer Y or *yes* to complete the command; otherwise, the command aborts.

Since the computer stores data in the order in which it is entered, you can erase in the opposite order on most CAD systems by removing the last item first; called backspacing. You should be able to backspace only once or as many times as there is drawing data. This edit erases the last item, regardless of layer, boundary, or selection criteria.

One of the worst feelings is watching a

terminal wipe away work you mistakenly erased. Fortunately, you can recover from an unwanted erasure with an **Oops**, **Undo**, or **Recover** key. The Oops key works because everything you erase from the screen is stored in a temporary memory buffer. When you press Oops, the contents of the buffer are reinserted in the drawing. Everyone likes this command.

In each of the following examples (Figures 7.4–7.7), unwanted data is removed. Each figure shows a different boundary condition. First, review the steps in editing: (1) select the edit levels, (2) define boundary criteria, (3) enter edit window, and (4) execute the command.

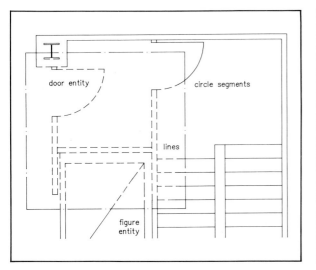

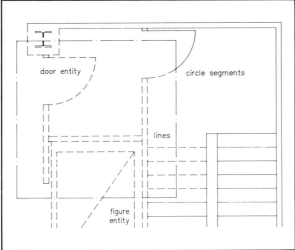

7.4 (far left) Window erasure works like a cookie cutter: all data within the edit window (or fence) is "cut" away.

7.5 (left) Intercept erasure is subtle, and puts the erasing shield to shame. Entities that intercept the edit window are deleted.

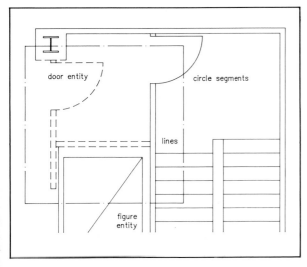

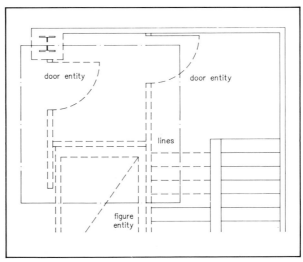

7.6 (far left) Entity erasure removes only those entities completely contained within the window.

7.7 (left) End-point erasure removes any entity whose end points fall within the window.

7.8 *The core is copied into a new drawing file. Copying sometimes duplicates the original, but sometimes removes the original. The convention depends upon your software.*

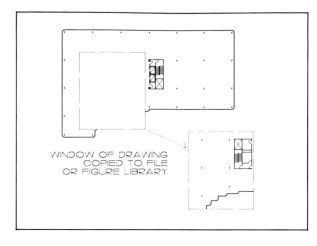

WINDOW OF DRAWING
COPIED TO FILE
OR FIGURE LIBRARY

7.9 *The doughnut copy saves everything outside the edit window.*

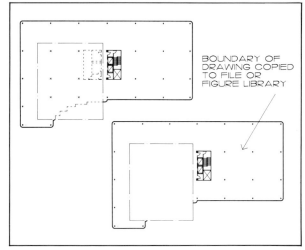

BOUNDARY OF
DRAWING COPIED
TO FILE OR
FIGURE LIBRARY

The **window erasure** (Figure 7.4) removes everything within the edit window on the selected levels (it is sometimes called a cookie-cutter edit because it removes all data within the edit boundary).

Any line that intercepts or falls within the edit window will be removed (Figure 7.5). The **intercept erasure** thus is the most frequently used form of erase and edit. As the figures shows, some data outside the edit window is also erased.

With **entity erasure**, any entity fully enclosed is erased (Figure 7.6). In this example, the entities are the three lines enclosed within the window, and only those lines are removed.

End point erasure: Any entity, whose end point or figure origin falls within the edit window is erased with **end point erasure** (Figure 7.7).

Figure 7.8 demonstrates how the building core is saved by moving it to another drawing file, using an entity edit. The balance of the drawing is discarded. In Figure 7.9, the process is reversed: The drawing is saved, except for the core.

EDITING: REVISING DATA

In the previous section, you learned the first method of editing: erasure. Now you'll learn how to edit by: changing, duplicating, and substituting graphics.

You'll recall from earlier sections that some edits work with general graphics, while other edits can be performed only with entities, figures, or intelligent graphics. General-graphics changes are controlled by level- and boundary-edit criteria. Entities, figures, and intelligent graphics are controlled by the selection list.

Changing Graphics

Erasing removes, while **changing** modifies a drawing. You'll find 11 different changes described below, beginning with simple moves and progressing to more complex or special-use changes.

Graphics moves

A **move** is akin to erasing and redrawing, except that you erase and the computer automatically redraws. To move general graphics, surround the graphics within a boundary, designate a starting origin point, establish the target origin point, and move. The procedure for moving graphics parallels erasing described in the previous section. Figure 7.10 shows a window move: All the data within the boundary is cut along the line of the inscribed rectangle and moved to the new location. In Figure 7.11, the intercept moves all the graphics falling within or intercepting the boundary. An entity move, shown in Figure 7.12, is similar to Figure 7.11, except that the complete entity must fall within the boundary to be moved.

You designate the distance of a move by entering two points on the CRT or by accepting the origin of the figure and designating the target with a relative point or polar point move. When the move (or stretch or shrink) is a simple translation, say $4' - 2''$ in the X direction, select any convenient location as the origin and enter the target reference point anywhere on the drawing. To insure accuracy in determining the target reference point, enter a relative or polar point on the keyboard. Alternatively, you can enter the two points graphically—as long as you have positive control—either by snapping or reading the incremental move distance displayed in the reference data on the CRT. There is no way to eyeball accurately.

There's a special kind of move—more precisely, a move-in-place—that works on at least one system. Actually, the graphics move to the buffer and return to their original location. In between, other edits can take place. As often happens when drawing, different parts of the drawing overlap or fall too close together (walls,

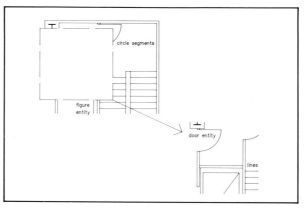

7.10 *A window move copies all graphics to a new location.*

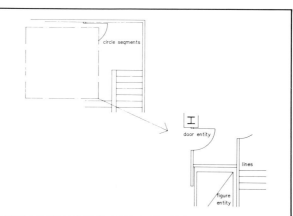

7.11 *An intercept move copies any and all entities that cross the edit window.*

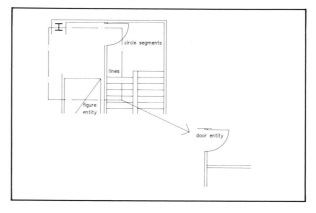

7.12 *An entity move copies entities completely contained within the edit window and moves them to the new location.*

dimensions, notes, reference lines, and so on), making editing difficult, even impossible. To avoid unintentional editing, you protect a drawing segment by windowing it and then **moving-in-place**. You then queue other edits that overlap the move-in-place and execute the command. The edit will change all but the segments you protected.

Rotation

You'll recall that $+X$ is to the right, $+Y$ is up, and $+Z$ is toward your eyes. Rotation may occur about any combination of or all axes. Rotation can be applied individually to entities, figures, or intelligent graphics. In two-dimensional work, rotation is often limited to the Z axis. You select an entity and determine the rotation angle, and the entity is modified. If you don't specify to the contrary, rotation will occur about the figure origin. (You can also rotate the entire drawing, but that will be covered in Chapter 9.)

Scale

Changing the **scale** of a figure functions identically to modifying figure rotation. You select a figure, determine the figure scale, and execute the change. (Return to Chapter 5 for a discussion of scale, if you need to refresh your memory. Look at the two men in Figure 5.4, differentially scaled.)

Stretching and shrinking

One of the more interesting changes is a move that makes drawings bigger or smaller in one direction only. Look at Figure 7.13. **Stretching** enlarges the graphics unidirectionally, whereas **shrinking** reduces. Before attempting such a major edit, make certain that a back-up file exists or that you save your current drawing— even experienced users can make mistakes. This edit is powerful, but it requires some practice to master.

Mirroring

This change reverses the image about one or two axes. You can review the details of mirroring on page 94 and in Figure 2.7. Figures can also be mirrored by changing a scale value to a negative number. Test first, however, to determine the effect of mirroring on text.

Line and fill textures

Line texture is a term that describes the thickness of a line or the pattern of dots, dashes, and spaces that constitute a broken line. You'll find that changing line texture is a great help and time saver, particularly when changing work in a dense area of the drawing. It's especially useful when you're dealing with demolition and remodeling work, where dashed lines mix frequently with solid lines. Look at Figure 7.14. Changing line weight improves readability, especially for monochromatic CRTs and pen plots.

Line and crosshatch changes follow the same procedure: Select the boundary and crosshatch fill texture and execute the change. Changing is considerably faster than erasing and redrawing new lines or textures.

Levels

Regardless of how many levels (layers) your CAD system has, there comes a time when you want to move graphics from one level to another. You might have placed the data on an incorrect level, or you might have just changed your mind. On a monochromatic monitor, you have no visual confirmation of which level contains which data because there's no visual way to distinguish one level from another, unless you redisplay each level individually (a time-consuming, tedious task). Here's a powerful reason for buying a color monitor: to be able to distinguish levels quickly (a specific color being designated for each level). In some cases, you can move data from one level to another during the process of loading a drawing, which is an efficient procedure.

Changing intelligence

Chapter 6 described how changing intelligence

changes the tags (fields) of an associative figure. Since neither general graphics nor entities contain data fields, only intelligent graphics are candidates. You select the intelligent graphics by enclosing the item within a graphic window or by matching the contents of a specific data field with a specific text string.

A door schedule provides a good example. Assume the first field contains the door number (say, door 101), the second field represents the door width; the third field, door height; and so on. Changing the plan view of a $3' - 0'' \times 7' - 0''$ door to a $3' - 0'' \times 6' - 8''$ door requires no graphic changes, only a data change in the third field, the door height.

First, select the door, either by enclosing it within a graphics window or by asking the computer to match the contents of a specific field with a known string. You might search for all doors with the number 101 in field 1. If only one door meeting this criterion exists, only one will be selected. On the other hand, a search for all $3' - 0''$ doors in field 2 might yield many candidates. Your search can be as broad or specific as needed. Once selected, the height is changed from $7' - 0''$ to $6' - 8''$ by substituting one text string for another. You can also search based on the contents of one field, but change another field.

Text

Another CAD feature you'll find extremely useful is editing text that is part of a drawing. Don't confuse text found in graphics files with that found in text files: A text file contains words, characters, and numbers, like a typed page. (You may want to refresh your memory by looking at Chapter 4 again, starting on page 48.

Text can be inserted into a drawing in graphic or ASCII format. In graphic format, text is drawn and manipulated like any other graphics and can be edited accordingly. But text editing works best when entered in ASCII format. Then the text is treated like a string entity and can be

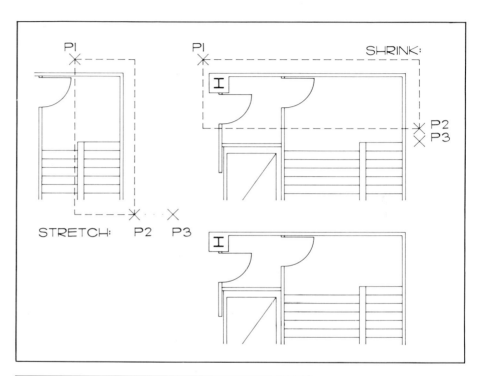

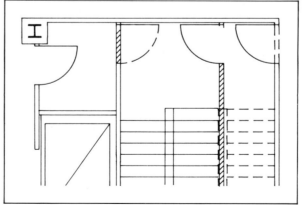

7.13 (above) *Stretching makes life easy when the client says, "Can I make that stair wider?" Shrinking works equally well.*

7.14 (left) *Changing line texture may also be automatic. Here, a door opening is cut into the wall simply by substituting a dashed line for a solid one.*

edited using techniques common to word processing. A part or all of the present text string can be changed. For example, you might edit the line "Paint all ceilings with floor paint" by windowing the entire line and substituting the word *red* for *floor*. The correction will substitute the new word and close the gap left by the two unused character spaces. You need not edit a complete paragraph to make a change, only a contiguous line. New text will be entered using the existing parameters: If the original was left-justified, so, too, will be the replacement.

More advanced editors allow you to change not only text content but text parameters: fonts, height, spacing, or justification. Because you can change or correct notes so easily, "lettering" ceases to be a production chore.

Duplicating Graphics
The second form of editing is duplication. During a change edit, the selected drawing is copied into the figure buffer, modified if requested, and automatically reinserted into the drawing. The process is not obvious (it is **transparent** to the user). When you duplicate graphics, the selected copy often appears under the cursor and can be reinserted (perhaps modified) into the drawing as many times as needed. The buffer copy automatically disappears when you finish. When you copy graphics, a permanent copy is created from the buffer contents and saved directly into the figure library on the disk for future use.

When you copy general graphics, you duplicate a section of the CRT screen, based on level selection and boundary conditions, like those used to erase or change general graphics, as discussed earlier.

Duplicating an entity
As with erasing and changing, it is easier and quicker to select entities and intelligent

graphics than general graphics. You select the item and bring up the figure in the cursor. Move to the new location and insert the figure.

Substitution
Refer to Figure 2.9. In order to substitute one element on a drawing for another, the CAD system must be able to isolate each item so that one element can be erased and another inserted in its place. Consequently, the element in the drawing and the substitute element must both be entities, figures, or intelligent graphics residing either on the drawing or saved on disk.

Select the element to be replaced, enter the SUBSTITUTE command, name the new figure, and the computer will replace the old element with the new one, duplicating origin locations. You should be able to simultaneously change scale, rotation, or origin location of the new figure. The next time your client wants to substitute low-back chairs for all the high-back executive swivel chairs, don't panic. You can make the switch with one global substitution. But there's more.

After having made the high back-to-low back substitution (or any other change, for that matter), you regenerate a new bill of materials (the computer recalculates the quantities). In a few high-end CAD systems, the regeneration is automatic. Best of all, creating a bill of materials on a CAD system forever ends manual counting.

The first step in mastering CAD is to master *all* of the editing features. Spend extra time here, and study everything the user's manual has to offer. The best source for expert help and advice is your technical representative. If you take him or her to lunch, you're certain to get tips on little-known techniques.

Now that you know about graphics editing, it's time to look at architectural design and design software.

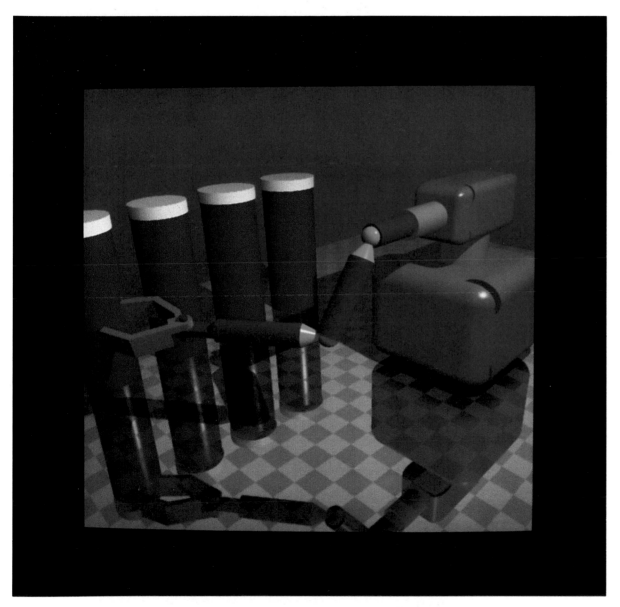

Color Plate 1
This graphic was produced on a very-high-resolution CRT, capable of generating images with extremely fine resolution. It is ideal for presentation-quality renderings and motion picture graphics. (Courtesy of Apollo Computers, Inc.)

Color Plate 2

Multiple layering is the electronic means for separating drawing elements graphically. In principle, it works exactly like overlay drafting. Each layer is distinguished by a discrete color: columns are on the "orange" layer, walls on the "raspberry" layer, and furniture on the "blue" layer.

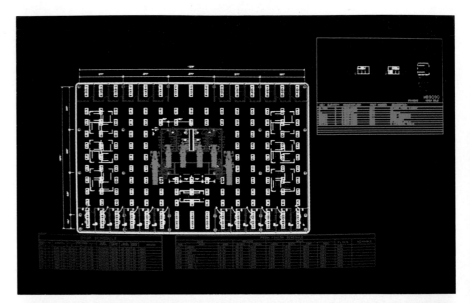

Color Plate 3

Standardized layers for graphics data may soon become a reality. Displayed here is the standard the author developed which integrates graphic layers with CSI/AIA specification sections and assigns standard colors to each of the 250 layers: Section 9, Finishes, is assigned to layers 90 through 99, with ten shades of red-purple.

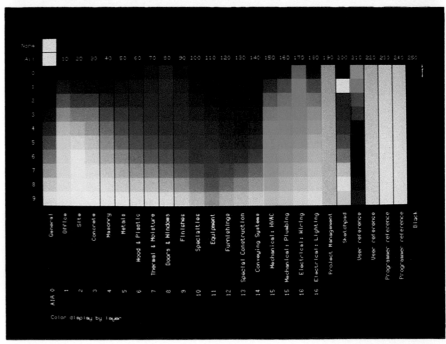

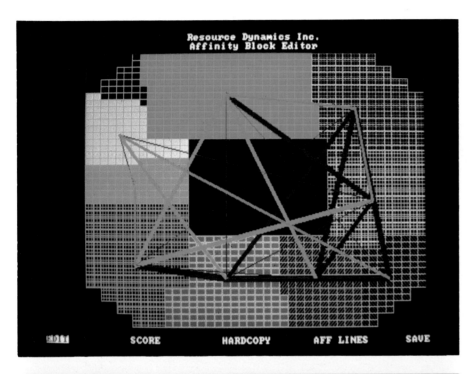

Color Plate 4
This proximity plan was automatically generated from data provided in the forecast report (see Figure 6.10) plus adjacency criteria. (Courtesy of Resource Dynamics, Inc.)

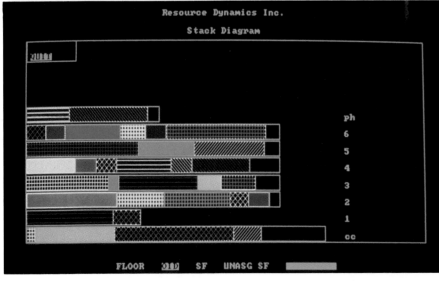

Color Plate 5
Space utilization can be depicted quite effectively using a bar chart. In this stack plan, each bar represents one floor on a multistory building and shows graphically which departments are where and how much space each is programmed to occupy. (Courtesy of Resource Dynamics, Inc.)

Color Plate 6
Interference checking begins with a composite plan. (Courtesy McDonnell Douglas AEC Systems Company)

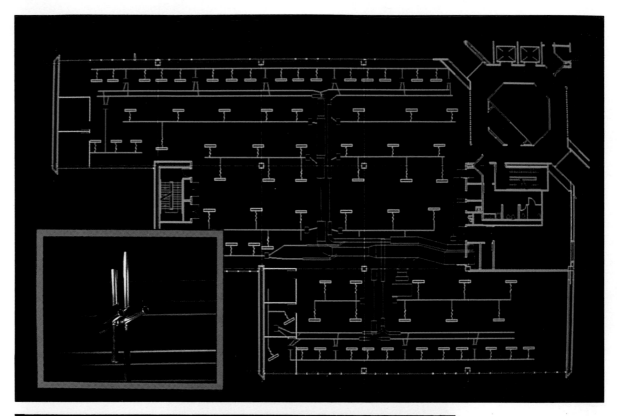

Color Plate 7
Interference was determined, and is shown here. (Courtesy of McDonnell Douglas AEC Systems Company)

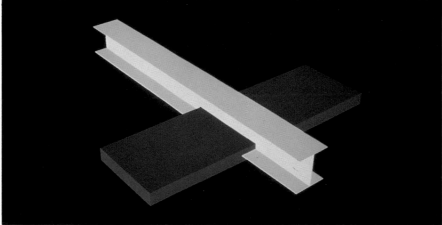

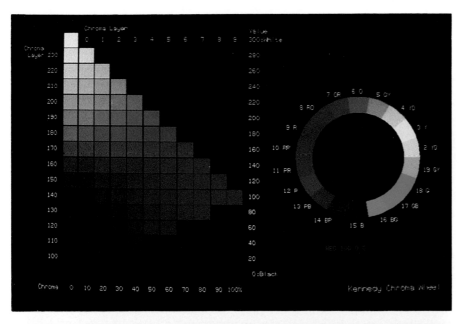

Color Plate 8
Kennedy chroma chart divides the spectrum into 18 equal visual hues (right). Each hue (left) ranges from 0 percentile of chroma (black) to 100 percentile chroma (natural hue) to 300 percentile chroma of chroma (white). There are approximately 75 colors per hue.

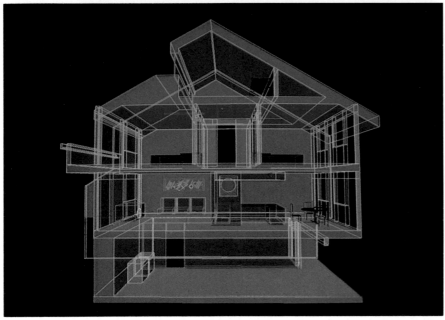

Color Plate 9
Wire-frame three-dimensional construction that exposes rear plane edges may not affect the designer's understanding or appreciation of the form, but the client may find the drawing confusing. Here's a drawing with all lines shown. (Courtesy of Hans Christian Lischewski)

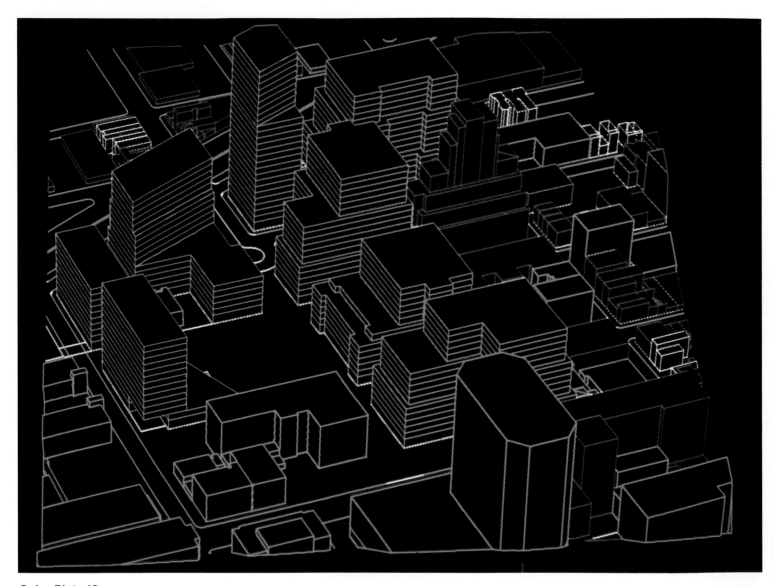

Color Plate 10
Hidden lines removed.
(Courtesy of Haines
Lundberg Waehler,
Architects, Engineers,
and Planners)

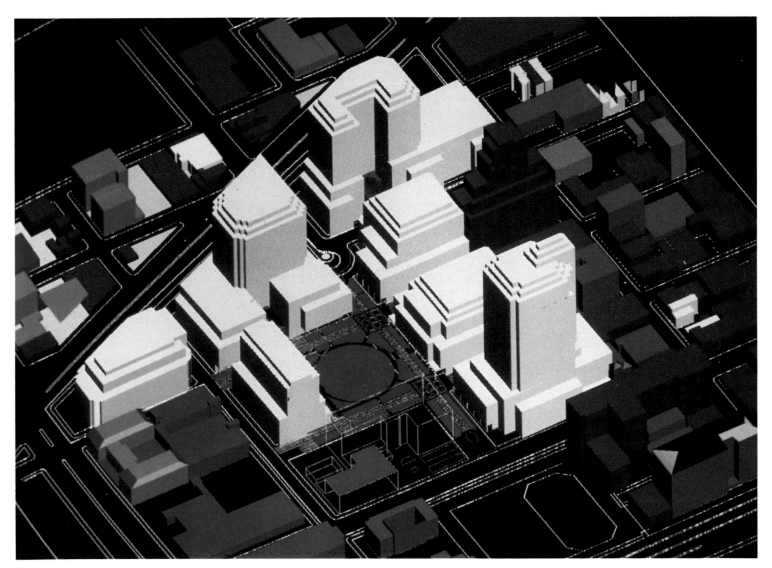

Color Plate 11
Planar surfaces are required for rendering. Here the wire-frame geometry has been replaced with polygonal surfaces. (Courtesy of Haines Lundberg Waehler, Architects, Engineers, and Planners. John Back, photographer)

Color Plate 12
Rendered building. Light-source shading has been applied. In order to intensify the quality of "sunlight" on the side, the sun was directed horizontally at the surface. The building could have been lit from any side.

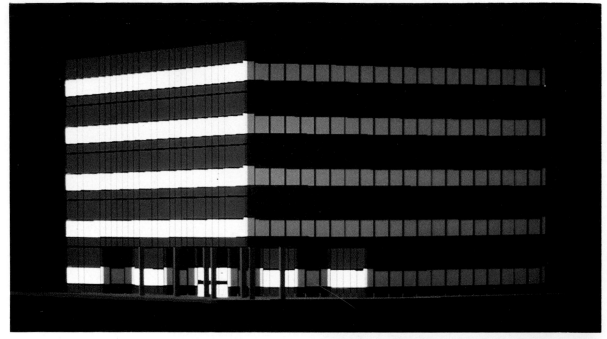

Color Plate 13
Advanced light-source shading allows for specular reflections, shadows, transparency, and refractions. All the advanced features are shown here. (Courtesy Apollo Computers, Inc.)

Design

Many people want computer-aided design—or think they want it. The difficulty lies in distinguishing between computer-aided *design* and computer-aided *drafting*. Architects often ask, "Can this CAD system design as well as draft?" It's a perfectly valid and important question. But when asked in return, "How do you define CAD design? What design work do you want CAD to perform?" the responses are uncomfortably vague.

In a profession that prides itself on understanding and defining problems with clarity and perception, it poses an interesting dilemma. Design philosophy is often perceived and stated with precision, but quantifying and articulating the design process, however generic, remains elusive. We want CAD to design for us, yet we remain trapped by our inability to define what it is we want from CAD as a design tool.

In this chapter, you'll learn what I believe to be the difference between computer-aided drawing (or drafting) and computer-aided design and how you can use both with CAD.

CAD DRAFTING

Fundamentally, **computer-aided drafting** is data entry. You enter two points, instruct the computer to draw a line, and the computer complies. You tell the computer to execute your instructions, and the computer displays the line graphically. You're drafting on a graphics terminal. That is what most of CAD is today: drawing electronically exactly what you drew manually before. It's an evolutionary change—from a wood-and-graphite pencil to an electronic pencil.

The full-color, three-dimensional shaded images the vendors show during product demonstrations are seductive, but the focus of most drawing in a design office is on drafting construction documents (drawing blueprints, as some like to say). Since this segment of work represents 30–40% of the design fee and is highly standardized drawing, CAD can be an excellent tool for reducing the cost of producing drawings. Most CAD software provides mainly computer-aided drafting.

CAD DESIGN

On the other hand, **computer-aided design** is a tool for making decisions and solving problems: You instruct the computer to connect two points, the computer finds the points, suggests available solutions (connect with solid line, broken line, or irregular line; quit; and so on), asks you to select an alternative, and then draws a line. You're designing on a graphics terminal, making decisions about your design work. Computer people call this process **interactive**.

Whereas drafting software is general in nature, design software is quite specific, almost always very complex, requiring considerably more memory, and, because of its necessarily limited market, expensive.

Since most drafting techniques have been quite suitably incorporated in the drafting software available today, the question is why there isn't more design software available.

DESIGN METHODOLOGY

Historically, programs that calculate engineering information comprised the first design programs. Look at Figure 8.1. Many structural, HVAC, and electrical programs have been with us for some time now and are well known to the professionals who use them.

8.1 *Area and dimension calculations are a natural by-product of CAD. Since the coordinates of each entity are stored in the system, these calculations can be readily extracted and manipulated. (Courtesy of The Miller Organization)*

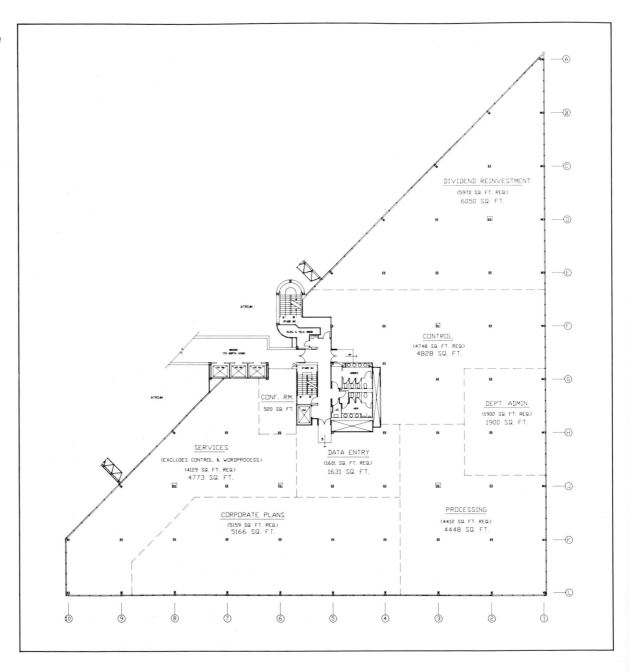

There are many electronic drawing techniques that are employed in design. Some of them parallel manual yellow-tracing-paper methods, while others are exclusively CAD techniques.

Backgrounds can be temporarily referenced under your current drawing as ghost levels. Figures are sometimes inserted in the drawing to verify a location or dimension and erased by backspacing, which erases the last item. Figures can replace the cross hairs and be moved about the screen. Some systems will let you insert any graphics temporarily, including text and figures, and preview the results. If you like what you see, you insert the contents; otherwise the temporary graphics are removed. It's possible to bring a reference drawing up with the graphic cursor, which eliminates having to refer to a print. And it's faster than saving your present drawing, loading the reference drawing, and then reloading the original drawing.

Another very successful use of CAD in design is for detailing, particularly when used with similar cross sections, discontinuous components (such as clip angles), interference verification, or complex joint conditions, especially angled joints. You can sketch these conditions manually, but only with the three-dimensional accuracy of CAD can you easily draw and resolve the geometry of joint conditions.

DESIGN SOFTWARE CHARACTERISTICS

The major advantages in using CAD to design come from being able to repeat complex calculation sequences and to structure a pathway through complex design processes, such as those found in exit width calculations for various occupancy groups.

Design programs fall into four categories. The first is calculations programs, which "crunch numbers" for such tasks as area or volume take-offs, engineering loading conditions, or determining the midpoint of a line. Second is database management programs, which include all inventory programs and crunch data. The most common are space planning and furniture inventories. Third, interactive design programs ask you to enter data, and the computer calculates the answer and displays design alternatives for your approval. Given a total program area and the site area, for example, an interactive program can determine the number of floors in a building with a net-to-gross efficiency of 75%. Last is the design utility program, which performs very useful and timesaving housekeeping functions, automatically generating elevations from plans or assembling several smaller drawings onto a full-size sheet with border.

Because drawing applications are fairly universal, excellent drawing software is widely available. But most **design** applications have a limited audience. Design applications are so specific that most are written by the user for in-house use. In this section, you'll look at the characteristics of specialized software to help you evaluate and decide when specialized development is justified.

Specialized Software

Most design software is created to fill a need of a specific user because no other software is commercially available or because major revisions to present software would be prohibitively expensive. It is usually more effective to write your own, using the computer or macro language that comes with the basic software.

Too often, design software is so specialized that its marketability is limited. The recent New York City Zoning Code provides an excellent example. The section applicable to Manhattan midtown office buildings incorporates a sky exposure plane defined by an exponential curve. Building mass that penetrates the allowable zoning envelope must be offset by other setbacks within the envelope. Here is an ideal candidate for design software: It is complex and full of calculations, it lends itself to automation, and it is ideal for design modeling. But the software is too complex and specialized to become a viable commercial product, although several New York offices reportedly have computerized the code.

Time Factors

Writing a software program (sometimes called writing code) requires close attention to the logic and the precise rules of grammar (**syntax**). Writing software is labor intensive: To determine how long a programmer needs to write a program, you allow one hour for each computer instruction (called a **line of code**). Even though this includes program design, coding, debugging, and documentation, time adds up quickly. Forty lines of code—a small program— requires 40 hours to write. In deciding whether to invest in specialized software, you need to evaluate the value of the finished product versus the time required (or available) to write the software. Does the anticipated return justify the investment?

Cost

Most professional billing rates are approximately salary times three. Consequently, 40 hours represents about $600 per $10,000 annual salary. Does the value of the 40-line program justify the expense? By comparison, writing the New York City Zoning Code software could easily have required 1000 lines, or 1000 hours, written by a good programmer. That's six months programming at a cost approaching $75,000. Still, an architectural practice regularly engaged in designing Manhattan office buildings might decide that the volume of their work would justify the expense.

Development costs must be recovered from within your organization through efficiencies achieved by introducing more effective software. For the software to be cost-effective, you must not only break even on development costs but realize reasonable profits. After all, drawing better, faster, and cheaper is the raison d'être of CAD. The profit break-even point on software development costs should not normally exceed two years. You should break even in two years because the software will probably be obsolete by the end of three years.

How many other architects who use the same CAD system as you do might be interested in your program? Sales of software for the New York City Zoning Code would be limited to a relatively small segment of the profession, but an egress-and-stair design/detailing application developed to run in concert with widely distributed microcomputer CAD software might find a wide market.

Purchasing Specialized Design Software

Although considerable design software exists, finding the right software to run on your computer can prove to be exasperating at best. Where do you look? Call the customer service representative of your CAD system or ask your local technical representative for the names of other customers known to be active in design software development. Published lists by professional trade journals focus on major software. There also needs to be a central information source that critically evaluates available specialized software.

Once you've identified software that you believe meets your requirements, contact the vendor to confirm that the software will indeed perform most of your major tasks. If you find any software that performs *all* of your tasks exactly as you expect, consider yourself extremely lucky. There are things you can count on happening every time you purchase software: You'll be disappointed with some parts; others will out-perform your wildest expectations; and you'll also find some unexpected strengths.

Calculation power

Many design application programs calculate answers without interpreting the results. Equations that involve intricate mathematics, exponentiation, or decimal locations are best left to the computer. Some of you may remember calculating beam deflections with a slide rule and the inherent frustrations involved. No longer. Structural, HVAC, electrical, or load tables are ideal applications.

Memory capacity

Most design applications require large amounts of RAM and/or disk memory, not only to store large drawings but to store the design application software. Since there's considerable interaction between the designer and the computer, the program must be understandable to the user, be visually easy to follow, and prevent the user from entering the wrong key (called **error trapping**), whenever possible. Making the program user friendly and interactive can double the length of the software program.

Speed

While fundamental drawing software is often written (**compiled**) in machine language (a high-speed computer language, most user-developed software applications, such as design programs, are written in a less difficult quasi-macro language (see Chapter 13). Since each macro language instruction must go through several more steps than its machine language counterpart, the added computer processing time becomes quite noticeable.

WHAT DESIGN SOFTWARE CAN DO

Here is a look at some available types of interactive design software.

Facilities Management

Software programs for space planning and programming are a mix of graphics and a database, ideally suited for CAD. Facilities management software is truly design software. You enter data, and the computer evaluates it and presents you with options, both alphanumeric (everyone in Department A is grouped together in descending order of workstation size, for example) and graphic (Department A requires 7235 square feet next to Department B, both on the 22d floor). The proposed solutions are derived from the data you enter, tempered by your own restrictions. The computer matches the data against the restraints and calculates the best solution, based on your determination of best.

Space planning

Space planning, the initial phase of facilities management, is essentially alphanumeric. The current space, staff, equipment, and occupancy costs are inventoried. You add projected staff changes (growth or reduction), proposed space standards, and changes in equipment. From this data, future space, staff, and equipment needs and costs can be projected. Traditionally, this work is undertaken when the client is analyzing long-term growth or considering a move to new quarters. Simple space planning is possible with a spreadsheet program and a microcomputer, but major planning should only be attempted with professional-quality database planning software. Figure 8.2 shows an example of a typical space projection report. Good software is available today for space planning and facilities management.

Planning diagrams

What separates sophisticated space planning software from the rest is the ability to digest the data developed earlier and generate graphic design solutions and alternatives. Using scaled plan and section drawings that you've entered on the system earlier, the software generates increasingly sophisticated diagrams of your needs.

The first diagram shows the locations of all departments, the relative size of each, and the relative importance of locating one department close to or away from another. The diagram is automatically generated by the software from a combination of the space planning data and a relationship matrix in which the relative need for proximity of all departments is evaluated and ranked. The relationship matrix is translated into a bubble diagram of the ideal condition. As with any design software, you may revise this bubble diagram.

Proximity plans

While a bubble diagram shows the relative proximities of departments, it is too abstract for planning or design. But translated into a diagrammatic plan like the example in Color Plate 4 (page 99)—a **proximity plan**—each department is placed, and a major segment of the work of space planning is complete. You can revise the plan and generate alternatives. The transformation from bubble diagram to a proximity plan is an impressive design software application.

Stack diagrams

Once you've established the proximity relationships, multistory building data can be translated to a diagrammatic vertical section known as a **stack diagram** (Color Plate 5, page 99). Each department on every floor is identified. Now the designer can review and refine vertical circulation. A campus plan with multiple buildings can be scrutinized in a similar manner. While the graphics are basically business bar charts, the technique works well in solving circulation between departments.

Departmental plans

When planning is complete, design begins. What started as numbers in an inventory of people and space has become a diagrammatic set of plan and section drawings, indicating where every department belongs. Now a designer can develop **departmental block plans**, using the outline floor plans drawn earlier and the planning information developed with the proximity plan and the stack diagram.

Dual data flow

The ability to transfer data from one design module to another, as from stack diagram to departmental plan, or to transfer the data in reverse from departmental plan back to, say, a proximity plan, although a simple computer database procedure, is an enormously sophisticated design programming feature. Because the computer automatically updates all other relevant data, you don't have to.

Schematic Design

With the planning complete and space standards developed during the early phases of space planning, the designer or architect now has all the tools at hand to actually conceptualize the space, selecting workstations and office planning standards from the figure library. You can develop schematic design documents with or without the use of intelligent figures, depending on the furniture and panel figures you insert. If the figures contain associative data, you can automatically generate an inventory of all the furniture and panels and an estimate of the total cost.

As you progress from schematic design to design development and finally to construction documents, the same base plans can still be used. And at each stage, appropriate drawing information can be added.

Zoning Envelope

While many large cities have zoning codes developed to cover their specific urban needs, the approach of most zoning codes is remarkably similar, covering, among other things, use, height, floor limits, setbacks, lot coverage, sky exposure plane. Such an application would be based on a generic—more or less typical—zoning code with selected cities as options and, of course, the option for the user to modify or add any particular zoning requirements to accommodate particular needs. Unfortunately, very little has been done in this area.

Site Work

Most software for site work covers land measurement, topography, and contours. Since topographic work requires full three-dimensional capability and very high numeric precision, sufficient capacity to calculate many coordinates and adequate memory to store the calculations are required. All this suggests high-performance CAD for a limited market. Most of this software, despite necessarily limited production, is well written and impressive. Just being able to calculate cut-and-fill quantities should make these welcome in the profession.

Building Code Compliance

Researching a building code is a little like searching the Manhattan telephone directory for someone named Smith in the 100 block of East 84th Street: It can be a long, tedious process, and it would be easy to overlook the sought-after name. You should be able to enter such data as occupancy type, construction type, floor area, and heights; calculate all the egress requirements, stair sizes, and exit widths; determine fire-resistive ratings and sprinkler requirements; calculate compartmentation requirements for horizontal separation; identify key code sections, such as nailing schedules or tie-downs for wooden structures in seismic zones; and identify minimum dimensions of horizontal passageways, habitable rooms, air changes, minimum sanitary facilities, and so on.

Software programs like this have been rumored. Expect to see them soon. While codes differ in each municipality, each addresses the same issues. Most U.S. cities use one of the few major codes or model their code after key regional or city building codes.

Architectural Massing

By entering the building area, floor dimensions, and floor-to-floor heights (perhaps generated from other structural, HVAC, and zoning considerations), a three-dimensional wire frame structure is generated. Information from the building code analysis and site analysis can generate alternative massing schemes. Light-source shading could permit architectural mass studies. Coupled with polyoptic-perspective drawing techniques and animation, schematic design could take on an entirely new meaning and become a truly productive design tool.

Engineering Massing

There are any number of architectural decisions that could be influenced by the volume and surface of the building, both of which affect construction costs and BTU loads. Being able to calculate the total building volume and skin perimeter area to estimate BTU gains or losses for various configurations, to estimate total structural dead loads and electrical loads, and then to apply these findings during early massing presents options to the architect, engineer, and, of course, the owner. Life-cycle costing, depreciation, capital versus operating-cost considerations, interest rates, and price indexes could also be factored into the calculations.

Building Core Design

For a building core design, you must calculate stair, elevator, and escalator requirements and translate the results into floor plans, identifying design configurations that use the least floor area. Next, translate the requirements into schematic design dimensions and alternatively create detail plans and sections of these elements. Too little has been achieved here, where considerable savings in the production of

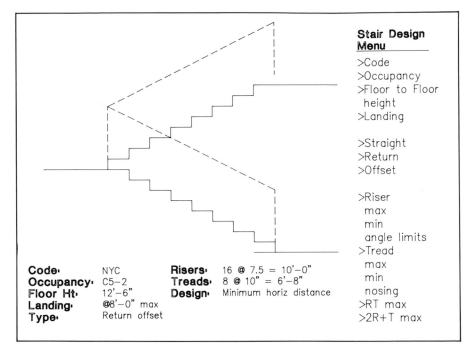

Stair Design Menu

>Code
>Occupancy
>Floor to Floor
 height
>Landing

>Straight
>Return
>Offset

>Riser
 max
 min
 angle limits
>Tread
 max
 min
 nosing
>RT max
>2R+T max

Code·	NYC	Risers·	16 @ 7.5 = 10'-0"
Occupancy·	C5-2	Treads·	8 @ 10" = 6'-8"
Floor Ht·	12'-6"	Design·	Minimum horiz distance
Landing·	@8'-0" max		
Type·	Return offset		

8.2 *Stair design is an ideal CAD design application.*

design development and construction documents could be affected. Figure 8.2 shows a design solution.

Engineering Design

Specialized software exists for almost every engineering aspect of any building design, especially for civil, structural, mechanical, and electrical engineering. Speak to your CAD technical representative for a complete list of software available for your system.

Interference Checking

This currently available design application should give you an idea of what a truly powerful program can be. If you examine the plan shown in Color Plate 6 (page 100), you will readily concede that identifying an intersection of two unintended items is extremely difficult. This program application checks for any two volumes that occupy the same space—interference checking—and reports the results. In this case, it's clear that the duct doesn't belong in the middle of the beam's flange, as shown in Color Plate 7 (page 100).

Cost Estimating

In order to estimate any element on a drawing, that element must be an entity and contain sufficient intelligence to identify what material it is, what CSI/AIA specification section applies, the units, and the units measure. A line therefore, might represent a number 6 reinforcing bar, section 5, 14 feet long. A rectangle might represent a 3500psi 4-inch reinforced concrete floor slab on metal deck, section 3,900 cubic yards. As you can see, this adds a significant amount of information to the drawing, but the fact that an estimate can be automatically generated opens so many possibilities for project management.

Specifications

If your CAD system supports intelligent drawings and you assign drawing data to active levels in accordance with CSI/AIA standards, then specific material data can be extracted by CSI/AIA section, converted into a data file, compatible with your word processor, and merged into the appropriate selected specification sections. Spec writing should be as creative a process as the design process, directed more toward product selection and less toward assembling and writing volumes that look and read like telephone books.

Project Management and Construction Administration

Project management software is very specialized, limited to fee and manpower projections, for the most part, and custom designed. Much could be achieved here. Construction administration software is equally scarce, being limited mostly to shop drawing logs. In due course, you can expect to see a CAD terminal at the construction site, connected by a modem to the designer's office, but for now, the bulk of construction administration work will be done manually.

Utility Programs

Last, but by no means least, is a potpourri of **utility programs** designed to make your CAD life easier. These utilities might also be called **housekeeping programs** because they perform those tasks you take for granted, such as alphabetizing a directory or loading, saving, or renaming a file. Some utilities will automatically copy your current day's work into a duplicate file and print out a list of all files moved, and others will generate time sheets.

Yet other utilities guide you through complex procedures, such as plotting drawings, so that you don't have to memorize them. A particularly welcome utility is one that assembles multiple small drawings onto a larger sheet and prepares the sheet for printing. Others read plan data and generate elevations.

Chapters 3, 4, and 5 showed you how to draw; Chapter 6 covered intelligence and data management; and Chapter 7 taught you editing. With Chapter 8, you concluded the CAD basics with CAD design. Now we turn to three-dimensional computer graphics.

Three Dimensions

Drawing really gets to be fun when you enter the world of three dimensions. For many professionals, CAD has been too expensive to buy solely for its three-dimensional capability, but software for professional three-dimensional rendering emphatically separates CAD as a *design* tool from CAD as a *drawing* tool. You may not buy three-dimensional drawing software at first, but you'll soon discover that the ability to draw any three-dimensional projection with shaded surfacing and a minimum of 16 colors is more than a fancy advertising claim; it's an essential design tool for the serious designer.

With professional-quality three-dimensional software, you can critique forms, spaces, lighting, scale, and any other aspect of a design in an accurately simulated environment. You can also test human response with animated sequences that "walk through" the space. Short of being there, it's the best way to experience the building and study alternative views.

THREE-DIMENSIONAL GEOMETRY

Not all CAD software has full three-dimensional capability. Some software can only draw plans or elevations, is strictly two-dimensional, and is incapable of combining them in a useful three-dimensional display. You'll understand why shortly. Many two-dimensional software programs do, however, accommodate optional three-dimensional capability, which you can add later. The CAD systems that are entirely three-dimensional are powerful and versatile, but they require more memory to store their larger and computationally more complex drawings.

Because little of professional training focuses on three-dimensional geometry, everything you learned in high school mechanical drawing class, college solid geometry, trigonometry, and

perspective drawing will prove valuable in working with solids in space. Three-dimensional geometry is not difficult to understand, but it can be confusing as you work to keep complex plans straight in your mind. Start your three-dimensional education with simple elevation rotations, move to orthographic projections, then to perspective drawings, solid modeling and color, and finally to shades and shadows. Since documentation in three-dimensional architectural drawing tends to be limited, make sure you progress through each step carefully and document your work for future reference.

Adding Height: The *Z* Coordinate

The Z coordinate adds height, or volume, to your drawing. The universal definition of three-dimensional space is: $+X$ extends to the right, or "east," of the origin point, 0; $+Y$ extends up, or "north"; and $+Z$ extends from the origin out toward the astronomical zenith. For example, you might want to add an emergency light to a floor plan at 8'-0" above the floor. You activate the figure in the cursor, designate the height as $+Z$ 8'-0" (or 96 inches), and insert the figure. But what if you're looking at a rotated projection of the plan? Where, then, is the fixture inserted? You might be surprised to see the light fixture inserted where you didn't expect it. Before looking at the two methods of referencing three-dimensional coordinates, look first at how XYZ coordinates are entered.

Point Entry

Three-dimensional points, like their two-dimensional counterparts, may be entered with a puck, pencil, or keyboard, depending on the configuration of your particular CAD system. You can enter each coordinate element—X, Y, and Z—individually or, in some cases, set a value for Z. As you enter subsequent X and Y values, each point accepts the default Z value.

Because of the complexity of calculating planar surfaces and spatial angles, polar point entry is infrequently used. Later in this chapter, you will learn about the normal vector, a polar line, that passes through and is perpendicular to a plane. It is used in shading and shadow calculations.

Adding Rotation

The angular and rotation conventions for locating an object vary, depending on the application. Unlike Cartesian conventions, a common definition has not emerged. Navigators and surveyors start at north and calculate angles clockwise. Architectural solar charts use **azimuth** to describe the direction of the sun east or west of south, and they use altitude to locate the angle of the sun above the horizon at a given azimuth. Astronomers locate stars by a measure called right ascension and declination, a method best left to be discussed elsewhere. As though this lack of uniformity were not enough, computer-aided manufacturing (CAM) designers use yet another angular convention.

To remove any confusion, you should start fresh. There are two methods used to locate an object in space: One uses the viewer as the reference origin, manipulating objects relative to this viewpoint. I call this **view coordinate geometry**. The companion system fixes the object in space and moves the viewer relative to the object origin. I call this **object coordinate geometry**.

View Coordinate Geometry

The viewpoint lies at the center of the universe: The eye always looks away from the origin along the Z axis toward −Z, looking through the XY plane, represented by the CRT face. All object manipulation is based on Cartesian translation and XYZ rotation relative to this viewpoint origin, which resides on the plane of the CRT. A crankshaft, for example, has no north or south, and presentation of CAM piece parts is easier using view coordinate geometry than object coordinate geometry.

X and Y angles commence in the XY plane, and the Z angle begins along the +X (east) axis. Rotation of the object is determined to be positive or negative according to the right-hand rule: If you hold your hand in front of you with the palm open and point your thumb along the positive direction of any axis, then positive rotation occurs about that axis in the direction of the curl of your fingers as you close them toward your palm. Try holding your hand in front of the CRT with your palm facing left (your thumb points toward your nose, +Z). As you close your fingers about your palm, your fingers rotate counterclockwise. Consequently, positive rotation about the Z axis is counterclockwise (the only rotation recognized in two-dimensional work). So the next time you see someone in front of a CRT doing strange things with his right hand, he or she may be creating a masterpiece.

Follow this example. Load a plan onto the screen. Rotate the plan drawing Z − 45, X − 35.27. The drawing first rotates 45° counterclockwise, and then the top of the plan "folds back" 35.27° to display an isometric view. If you then rotate the drawing 180° about the Y axis, your drawing will appear reversed, or mirrored. Just remember that X − 45 always rotates the currently displayed image away from you 45°. Also, you will alter the result if you reverse the entry sequence: entering X − 35.27, followed by Z − 45. See Figure 9.1.

9.1 *View coordinate geometry. Rotation in the X and Y axes are always about the surface of the CRT, and Z rotation is always about a line extending toward the viewer.*

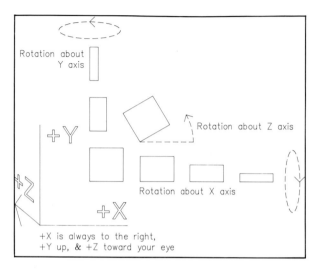

Rotation about Y axis

+Y

Rotation about Z axis

+Z

+X

Rotation about X axis

+X is always to the right, +Y up, & +Z toward your eye

9.2 *Object coordinate geometry. Rotation is calculated relative to a fixed object in space.*

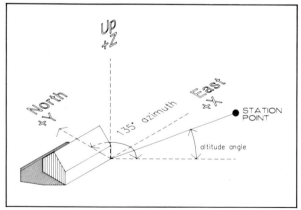

UP +Z

North +Y

East +X

135° azimuth

STATION POINT

altitude angle

Object Coordinate Geometry

In this reference system, the object has finite coordinates and keeps them. All rotation and translation takes place relative to the building origin. Since most buildings are designed for a fixed location on a fixed site, it is natural to think of a building in its planned setting and therefore to view it three-dimensionally in the context of its known coordinates. Object coordinate geometry uses two angles and one distance measurement to define a location. The azimuth measures the angle along the earth's surface clockwise from north, and **altitude** measures the angle above or below the horizon. Both angles and distance are measured from the drawing origin.

The azimuth of a building is established by aligning a building axis relative to north and by fixing a known building coordinate at the drawing origin. No altitude or distance setting is needed, since both are 0. To view the drawing, establish the point from which the drawing will be viewed, the **station point**. Set this point by entering the azimuth, altitude, and distance from the origin or by entering the *XYZ* coordinates for the station point. You change the view by changing the location of the station point.

If you want to "look" from the southeast, for example, set the azimuth angle at 135°. To look up or down at the building, set the altitude angle accordingly. You can change azimuth without changing altitude and vice versa. More important, by working with object coordinates, you can manipulate the drawing in a manner consistent with the methods you learned as part of your professional training. Look at Figure 9.2. By contrast, a change in the *Y* or *Z* angle using view coordinate geometry rotates the object in all three axes, producing unpredictable results.

Although each method has advantages, **object coordinate geometry** is better suited for architectural and engineering applications than **view coordinate geometry**. But since some architectural software is derived from CAM software, your computer may use **view coordinate geometry**. If so, you should be aware of the differences and be prepared to take corrective steps to make it suitable for architectural purposes.

Rotation Versus Translation

Because rotation angles can sometimes be entered as trigonometric functions, it is often easy to confuse multiple angular rotation with multiple *XYZ* coordinate translations. Angular rotation is cumulative, and the final location of a point is determined not only by the individual *X*, *Y*, and *Z* angular rotations but by the sequence in which the angles are entered.

Coordinate translations are noncumlative. You can apply them in any order, and the resultant point always ends up at the same place. An example explains best. Coordinates are transformed as the figure is rotated:

	X	Y	Z
Start with point at:	1	0	0
First rotate $Z+45$:	0.707	0.707	0
Then rotate $Y-45$:	0.5	0.707	0.5

Now interchange *Y* and *Z* rotation:

	X	Y	Z
Start again at the same point:	1	0	0
Rotate $Y-45$:	0.707	0	0.707
Then rotate $Z+45$:	0.5	0.5	0.707

The final location of the first point is: *X*.5, *Y*.707, *Z*.5, but it ends up at *X*.5, *Y*.5, *Z*.707 when the rotation sequence is reversed. On the other hand, point translation may occur in any sequence without affecting the final location of the point.

THREE-DIMENSIONAL CONSTRUCTION

Drawing in three dimensions can add power and sophistication to your drawing, but drawing in three-dimensional architectural space has some limitations. For example, you can draw a spherical surface easily in CAM software, but only with skill and patience in architectural CAD software.

Consider the following anomalies in graphic construction. Drawing a line in three-dimensional space can be achieved quite easily by connecting two separate points, each with different *XYZ* coordinates. Irrespective of the *XYZ* coordinates of both points, a line drawn between the two points will always appear to be a straight line. But drawing a circle or polygon does not offer the same freedom; these objects must generally be drawn in an orthographic plane and rotated into position.

Orthographic Construction

The computer can construct any planar surface, crosshatching, or text at any angle, but it will construct all of them more quickly when drawn parallel to the face of the CRT, an orthographic construction. You can then rotate the display and work on other surfaces. It's a very efficient way to construct surfaces accurately, but it's not always the most convenient or elegant solution. In some systems, you can only construct planar surfaces in the plane parallel to the CRT face.

Nonorthographic Construction

Drawing a circle rotated in space at a compound angle requires the computer to recalculate the circle as an inclined ellipse. And while this may be possible on your system, you'll find that most of your three-dimensional drawings can be constructed as orthographic planes and later assembled into a three-dimensional object. Linear shapes, such as lines and rectangles, however, can be constructed outside orthographic limits.

Three-Dimensional Figures

See Figure 9.3. The fundamental method of creating three-dimensional volumes is to draw (or insert) multiple surfaces, rotate the view, and

9.3 *Three-dimensional figure construction is diverse. These samples show various means of construction.*

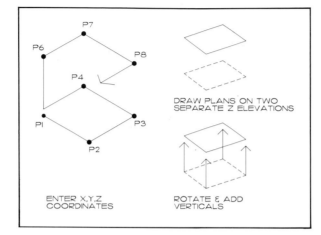

9.4 *Three-dimensional substitution for a two-dimensional figure can provide an efficient means of creating and saving a drawing in two dimensions, followed by a three-dimensional substitution at rendering time.*

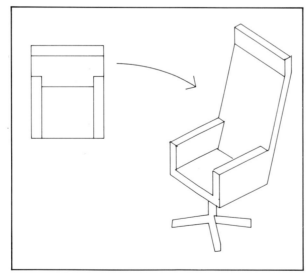

complete the boundaries of the solid shape by connecting corner points with additional lines. By snapping to corner points, you can construct any solid shape. It's a simple and reliable method.

Storing Three-Dimensional Data

While three-dimensional drawing capability is ideal for massing, spatial studies, and presentations, not every application needs three-dimensional drawing. In fact, two-dimensional geometry is adequate for most drawings. You might imagine that it would be nice to insert a three-dimensional figure of a window wall into your plan drawing so that you could readily develop elevation drawings merely by rotating the plan 90°. While you could do that, you would be adding a substantial burden to your database, even if all Z coordinates are the same. In exchange, loading time and display (repaint) time would increase every time the drawing is redisplayed. Consequently, you don't want to add unnecessary data to a two-dimensional drawing unless three-dimensional drawing is necessary. There is another way to draw in three dimensions.

Three-Dimensional Figure Substitution

The concept is simple: Draw in two dimensions. Then when you need a three-dimensional drawing, substitute a three-dimensional figure for the original two-dimensional one (Figure 9.4). Methods for accomplishing this vary, but the principle is the same. This is a highly productive technique and can be used to develop standard elevations from standard plan elements, such as window walls, retail displays, and garden apartments. The select-and-search concept is fundamental to any database.

The most efficient graphics database systems maintain a pair of sister files: One contains graphics data (points, levels), and the other contains the intelligence (all the descriptive fields). The graphics information is maintained in RAM, while the intelligence is contained in a separate text file on the disk.

THREE-DIMENSIONAL PERCEPTION

Three-dimensional drawings should recreate accurately what the eyes see. A visual scan of a drawing or photograph reveals the view in approximately the same proportions as a scan of the real items. Even though the eyes perceive a relatively broad view through their peripheral vision, they focus on a comparatively small region, forming a **view angle** of no more than 5°–10°. The narrowness of this angle sets our criteria of visual accuracy; it maintains the perception of straight lines as straight. Beyond this limit, we perceive distortion. At work are a series of anomalies between the dynamics of eye movement, the actual view registration (view angle), and a perceptual notion of accuracy and distortion (keeping lines straight).

A simple example explains the anomaly (see Figure 9.5). Stand in the middle of a ring of equally spaced flagpoles. If you construct a traditional one- or two-point-perspective drawing of this scene, the flagpoles at the center of your view will be drawn shorter and closer together than the flagpoles at the periphery, creating the illusion of the poles being in an arc. But since the poles are equally spaced, no one pole should appear closer to another than any other. And since all are the same distance from the viewer, all should appear the same height. Only if the flagpoles are drawn "inaccurately" are they perceived accurately.

Actually, the eye is quite forgiving: It accepts a wide range of distortion as being accurate. Commercial artists and stage designers have long recognized and capitalized on the extended limits of visual acceptability. Look, for example, at the elongation of body proportions

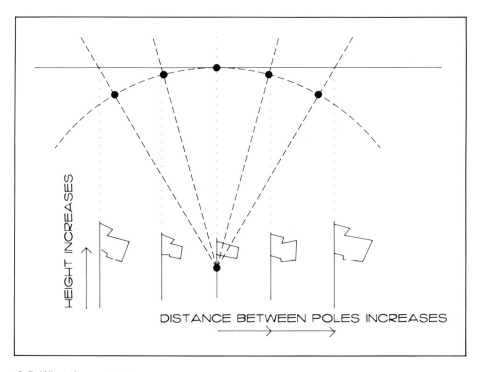

HEIGHT INCREASES

DISTANCE BETWEEN POLES INCREASES

9.5 *What the eye sees and what looks correct aren't always the same thing. Although the flagpoles are equidistant from one another and from the viewer, drawing them this way fails to convey the sense of the half circle.*

9.9 *The one-point perspective hardly needs an introduction. Perspective drawing generation is capable of producing a perspective from any angle looking in any direction. Care must be exercised in setting up a view to ensure that vertical and horizontal lines remain parallel to their respective axes. Here the horizon line is set at 5 feet above the floor, and a wire frame one-point perspective drawn.*

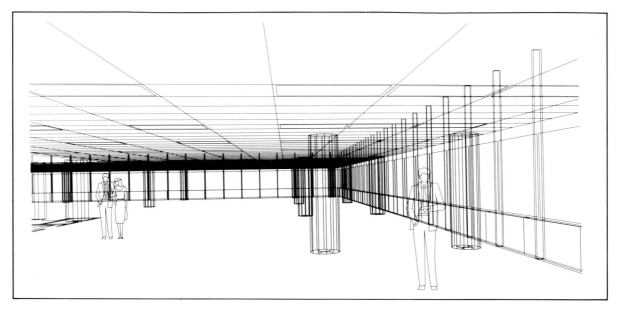

9.10 *The two-point perspective shares some common display subtleties with the one-point. Note the line detail available with computer-generated perspectives.*

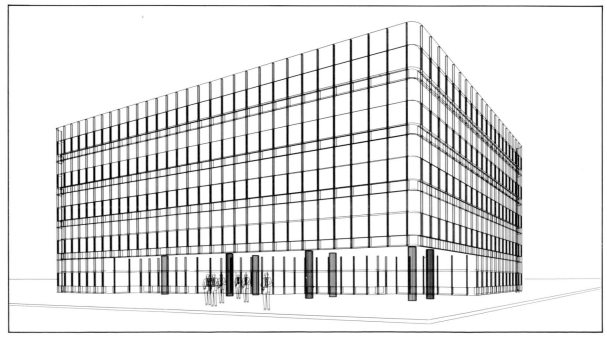

computer-generated perspective. The computer calculates the perspective and then places the full image on the screen. Later, you scale the drawing to fit any final presentation size.

Most of what you already know about plotting each of the common perspective views applies to CAD. To verify which projections are available on your CAD system, zoom in close on the test cube and modify the vertical view angle so that you are looking down (or up) from the horizon. If the perspective you generate curves or facets straight lines, you can plot **polyoptic** (fish-eye) views and correct perimeter distortion. If the same projection creates three vanishing points, you can plot the three classic views: one-, two-, and three-point perspectives. If the vertical lines remain vertical even though your line of view is not horizontal, your system will plot one- or two-point perspectives only.

One- and two-point perspective

One- and two-point perspectives are the most commonly plotted views, although both are forced perspectives: graphic accommodations that are not optically correct (see Figures 9.9 and 9.10). If your building is particularly wide or tall, you may have to experiment with several views to overcome excessive distortion at the edges. As in manual plotting, the vertical view angle must be perpendicular to the vertical lines on the building to maintain these lines as vertical and parallel; otherwise, you will be generating a three-point perspective. If this forces your station point back too far, you can compensate, in part, by generating the perspective off center. Then, recrop by panning the shifted drawing into the center of the screen—something you can't do manually.

Three-point perspective

The view shown in Figure 9.11 has never been popular with architects because the sloped faces (particularly on high-rise buildings) proved visually more objectionable than keeping

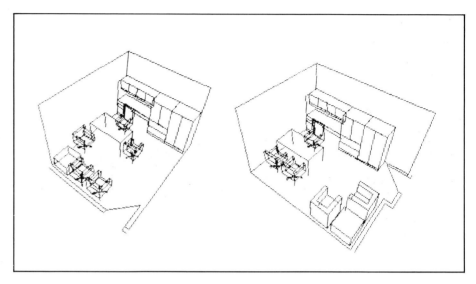

the distortion in a two-point perspective, which the three-point sought to correct. With CAD, you can experiment by tilting the altitude of the view angle up or below a line parallel with the earth. Distortion in a two-point perspective can sometimes be corrected by regenerating the drawing with a small amount of three-point rotation.

Polyoptic perspective

In the early 1970s, I developed **polyoptic** perspective drawing, a multipoint perspective drawing system based on optics and real distances, rather than the traditional flat picture plane methods. The system uses a multiview plotting graph called Perspectigraph. Lines are drawn from points located in space rather than by projecting them from a vanishing point. The key to correcting distortion lies in varying and controlling the vanishing points of parallel planes. Optically corrected perspective with view angles of 120° can be plotted without distortion. Since traditional perspective drawing suffers from edge distortion when the view angle approaches 45°, the gain is significant. For

9.11 *Most CAD systems generate three-point perspectives automatically (by default), unless the computer is "forced" to draw one- or two-point perspectives.*

9.12 *This polyoptic perspective drawing of the
State University of New
York at Purchase was
manually created using a
perspective drawing sys-
tem developed by the
author in 1972. Duplicat-
ing the pencil technique
on the computer would
be difficult, but generating this complex cur-
vilinear perspective is far
easier on the computer
than constructing and
plotting by hand.*

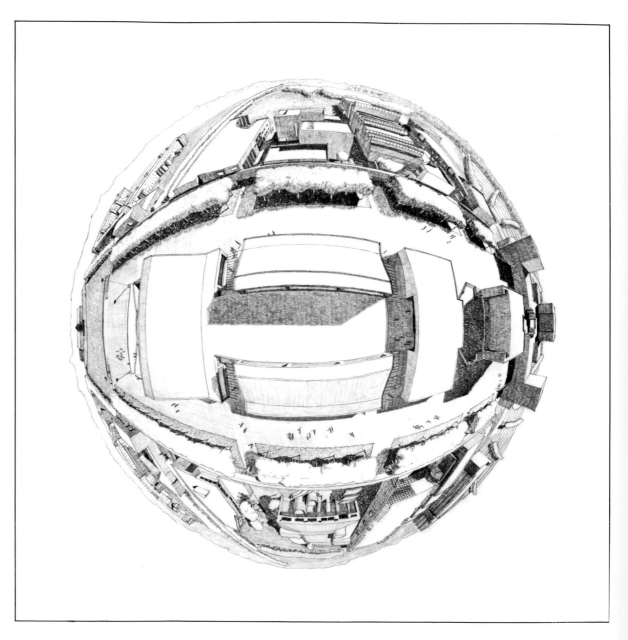

example, all four walls and the ceiling and floor tiles of a room can be shown without distortion. The most ambitious polyoptic perspective drawing, however, is the fish-eye, which combines the polyoptic concepts into a 180° hemispherical drawing (Figure 9.12). Although I've been able to emulate the polyoptic effect on some computers, these optics are not generally available on commercial CAD systems.

COLOR

Most architects and designers have experience understanding and working with color, its interaction, and its properties: **hue, saturation,** and **value**. But the color you see on the CRT is mixed from three light sources (red, *green*, and blue) rather than from three paint pigments (red, *yellow*, and blue), so you may find that some classic notions of color must be revised.

Mixing Colors

Like every schoolchild, you probably learned how to mix colors with poster paint. The colors weren't very elegant, but red and yellow produced orange, and green mixed with blue produced a dark turquoise. By varying the mixture of each primary hue, you created a new hue. With light, the primary hues are red, green, and blue (often referred to as **RGB**). You still control the intermediate hues by varying the amount of the primary hues, but mixing red and green to create yellow may seem unsettling.

When the CRT displays a hue in its purest form, without any white or black, you see the color at its maximum chromatic saturation. This **natural hue** contains the hue definition: 100% of one primary hue plus 0%–100% of one additional primary hue. The natural hue of orange contains 100% red, 67% green; yellow is 67% red, 100% green. Six hundred different hues can be defined, but the 18 shown in the right half of Color Plate 8 (page 101) represent enough hues to accommodate the 16 CSI construction divisions while maintaining enough hue separation to be easily distinguishable. The left side of Color Plate 8 shows the full hue spectrum or red, a triangle with white, black and the natural hue at the right vertex.

Black is the absence of any hue, or 0 percentile. White contains 100% of all primaries, or 300 percentile. Look at the left half of Color Plate 8. Saturation is displayed horizontally in ten convenient divisions ranging from 0% saturation, which contains no hue, to 100% saturation, the maximum saturation of a natural hue. Grays contain equal amounts of each hue, increasing from black to white, as shown on the left boundary. Black is added to a natural hue to create a **shade,** shown on the lower boundary of the hue triangle. Black is "added," however, by reducing the saturation of the natural hue. A **tint** consists of a mixture of white added to the natural hue, shown on the upper boundary. "White" is added by increasing the concentration of the **complement** (the hue directly across the **hue wheel**). Thus the complement of red—cyan, a hue containing equal parts of green and blue—is added to make pink. A tint of yellow contains the complement red-purple in the relative proportions 33% red, 100% blue. Finally, a **tone** contains gray mixed with the natural hue. Each chromatic designation inside the perimeter of the left chart in Color Plate 8 is a tonal variation.

Value (the degree of lightness) ranges from 0 (black) to 300 (white). It is separated for convenience into 16 vertical divisions on the left side of Color Plate 8, each corresponding to 30 percentiles of increasing lightness. Neutral 100 (33.3% each of red, green, and blue) lies on the same horizontal value as red 100. An individual designation of hue-saturation-value is called simply, a **color**.

Hue Anomalies

As every artist and designer knows, subtle color shifts occur when two hues are placed next to each other. Hues adjacent to one another in the spectrum appear to separate or subtract from each other. For example, vermilion seen next to red looks orange, whereas red next to vermilion appears to turn purple. As the hues move away from one another in the spectrum, they separate less, becoming briefly neutral until, as complementary hues (on opposite sides of the spectrum), the colors appear to add the color of their counterpart. Yellow and purple borrow from each other, producing a graying effect on both.

Visual and RGB Spectral Anomalies

Look at the hue wheel on the right side of Color Plate 8. The visual spectrum divides the hue wheel evenly into six primary and secondary hues: red, orange, yellow, green, blue, and purple. But the primaries of light—red, green, and blue—fall unevenly around the visual spectrum. While a mixture of green and blue produces two very similar tertiary hues, a mixture of red and blue generates five intermediate hues, one secondary and four tertiaries. With the spectral distance between red and green the greatest of the three primaries, these two primaries must produce both orange and yellow, as well as six intermediate tertiaries, in order to balance the visual spectrum. As you might imagine, blue-green hues are easily defined, while yellows and oranges are both difficult to define and to display consistently.

Value Anomalies

Because colors are created by mixing light, some natural hues are lighter or darker in value than their spectral counterparts. The light energy of red combined with blue phosphors creates not purple but a rather electric lavender that is popular among computer people because of its brightness. Cyan, a combination of blue and green, should also be a dark-value natural hue, but it ends up as a pale irridescent blue-green. If you have difficulty with either color, reduce the saturation (effectively adding black) to bring the colors to their proper value. Yellow and orange are tricky. Natural-hue yellow is often dark and dull, but it can be corrected by adding some "white" (a little purple). Build a test color pattern to display your favorite palette. See Color Plate 8.

Color Resolution

The color you see on the screen is made by combining the brightness of three grouped pixels, one each for red, green, and blue. A filled area of yellow, for example, consists of the light from many pairs of red and green pixels. Because the color capability extends to many drawing levels, you may see some inconsistencies in color resolution. Primary hues sometime spread out, spilling over boundaries and creating fuzzy edges. Line width sometimes varies between hues. On one system, I found that red lines always displayed two pixels wide, whereas brown lines displayed as alternate pixels, one pixel wide. You may also find that fine colored lines (and text) physically change color on a complementary background: On one occasion, red lettering on a pale-green background actually turned black—the pale green obliterated the red. Since each CAD system has its quirks, color tests are always in order.

Selecting the Right Color

If your CAD system is limited to six or eight colors, you may not have any control over the selection or changing of hues. But CRTs capable of displaying 16 colors usually permit you to define at least 64 colors, whereas 256-color displays often support 1000 or more color definitions. In some cases, you must enter the

RGB values from the keyboard. But better software lets you change hue, saturation, and value by moving the cursor over a set of on-screen color scales. As you move the cursor, the color changes on the CRT.

Adjusting Color on the CRT

How do you know the color adjustments on the CRT are correctly set? As with tuning a color television receiver, a slight change can shift all colors. Use a test block or hue wheel like the one shown on the right side of Color Plate 8. The telltale colors are orange, yellow, and gray. For best results, the hues should be equally spaced and follow the natural rhythm of the visual spectrum (start at red, then orange, then yellow; don't jump from red to green to orange). Use colors in multiples of six, with a minimum of 12 preferable. Be sure to include black, white, and several neutral grays. If several adjacent colors look alike, or if the yellows aren't clear, or if the grays look like any hue other than neutral gray, then ask your technical field representative to realign the color adjustment while you watch the test diagram on the CRT.

RENDERING: SURFACES, SHADES, AND SHADOWS

Rendering is the most exciting visual product of CAD, creating a surface model of your design that is complete with shades and shadows. Once the basic data about the object is entered, you can generate multiple renderings by varying the view direction, surface qualities, and lighting conditions. Professional CAD renderings require advanced hardware and software to accomplish this task, but the results can be spectacular. In this section, you'll learn the principles of rendering: how **surface drawings** are developed from **line drawings**, the principles of shading, and the generation of **shadows**.

Surface Development

You begin with an outline of the object or building. Start with a perspective you developed earlier in this chapter.

Wire frame drawings

See Color Plate 9 (page 101). The wire frame drawing looks like a model made from sticks or wires. The boundaries of all planes, both visible and hidden, are shown. Because of the transparency, many people find these drawings difficult to read and understand. During this first step, generate as many outline perspectives as you like, saving one or several for final rendering.

Line drawings

Look at Color Plate 10 (page 102). Once you've settled on several wire frame perspectives, the next step is to remove the unwanted lines on the "back" side of the drawing, the **hidden lines**. Professional-quality drawing software removes hidden lines automatically, but the process is often slow. The computer must analyze each line on the drawing, determine which part, if any, is behind another line, and regenerate the corrected drawing. The process requires considerable computation and processing. The delay will be apparent, but the result is a finished line drawing.

Surface drawings

Up to now, drawing with CAD has involved drawing lines and shading between lines. Three-dimensional drawings have remained two-dimensional representations. In the process of drawing a perspective, the computer calculates the location and draws lines in space.

In order to draw surfaces, the computer must be able to recognize lines as boundaries of a plane, not just as lines. A plane is flat. A surface, however, is a geometric entity and may consist of many planes. A sphere, for example, has one surface but is depicted on a CRT as having many planes. Every plane contains at least three boundary lines, contains only straight lines drawn from any two points on the surface, and is in no way curvilinear. In the process of drawing a solid surface model, the computer calculates the boundaries of all planes, filling each with solid color (Color Plate 11, page 103). A solid is represented by planes and surfaces: a tetrahedron by four planes, a cube by six. A cylinder contains two flat planes at either end and one curvilinear surface, which the computer separates into many flat rectangular planes. An architectural rendering contains many surfaces but many more planes.

Software varies in the manner in which the user defines or identifies planes. In some programs, you can collect lines into a planar boundary. A cube contains 12 lines, but as you've learned, you can't render 12 lines. By converting these lines into six planes, each consisting of four lines (a total of 24 lines), the planes can be shaded, giving each the appearance of being solid. Later in this chapter, you'll see how the angular slope of the plane is used to calculate light and shaded surfaces. In another method, planes are automatically created every time a rectangle, circle, ellipse, or polygon is created.

One system uses a shortcut that creates surface renderings by taking advantage of the sequential method of storing graphic data. You create the drawing by constructing polygons in the background first and working toward the foreground. As the drawing displays on the CRT, the planes load in the same sequence as created. Consequently, the planes in the foreground paint over the section of those in the background, effectively hiding the background planes. It's a little tricky, but it works as long as you don't change the view angle and display the background in front of the foreground.

Shading
See Color Plate 12 (page 104). Shading turns a surface drawing into an architectural **rendering**: a lifelike image that depicts the reflected light and texture of each surface. Shading adjusts the saturation and value of the hue assigned to each plane on a surface. For example, the surface of a round yellow column will be redrawn as a series of planes in various colors of the hue yellow, starting with white (reflecting the light source and obscuring any yellow), progressing through pale tints to bright yellows (the lighted planes), and turning into dark shades of yellow and then brown (the shaded side of the column). The range of colors makes up the **shading spectrum**. To better understand, look at how planes are located in space.

Vector definitions
The orientation of every plane must be calculated in order to shade, so the computer needs a simple, efficient way to locate each plane in space. Line endpoints easily define the boundary, and the angular displacement of a plane is best defined by the **normal vector**, a line passing through and perpendicular to a plane. The direction of the normal vector is determined by two XYZ coordinates: an origin, assumed to be at 0, 0, 0, and a terminus at another point relative to the origin, defined by unit distance, ranging from -1 to $+1$. The direction can then be expressed as a value for the terminus of the normal vector. For example, the normal vector 0, 0, 1, "originates" as 0, 0, 0 and "terminates" at 0, 0, $+1$, passing through only $Z+1$, which defines a plane parallel to the XY plane. A normal vector of 1, 1, 1, passes through $X+1$, $Y+1$, $Z+1$ and defines a plane on a northwest–southeast axis whose face is inclined at an angle of 45°. The direction of the normal vector is from "below" in the "southwest" toward "up" in the "northeast."

How shading works

In determining the shaded color, the computer considers the surface characteristics of the plane, lighting conditions, and the three construction vectors: (1) the **planar vector**, the direction of the plane; (2) the **light vector**, the direction to the light source; and (3) the **view vector**, the direction to the eye's viewpoint (see Figure 9.2). In order to simplify the calculation of color content, shading is often confined to half of the hue spectrum, a range of colors derived by mixing black with the natural hue (called a *shade* in the earlier section on color and not to be confused with the term *shading* used here). Black, as you may recall, is "added" to the natural hue by reducing the saturation of a hue. In order to provide a full range of shading in rendering, the software must support the addition of white with the natural hue to create tints. Tints are essential to show brightly lit or highly reflective surfaces. Otherwise, the shading spectrum is limited (see Color Plate 12).

Refer to the earlier example of the yellow column. Without full shading capability, the colors range from yellow to black only. Darker hues, such as blue and purple, have limited use because of the limited shading spectrum (unless you're using that ubiquitous irridescent lavender euphemistically called magenta). Without the ability to add white, colors appear flat and dull, as though under a cloudy sky, and of course, specular (mirror) reflections cannot be indicated. Many software shading programs cannot tint, but professional-quality software will both shade and tint. You may find it necessary to supplement your computer with a special graphics processor in order to draw high-quality renderings.

Surface characteristics

Look at Color Plate 12. Surface characteristics determine how much light is reflected and the quality of the reflected light. The ability of the software to accommodate these characteristics varies considerably.

Textured surfaces reflect less light than smooth ones, but as you move away from a highly textured surface, the relative texture diminishes. An otherwise rough brick surface can become substantially reflective when seen reflecting a large light source, such as the sun. And smooth surfaces can become as reflective as mirrored surfaces.

Light source

Lighting conditions that occur in nature are very complex. For the most part, these subtleties add little to an architectural rendering, as most depict daylight scenes lit by the sun, a single-point source of light. This simplicity lends itself well to computerized rendering.

There are three light qualities to consider: direct light, ambient light, and reflected light. **Direct light** is any primary source of light; for most rendering, it is the sun. Direct light, when reflected into the eye of the viewer, produces a specular reflection, creating a white highlight.

Ambient light is diffuse light that backfills and softens contrast. It is the ambient light that comes from the sky and fills shadows. High-level ambient light reduces contrast to a minimum, eliminating shade and shadows. Thin surface fog, snow whiteouts, and luminous ceilings produce high ambient light levels. Low-level ambient lighting creates high contrast between lit and unlit areas. Accent lighting projected on dark surfaces and lighting on the lunar surface (there is no atmosphere to diffuse the light) produce low ambient levels. **Reflected light** brightens an adjacent plane, typically a neighboring building.

Direct light accounts for the major segment of shading calculations. When you set the azimuth and altitude of the light, you are really defining the light vector of a direct light source. The process of shading calculates the **shading coefficient** of any plane by interpolating the light, planar, and view vectors. The ambient light factor will determine the upper and lower limits of the shading coefficient, but the overall effect is small in comparison with the direct light calculations. The total palette of shading coefficients is limited to the total number of displayable colors. The range of shading coefficients from dark to light will be divided equally among a given set of surfaces. The brilliance and contrast of specular reflections will be determined by the surface texture, modifying only those planes affected.

Most software assigns one shading coefficient to all planes that share the same planar vector. This speeds processing, but it can make the drawing look rather sterile. A glass facade that might otherwise reflect in sunlight in several central spandrel sections will appear as one large, uniform plane.

The mechanics of surface shading are an ideal and efficient application for a computer, but the concept has been around for some time. The pencil drawing in Figure 9.12 was rendered using a set of manual light-source shading algorithms I developed in the early 1970s. The shading coefficients are based on five lighting/viewing conditions: reflective, lighted, edge-lighted, unlighted, and unlighted surfaces seen on edge; these are adjusted for surface texture, color, size, and importance. The palette consists of white, black, and six intermediate grades of pencil gray. Look at what is possible now in Color Plate 13 (page 104).

Surface and lighting anomalies

Glass is a material with extraordinary properties. It is transparent as long as the illumination level on the opposite side is higher than the level on the viewing side—otherwise, glass becomes reflective. And regardless of the lighting level, glass (and water) becomes reflective when seen at angles nearly parallel to the surface.

Planes closer to the viewer appear lighter and brighter, containing a higher saturation of a hue, whereas planes farther away look grayer, becoming dark and dull. While a nearby white wall may reflect 95% of the light, a distant landscape reflects no more than roughly 19%. Larger surfaces also tend to be lighter, primarily because their size dominates the view. Smaller surfaces, on the other hand, tend to shift, sometimes matching, sometimes contrasting with the background.

The computer uses the "removed" hidden lines to draw surfaces seen behind transparent planes, mixing the surface colors of each plane. Although reflected images—such as those seen on the surface of a mirror or smooth water—can be calculated, software is limited. The same holds true for refracted images, those distorted when seen through curved glass.

Shadow Projection

Whether you call it plotting shadows (as architects do) or ray tracing (as computer programmers do), its meaning is the same. The computer projects an imaginary line from the boundary of a lighted surface (one with a certain minimum shading coefficient) until it intersects another surface. The interior of the resulting polygon is then filled with "shadow": a color with the same hue as the lighted surface, but with a value equal to the shading coefficient of a shaded plane. Matching the endpoint of an imaginary line with a planar surface and tracing the line requires considerably more computation than shading. While it's slow, the results are very effective.

Creating a Rendering

Here's how to draw a rendering. Look at Figure 9.2 and Color Plates 9, 10, 11, and 12. Three location vectors are used, one to locate the building origin and orientation; one, the light source; and one, the station point. The building azimuth is located on the site by aligning a wall or column grid relative to north and by fixing a known building coordinate at the drawing origin (all azimuth, altitude, and distance calculations commence from this origin point). No altitude or distance setting is needed, since both are 0.

You may establish either the station point or the light source next, adjusting both in the course of creating a three-dimensional drawing. I suggest that you establish the station point first: Set the azimuth, altitude, and distance or set the XYZ coordinates of the station point, being careful to control the viewing angle so as to limit perimeter distortion. If you want to look from the southeast, the azimuth angle is 135°. If you want to look up or down at the building, set the altitude angle accordingly, but keep in mind that any view angle other than parallel to the horizon will cause the vertical lines to appear in three-point perspective. You can correct this by setting the Z elevation of the station point the same as that of the drawing origin and the altitude angle at 0°.

Now establish the location of the sun, given as an azimuth and altitude for a given time at a given latitude and longitude. If you want to plot the sun at 3 P.M. on June 21 at 97°W, 35°N, you will determine its position to be due west at 50° above the horizon, locating it without guessing. The distance of the sun is assumed to be at infinity. From each of these coordinate locations, the planar, light, and view vectors are computed.

After you've finished generating as many views as you require, remove the hidden lines and save the drawings. Before you start to render, create a background and reinsert the perspective drawing over the background. Then select the hues you want (if your system is limited to 16 colors, select carefully) and the direction of the sun. I prefer to locate the sun at a very low angle above the horizon and off to one side. In this way, one side of the building is in bright sunlight and the front is shown in greater detail in shade. The horizontal angle insures that some surfaces are highlighted by specular reflections. After you've generated the rendering, you may want to correct some of the colors, adding highlights or modifying window colors to emulate reflections. Once you're satisfied, sign it, and save two copies.

Now that you understand the principles of drawing, design, and data management on a CAD system, you are ready to learn how to organize and control your graphics database.

Part IV

MANAGEMENT

A CAD system does not manage itself. Learning how to manage it and determining who shall be the manager is the subject of Part IV. You'll learn how to create and manage a library of electronic drawings. Chapter 10 shows you how to keep track of drawings and how to develop and implement office CAD standards. Chapter 11 teaches you how to manage the data you've entered into your CAD system and use that information to produce better drawings and more profitable projects. Chapter 12 covers the essentials of system management: what you need to know and do to keep your CAD system in good order.

10
Drawing Management

Drawing management for manual drafting is relatively simple. The project manager keeps a list of the drawings stored in the drawing plan chest. Since there's only one copy of each drawing, only one person at a time can use a particular drawing. When you need a drawing, you go to the plan chest, find it, and tape it to your drawing board. Your CAD plan chest, while physically much smaller, will contain both your work-in-progress and finished drawings. You'll keep most of your work-in-progress on the hard disk, some on floppy disks, and your record copies on tapes, cartridges, or floppies. As your "plan chest" of CAD drawings grows, you'll want to organize your drawing files for easy access.

FIRST LAW: SAVE TWO COPIES
Save two copies of everything. Single copies of computer data have a way of self-destructing, while multiple copies seem to defy Murphy's Law, which says that if anything can go wrong, it will. The first time you lose a major set of drawings just before a presentation, you will become a believer. Don't wait to learn the hard way. *Always make two copies.*

Second Law: Save Periodically
The sequel to the first law is: *Save work-in-progress periodically.* Your only "best" copy is the most recently saved drawing, so develop the habit of saving your work about once an hour.

Input Logs
One of the handiest lifesavers is the **input log**, also called a data log or keystroke log. The log records all your input—keystrokes (including errors and corrections) and cursor moves in the same order as entered. Typically, a log is opened and closed voluntarily, but it will close

automatically when the system is shut down. When you enter the command to open an input log, the computer will **prompt** you to enter a name. If the computer shuts down unexpectedly —called a **crash**, whatever the cause—you lose the ability to communicate with the computer. Since your current drawing resides in RAM, you lose your drawing because you can't save it. So if the power fails, the computer crashes; the loss of power, however short, erases all your data in RAM.

Input logs are the most valuable when the computer crashes because all your drawing is saved. To redraw, enter the command to replay the input log and then enter the log name. The computer re-creates the drawing in the same sequence as originally drawn. Remember that the input log simply repeats each input entry up to the point when the computer crashed or you terminated input. Watching your drawing being re-created on a CRT is an excellent training tool because you see how well you draw at a glance. If your computer permits, an input log should be built into your start-up routine to run automatically. These files use very little memory and do not affect performance—and they're excellent insurance.

Be Prepared for the Worst
If the power fails or the cord is inadvertently unplugged and the system crashes, what do you do? Two of my "favorite" catastrophes were saving an old, obsolete drawing over a newly completed revision and deleting a directory full of good drawings when I'd intended to copy or move the directory. The phone rings or someone interrupts with a question, and, distracted, you can all too easily enter the wrong command. So safeguards are in order.

SAVING DRAWINGS

Just as loading a file transfers a drawing from "drawer" to "drafting board," saving a file transfers your new drawing back to its electronic drawer. You can save a drawing anytime simply by entering a command like SAVE FLOORPLAN. A202. Let's look at some of the manual and automatic methods to save drawings.

File Names

Before you name a file, find out what the naming conventions are for your computer. This is usually determined by a program called the **operating system**, which you can learn about in your user's manual. Generally, a file must begin with an alphabetic character or one of several selected characters, such as the dollar sign ($) or the percent sign (%). It is normally limited in length from 6 to 32 characters.

Everyone develops a preference in naming. Some people like short coded names (often because they hate to type). Short names require careful planning, limit descriptiveness to general coding, are often en "coded", and are prone to confusion and errors. It is not difficult to mistakenly delete file J01601 instead of J01501. Longer names are more descriptive and easier to identify, but they require more typing. Some like a comprehensive name because finding the drawing in a directory list is easier and typing disasters like the file J01501/J01601 example are less likely. For instance, the file name ABCPLAN1.7049 describes a first-floor plan drawing for client ABC drawn on July 4, 1989. Each alternative has its advantages, so select the one that makes you comfortable.

Auto-Saving

If you load a drawing with an AUTO-LOAD program, the computer remembers the file name. The companion program SAVE.DRAWING not only recovers the name stored in the global variable but tells you the name of the currently loaded, unmodified drawing. You simply press the Return key, or Enter key, to save the revised drawing under the original name. If you know the name is supposed to be the same, you don't have to remember the actual name.

There are also ways to store the name of the drawing with the drawing. When you save the drawing, the computer reads the stored name and saves the new drawing under the old name, insuring that the drawing is saved under the correct name.

Saving Two Drawings with Identical File Names

Sometimes, but not always, you can save two drawings with the same name. But first, find out what your system is capable of.

Some CAD systems will save a new file over the old file by automatically replacing the old drawing with the new one under the same name. If your system functions in this manner, I suggest that you create (or ask your CAD vendor to create) a macroprogram that verifies the existence of the old file and asks you if you want to replace the current drawing with the new one or save the new drawing under another name. Otherwise, be very careful: Remember what happens to single unduplicated copies of drawing files.

If your disk supports a directory tree, you can save identical drawings with identical names in different directories. Thus, the floor plan PLAN-A202.DG might be saved in the directory //CAD/APPROVED-WORK and in another directory //

CAD/WORK-IN-PROGRESS. If you can save duplicate copies under identical names, you should be able to determine the directory from which you load PLAN-A202.DG.

If you want to keep the original and save a revision in the same directory, then the file names must differ in at least one character. Sometimes the original file is automatically renamed with a suffix like .BACKUP or simply .BAK, and the new file is saved under the original name. When the process is not automatic, you should append either a date or a revision number. Hence, PLAN-A202 could be revised as PLAN-A202-70486 or as PLAN-A202-1. You would then have two files: the original and the revision.

Saving All or Part of the Drawing
By default, the entire screen, visible or not, is saved on disk with the basic SAVE command. But you can also save selected parts of a drawing if you want. You may copy portions, selected levels, or entities of any type. Review the details in Chapter 7.

Pixel Saves
The graphic image you see on the CRT screen is composed of individual dots of light called picture elements, or pixels. Under normal circumstances, drawings are saved as data: A line is saved as an origin and vector or as two connected points. Consequently, graphics are stored as a list of instructions, each instruction identifying a specific graphic element of a drawing or an intelligent data element. It is this sequential file structure that allows the computer to extract any selected text, which subsequently becomes the intelligent data.

But some drawings require only the graphic information, not the intelligence. When you map the pixels, you save a description—called a bit map—of the color of every pixel. Typically, there are about 600–1200 pixels horizontally and 400–800 vertically, totalling 240,000–960,000

pixels. However, bit maps can often be compressed with utility programs to use less memory space and to display faster.

Creating a Temporary Record: Back-up
All drawings, files, and software should have at least one **back-up copy**, although you may feel more comfortable making two back-ups of your current work. Some firms make duplicates by rotating back-up copies: Last week's copy is stored for two weeks, when it is then updated; this week's copy is saved until the week after next, when *it* is updated.

Creating a Permanent Record: Archiving
All drawings wind up in the archives of municipal building departments as a public record of the construction. But don't rely on the building department for your **archive copy**.

With magnetic media, it is wise to archive copies of your work as the work progresses. Firms with large CAD systems use tape drives or high-density tape cartridges. Laser disks are finding their way into this area, and Bernoulli boxes are also being used for PC systems. If you don't have one of these high-speed or high-density devices, then you must archive with your floppy-disk drive, a comparatively slow process.

Archive copies should be made at least once a week and physically stored in a vault or in another building. It is unlikely that fires will occur at both locations at the same time.

GETTING DRAWINGS OUT OF A FILE
Now that you've saved a file, how do you get it back to work on the drawing again? If you know the correct file name, you can load the drawing. If you key an incorrect file name, your load command will be met by a curt "File not found." This is one error message that has never amused me, especially when I know the file exists. Then how do we find your drawing?

Locating the Correct File

To locate the correct drawing, you'll probably want to look at a list of the drawings stored in the computer. Whether it's called an **index**, **catalog**, or **directory**, it displays a list of all the files. Some will be drawings; others will be text files or input logs; and some will be software or utility files.

You'll soon discover how to organize the disk files that contain your drawings. Become familiar with how your system saves and manipulates drawings, as well as how you locate drawings. Does your directory contain all drawings on the system in one main directory, or are the files divided into **disk compartments**, **subdirectories**, or both? Many systems append identifying text to help you locate files: A drawing you named ABCPLAN1 might be saved as ABCPLAN1.DWG. The suffix will identify the file type, but its use is not necessary to locate the file.

Smaller disk drives show the entire contents of the disk or of a disk partition. Larger systems use a hierarchical naming system called a **tree**, which allows files to be placed in a subdirectory level under another directory. The result resembles an organizational chart or a tree's limbs. The top directory is called the **root directory**, under which, for example, you might establish a number of directories, perhaps called WORK-IN-PROGRESS, APPROVED DRAWINGS, and SOFTWARE. WORK-IN-PROGRESS contains two additional subdirectories for two users, Smith and Brook, each containing their current drawings. You could then review a directory of Brook's drawings by entering the directory command followed by a logical **path** down the tree until the file is located. The complete **pathname** might look like this: DIRECTORY //CAD/WORK-IN-PROGRESS/BROOK/ABCPLAN1.

Spend some time learning how your directory works. You may be able to display a variety of file information, such as the file name, type and length of file, date created, and last date modified—useful in identifying work created on a specific date or on the most recent date. Identifying files created after a certain time or date is a useful technique when saving recent work.

File size is expressed in bytes, **sectors** (256 bytes), or **blocks** (1024 bytes). If you have a 10MB hard disk (10 megabytes) you can load almost 10,000 blocks (10,000 × 1024 bytes = 10,240,000 bytes, called, by convention, 10MB) of data or drawings. Architectural drawings range in size from 100 to 500 blocks, although a rendering can reach 1000 blocks, and some urban studies require upward of 2500 blocks. Don't expect file sizes to diminish; rather, you can expect them to grow as more ways are found to add more information to a drawing.

Loading a File

You gain access to a drawing by loading a file. The computer copies the data in the file from your disk into the temporary memory area, that is, into the random access memory (RAM). Once the file is in RAM, you'll be able to view, add to, or change the drawing. The original remains safe on the disk just as you left it. You will be revising the duplicate copy stored in RAM. To prevent two people from working on the same drawing simultaneously, no one else will have access to your drawing until you save it. On some larger systems, your revisions are dynamically updated in the main copy, which can be viewed by, but not worked on by, anyone else on the network.

The drawing files on many systems save all the graphics and intelligence information sequentially in one file, while others separate graphics from figures and intelligence. The former is more direct, but the latter uses memory more efficiently.

Multiple Parts

Architectural drawings require relatively large quantities of memory. If disk memory space becomes limited, you can separate drawings into parts common to many drawings and parts unique to a particular drawing. Common parts, such as borders, grids, walls, and dimensions, are saved only once and then combined with unique parts, such as partitions, ceiling patterns, or duct layouts, to create three new drawings when needed.

Load Procedures that Remember File Names

The best way to insure that you save your current drawing under the correct name is to save the loading name or establish the new file name to be saved at the time of loading. Unlike word processing software, CAD software does not always maintain the name of the currently loaded drawing, although the need should be obvious. In the absence of such information, you can write a short macroprogram—let's call it LOAD-DRAWING—that asks for the file name (often written *filename*). After entering the name PLAN-A202, for example, the computer stores that name in a special memory place called a global variable and then loads and displays the drawing.

HOUSEKEEPING

When files are not in exactly the right place, when they have an incorrect name, need to be duplicated, or have outlived their usefulness, a little housekeeping is in order. Computer housekeeping does not change the data in the files, it changes only the file names, the location, or the number of copies.

Rename, one of the most versatile commands, allows you to revise the name of any file. In some instances, the selected file name is changed; in others, a copy is made under a new name, retaining the original file with the original name. Consult your user's manual for the procedures and syntax that your computer recognizes.

Files can be moved or copied within or between compartments or directories. Moving shifts the location of a file, while copying duplicates the file with or without a new name.

You can delete files. How? Cautiously. Once deleted, the file is gone. It is good practice to save any work-in-progress before you delete, just to be safe. Deleting a file, by the way, removes a **pointer** in the directory (the pointer tells the computer where to look for the file). It does not erase the file; rather, it makes the space on the disk available to be overwritten by a new file. On some systems, consequently, there are ways to recover deleted files, but the results are not always reliable, and knowing how to recover one requires skill and understanding normally only possessed by experienced programmers.

In saving the original file, both the name and the pointer are saved in a special location called the **volume table of contents** (**VTOC**), a directory the computer uses to locate files. When you load a drawing, the computer matches your file name with the file name found in the VTOC. Then it reads the corresponding address (location in computer memory) contained in the pointer, moves the read-write head on the disk to that address, copies (loads) the data into RAM, and starts the program.

CONTROLLING FILE SIZE

Drawings demand large amounts of memory, consuming space at roughly 100 times that of word-processing files. Although you won't want to restrict content, there are some techniques that will help you control drawing size that will, in turn, help control the amount of RAM and disk space available.

During a work session on CAD, you may be tempted to save every revision or scratch-pad drawing. Your directory will fill up with needed as well as many unneeded drawings, and you'll soon discover that you have used far more space than you intended, that little or no space remains to store additional work, or that the computer performs sluggishly because too little RAM remains for the computer to perform properly. Let's look at some techniques that conserve space without reducing content.

Save a Common Item Just Once

If you'll be using a common item for different applications, save the truly common part just once. For example, save the sheet border once, and you won't have to store the border with every plan, elevation, or detail. Save the sheet title information as required, and join these two with your drawing when you're ready to print. You apply the same principle with common architectural and engineering elements: the column grid, core, perimeter walls, and interior partitions. Since you reassemble the drawings relatively infrequently, write a macroprogram that loads and reassembles the specific drawing parts into a complete drawing. (You'll learn how to write macros in Chapter 14. If you're new to CAD or need help writing a macro, ask your CAD vendor for guidance.)

Packing

Drawings are saved in the most direct manner available, which may not be the most compact manner. Drawings that are saved as data (and reconstructed when displayed) generally store that data in the same sequence as created. As you work on a drawing, your changes and revisions will be reflected graphically, but they may not be automatically corrected in the database. In other words, a graphics deletion may not result in a data deletion, (just in skipping past the unwanted data leaving the file length unchanged). You reduce the length of the database with a system command that closes the data gaps. **Packing** can reduce the file size by one third. Consequently, you should pack a drawing before saving it. Drawings saved as bit maps employ special packing programs that identify repetitive patterns in the image and substitute a shorthand notation for the pattern.

Graphics Compaction

Some graphic forms require more memory than others. Drawings created using such data as a point and vector for a line require a data pair for every line. A solid line 5 inches long requires one pair, while a dashed line with ten dashes may require ten pairs on many CAD systems. Circles generally require more memory space than polygons, and three-dimensional objects require more space than two-dimensional ones. The differences are apparent during redisplay: Solid lines and polygons display more quickly than dashed lines, circles, or crosshatching. For general drafting, polygons can be substituted for circles and two-dimensional figures for three-dimensional ones. You can substitute a 24- to 32-sided polygon for a circle with little loss of visual roundness.

DEVELOPING OFFICE STANDARDS

Every office develops drafting, lettering, and dimensioning standards, along with standard titles and title blocks, so that construction documents drawn by different people look reasonably similar and are uniformly legible. Enacting standards such as these is a chore in manual drafting. On the other hand, enacting graphics standards for CAD can be easily established and mandated. Figure symbols, lettering, dimensioning, line weights, and textures require that you create a specific graphics figure or define the standards before proceeding. The standard then becomes an integral part of your drawing lexicon. Here are some samples to guide you.

Color and Level Control

While the use of color is most often thought of as an enhanced visualization tool, both for renderings and for two-dimensional line drawings, the use of color is visually essential in the identification of parts in complex drawings. Adding color to the display allows you to include more information on a common drawing. For example, furniture, walls, ceilings, lights, and power can be displayed successfully in color when they overlap and are completely unreadable in back-and-white.

The possibility of separating drawing data into levels that are compatible with the Construction Specifications Institute (CSI) standards for specification writing has intrigued me for some time. Such a standard would provide a cross-reference for drawings and would simplify specification writing. For example, a spec writer can display only gypsum board walls, identify the sizes and standards, and proceed with the writing. A project manager might display all the notes for gypsum board walls to verify uniformity and correctness.

Color Plate 3 is the result of my work in developing standards for layer designations based on the CSI/AIA format and integral color designations based on a spectral progression of color definitions. At first, I was concerned that separating construction information into 16 drawing sections would prove awkward or unworkable and that the color separation between adjacent layers would be too close to be distinguishable, both of which would threaten the simplicity of the concept. After testing, my concerns proved unfounded.

When you study Color Plate 3, you will recognize that each of the CSI sections has been assigned ten levels, beginning with level 10, corresponding to Section 1, Office Equipment. Dividing the CSI sections into subsections of ten numbers provides ten levels for each CSI section. The first digit(s) of each level number match(es) the CSI section number. Thus, Section 9, Finishes, is allotted levels 90–99. Ten levels are insufficient for Sections 15

and 16, Mechanical and Electrical, respectively, so they have been assigned 20 levels each. Section 0 is called General; it contains data common to all drawings, including borders, grids, dimensions, general notes, revisions in progress, and undisplayed graphics. Additional levels are assigned for project management use, for a color palette for general color use, for a scratch pad for temporary drawings, and for system or programming use. This full standard requires 200–250 levels to implement. You can, of course, reduce the number of layers (you'll be forced to if your system supports fewer layers), but it's extremely easy to remember that section 12 belongs on layers 120–129.

Colors follow the spectral rainbow, beginning with Section 1: cool yellows for office, gold for site work, oranges for structure, reds for architecture, purples for equipment and furniture, blues for special construction and conveyance, greens for mechanical equipment, and yellow-greens for electrical equipment. This particular array of colors was selected for display quality, frequency of use, logical groupings, and because of certain CRT color-spectrum anomalies.

On color monitors, the number of colors displayed is a function of the number 2 raised to some power: $2^2 = 4$; $2^4 = 16$; $2^8 = 256$. With 16 CSI/AIA sections, you need 16 hues plus two for the extra levels in Sections 15 and 16, for a total of 18—which works perfectly with the six primary and secondary hues. The hue wheel on the right side of Color Plate 8 shows the 18 hue divisions used with the 256-color palette. Section 0 and all non-CSI sections are assigned neutral grays, ranging from a black background to a white cursor, with temporary graphics between. The remaining colors are spread over the 16 sections.

Professional color work requires a monitor capable of displaying 256 colors. This color standard assigns 256 colors, one for each level, with the color number equal to the level number. Each of the ten levels within the CSI/AIA sections is assigned a progressively lighter chromatic variation of the basic hue. Thus, each level has a distinct color (Color Plate 3). On a 16-color monitor, I assign black to the background, white to both temporary graphics and General, leaving 14 colors to distribute among the 16 sections. I double up Concrete and Masonry (Sections 3 and 4) and Special Construction and Conveyance (Sections 13 and 14).

Figure Library
You can remove all those templates from your desk and put them away for your grandchildren. Even though your CAD vendor has supplied you with some standard figure libraries, you will want to create your own. Here, then, is an opportunity to standardize the office symbols commonly used on your drawings.

On some systems, you save a figure symbol like any other graphic entity; therefore, your **graphics library** can be anywhere you choose. On the other hand, that library might contain special graphics created in machine language and stored in a special binary shape table. Figures created with vectors require more time to create and are not as easily rescaled as are pure graphics files.

Everyone who uses a graphics terminal develops his or her own personal macros and figures. For those and other files, a personal library should be designated for each user. This library should be separate from all office libraries.

USING OUTPUT DEVICES
Creating CAD drawings is fine, but until everyone has a CAD wristwatch or a portable "CADman" on which to view drawings, we'll have to rely on more prosaic means to transmit copies of drawings, using what is

unglamorously referred to as an **output device**. The three main output devices to print drawings are printers, hard-copy devices, and plotters.

Printers
Dot matrix printers can produce written reports or graphic documents in one or more colors. They are ideal for quick-review drawings, known to designers as check prints. Most printers accept continuous paper or single sheets. Continuous paper is ideal for long reports, and single-sheet capability is great for letter quality mailings printed on letterhead stationery or on preprinted forms, such as a Standard Form 254, commonly used in selecting consultants for federal work. Most of the printing generated by a CAD terminal will be reports that require continuous paper. Letter quality printers can be used with CAD systems but, are not capable of printing graphic images.

Two sizes of paper are common: $9\frac{1}{2}'' \times 11''$ and $14\frac{7}{8}'' \times 11''$. The $9\frac{1}{2}''$-wide paper with $\frac{1}{2}''$ perforated edges can be trimmed to the standard $8\frac{1}{2}'' \times 11''$ size; it will accommodate a standard 80-column display based on ten characters per inch, (called **character pitch**). At the same character pitch, the wider paper displays 132 columns of text, useful for wide-format reports or graphics.

Hard-Copy Devices
These devices resemble photocopy machines because (unlike printers) they can only make a copy of the screen display (**screen dump**). They are capable of printing in both black-and-white and color and have high resolution (produce sharp details). Since the copy (dump) is limited to a single screen display, it is not practical for long reports.

Plotters
Plotter-generated drawings provide the greatest degree of accuracy of any medium, substantially exceeding the accuracy of any

manually created drawing. Pen plotters produce extraordinary line quality, but they do not have sufficient speed to support volume printing, which is best left to electrostatic plotters. Since printers and hard-copy devices produce drawings of limited size and variable resolution, neither is suitable for producing construction documents or architectural working drawings.

The plotter is an integral part of your CAD drawing system. Since the cost of quality plotters and electrostatic printers is high, one plotter will be shared with several CAD terminals. Running the plotter ties up a CAD terminal on a PC system, so you can't plot and draw at the same time. One way around the problem is to connect a stripped-down computer (sometimes called a **print server**) to the plotter to be used solely for plotting. More expensive systems let you draw and plot simultaneously. While you must own at least one plotter, reprographic houses can assist you by providing volume, overflow, or specialty plotting, using your disks or tapes.

Plotters accept all popular drawing media, including tracing paper and polyester film. Pen plotters will also produce extraordinary results on other media. I often plot on a glossy cover stock using ballpoint pens because the lines are crisp and the stock is sturdy, making it ideal for menus or presentation drawings. Be careful, however, not to use a medium exceeding the thickness set by the plotter manufacturer,

because gap and pressure tolerances are quite fine. Polyester film, like linen, is a better medium than paper for manual drafting because of its durability. But since you can plot a new drawing at any time, and since many building departments now microfilm drawings, you can use vellum for most CAD drawings and polyester film for manual or combination CAD/manual drawings.

Three types of pens are commonly used by pen plotters: technical, roller (ballpoint), and felt tip. Although technical pens are the classic favorite (they are available in many widths), they must be absolutely clean to insure constant ink flow and consistent line quality. Felt tips offer a wide selection of colors and are ideal for filling-in solid-color planes, which make them ideal for architectural renderings. But they wear out quickly, producing skipped lines or lines of varying thickness. A ballpoint pen is ideal for line drawings: The point is fine, the line quality is consistent, and it is clean and convenient to use.

In manual drawing, you can force an old pen to work reasonably well, but you're asking for trouble if you attempt to use an old pen in a plotter. Correcting a skipped plotter line manually is next to impossible.

Now let's turn to project management. You may be surprised to discover that project management takes on new meaning in a CAD-equipped practice.

11
Design Management

Traditionally, **project management** is the supervision of the creation of a set of drawings and the administration of a building's construction phase. With CAD in the office, the architect, engineer, interior designer, or facility manager now has the means by which to plan, design, build, and manage a building: an integrated building database. The use of CAD requires rethinking the scope of conventional design services and the role of project management.

CAD: THE KERNEL OF THE BUILDING DATABASE

In a conventional project, the owner brings the requirements to the architect, who designs the building that will be built by the contractor and occupied by the owner. In effect, the continuity of the project passes in segments through many hands. With the advent of CAD, the architect now creates more than a set of drawings. He or she creates a **building database**, a coherent base of information of vital interest to the owner's facility manager. It all becomes possible because of intelligent graphics, the ability to store data with graphics. If CAD provides the foundation for facilities management, can it not also aid in making predesign decisions? Of course. Now the design-build-occupy process is integrated from beginning to end. This integration, however, redefines the traditional roles and phases of service.

The Design Model

This phase starts with the idea to build. Everything that is germane to the real estate analysis, site, return on investment, occupancy, cost of money, life cycle, zoning and building code compliance, staff forecasting, and space programming contributes to the decision to build. This data is entered into a CAD terminal to generate the **design model**, a maximum-minimum envelope that defines the building in terms of geometry, costs, and returns. This phase joins analysis, predesign, planning, and schematic design into one integrated design phase. By embracing these nontraditional architectural services, architects can expand their practices.

The Build Model

Taking data from the design model, the professional design team completes the drawings and construction. During this phase, the designers finish the building database, a complete associative database of the building: its contents, occupants, and environmental and safety systems. And they produce CAD drawings: architectural, engineering, and facilities documents. This phase begins with design development and concludes with construction administration. Again, using production data from the building database, each professional can monitor costs and progress. (More details about this follow in the next section.)

The Occupy Model

While the building database contains the data necessary for the architect or other design professional to design and construct the building, all the data needed to manage the building after occupancy is also there: staff, furniture, telephone extensions of all occupants, and the entire electromechanical system. Each segment becomes a part of the smart building control system. For the architect or other professional, there is an opportunity here to expand the scope of his professional services. The key element is the CAD system, and the key ingredient of CAD is the associative database.

Everyone benefits from the CAD building database. The contractor uses it to build, the furniture installer to move in, and the client to manage the completed facility. But the design project manager benefits, too, using the data to manage the project.

PROJECT MANAGEMENT

The project manager is responsible for producing timely, high-quality construction documentation and for coordinating construction profitably.

Document Review

You may have considered CAD exclusively as a design or drawing tool and overlooked CAD as a supervisory tool. One of CAD's features is being able to review work quickly without the necessity of running a set of check prints. Sitting at a terminal, a project manager can review any work on the system, either noting revisions needed (which would subsequently be made by the person responsible for making the drawing) or making the revisions himself.

But when a project manager (or principal in charge, for that matter) is only annotating, not correcting drawings, it's an expensive use of a high-performance CAD terminal, since that terminal cannot be used for drawing. A CAD system makes money when it's being used, not when it's idle. One effective alternative is to connect a less powerful graphics node to the system to make these reviews and comments. This terminal (or node) will be used only for graphics display with minimal annotation: no drawing, computations, layering, or editing will be performed. The project manager reviews drawings, circles queries, and notes whatever corrections are necessary. The annotated drawings are saved, ready for revision. When the

CAD designer redisplays the drawing at the graphics terminal, it will include the project manager's comments about what should be corrected.

Alignment Verification

If you suspect a problem in the ceiling, for example, you might load several parts of several drawings concurrently to check for interference. Or you might want to confirm that certain revisions have been made on several drawings, such as changing a partition location. By simultaneously loading the partition and ceiling plans and displaying the pertinent layers, you can verify changes and alignments. (Dynamic interference was discussed in Chapter 8 and is shown in Color Plates 6 and 7.)

Specifications

How helpful it would be to automatically generate a set of specs from a set of drawings. Much of the time spent writing specifications is housekeeping: putting the set together, matching this boilerplate with that catalog, coordinating needs with specific code requirements, and so on. It seems like a poor use of resources for spec writers to spend so much time keeping house instead of analyzing new products or working more closely with cost consultants, designers, and job captains. Look at Color Plate 3, the level-assignment and color-coding standard developed for construction documentation (discussed earlier). The standard divides the 16 CSI specifications into blocks of ten levels (layers) each. Specialties, for example, can be found on layers 100–109. Your spec writer might call up a floor plan to display only those layers to verify chalkboards, lockers, etc., or he might create from layer 112 a bill of materials of all laboratory equipment. Did you ever think specification writing could be so easy?

Construction Coordination

Managing paperwork during the construction phase can be a real headache for everyone. "Why hasn't Smith returned the shop drawings?" "Where is Brook's resubmittal?" "Where is Change Order 17?" "Why doesn't the general contractor have his copy yet?"

To a great extent, the burdensome logistics of paperwork can be rendered all but painless. Instead of looking through reams of drawings, many of them out of date, you can retrieve any drawing you need within minutes. Considerable time can also be saved by computer-to-computer transmission of drawings between architect, engineer, contractor, and subcontractor via a **network** or via telephone **modem** connections. All the contractor needs is his own read-only terminal—connected to your CAD system—at the construction site. He can review drawings as needed and plot his own revisions at the site.

Shop Drawings

It wasn't long ago that architects drew full-size profiles of moldings, cornices, and details. How many times have you drawn profiles, contours, or moldings, only to discover that the shop drawings were so inaccurate that they required complete redesign and resubmittal? Real progress is being made with shop drawings prepared on a supplier's CAD computer from CAD profile drawings supplied by the architect (but verified by the supplier) and integrated into a truly complete drawing set. Expect to see more in the future.

On CAD, you can trace a profile at twice full size and then insert the profile into a detail at 3-inch scale, for example. More important, you might design a column with true entasis, drawn at any convenient scale. And although the profile might appear in the architectural drawings at 3-inch scale, the fabricator could extract a full-size template.

Changes in Professional Liability

Traditionally, the architect has been responsible for design intent, the contractor for methods of construction. As the level of detail and accuracy grows with CAD, the architect and engineer could become liable for having shown too much detail on a CAD drawing. Courts might be tempted to construe these drawings as describing methods of construction, incorrectly exposing the architect to new, unwarranted, and unnecessary liability.

INFORMATION MANAGEMENT

The purpose of inserting intelligence into a drawing is to be able to extract the information in a usable format at a future time, usually in some form of inventory. When the amount of data is small, a report like a door schedule for a residence will be small and can be generated using standard reports included in your software. Processing a small report places few demands on your computer.

On the other hand, processing a furniture schedule for a new office of 20,000 square feet represents approximately 1000–1500 separate items of conventional furniture and as much as twice that for open-office design. You'll recall from Chapter 6 that each descriptive element of each item of furniture constitutes a field, and each complete furniture description represents a record. For every field that you add to 2000 records, you increase the processing load by a factor of 2000. So you must weigh the merits of adding new fields of information against processing time.

Terminal Use

You can one day expect to own a CAD system composed of different terminals devoted to specific tasks (why use a graphics terminal for specification writing?) and connected by a communications ring, or local area network (LAN). In fact, you could be sending change orders to a contractor via telephone modem right now.

The concept is simple. You create data on one terminal—for example, associative data on a graphics terminal—move the pointer file(s) to a second, less-expensive and specifically formatted, computer, matching and merging the source file with a target file. The new file can then be manipulated to generate the desired reports.

Hybrid systems like this are being used today, but connecting different computers to one another, even in a local area network, is not foolproof. Yet one change is quite obvious: No longer is the mainframe off doing mysterious things in the back room. Personal computers are being linked with graphics minicomputers, which in turn are connected to other database computers (most notably in the accounting department).

The Facsimile Building

The most exciting developments ahead will be an outgrowth of associative-attribute management and three-dimensional graphics. First will be the use of CAD as a modeling and graphics presentation tool for schematic design (the design model). But the real prize will be the development of the **facsimile building**. For years, we have drawn plans, elevations, sections, and details. These drawings show features of your design work, but only selected views. As memory capacity grows, it will become possible to construct an efficient CAD facsimile of the actual building, using a combination of associativity and advanced three-dimensional software.

You will "enter" the entire building or its principal parts— not just selected views—onto your CAD system. When finished, you will have a three-dimensional simulation of the actual building. By rotating the facsimile, you will be able to view any elevation. You will generate a section or plan (horizontal section) by selecting the view direction, plane of cut, and depth of view to mask any construction that you don't want to see. All the design disciplines add to the same database. Interference and coordination are immediate. As processor speeds multiply and mass memory grows to a gigabyte (1 billion bytes), professionals will have the tools to manage an entire building and its contents from conception onward.

But looking at a two-dimensional image of a three-dimensional object on a CRT screen is not the same as looking at a truly three-dimensional image, which may become possible with a dynamically generated holographic display, using the composite information from the building database.

PROFIT MANAGEMENT

Project management might better be named profit management, because, for the most part, that's the project manager's real responsibility.

Financial Planning

One task over which most project managers labor is the allocation of time to various phases of a job. Two approaches are popular. Using the first method, you commence with gross fees, deduct consultant fees and overhead, project a target profit, and convert the available fee to man-hours. With the second method, you project man-hours, convert to direct costs, and add indirect costs, profits, and consultant fees to arrive at a total fee.

You can develop your own financial model on a microcomputer with the aid of any spreadsheet program, just like the fee-and-manpower projections shown in Figures 11.1 and 11.2. After creating the model on a micro, you can feed the data back into the network or directly to the accounting department.

Payroll and Invoicing

Any CAD terminal can be designed to incorporate a **log-in file**, which works like a time

```
**********************************************************************
P R O J E C T   F E E   &   S T A F F   B U D G E T            KENNEDY DESIGN ASSOCIATES
**********************************************************************
    ENTER      PROJECT NAME ))   SAMPLE          ((      COPIES:    ELK
    ENTER      ACCOUNT NUMBER )) 124              ((                 MS
    ENTER             DATE ))    121283           ((                 YS
    ENTER        PRINCIPAL ))    ELK              ((
    ENTER   PROJECT MANAGER ))   MS               ((             PROJ MGR
    ENTER     PROJ DESIGNER ))   BSK              ((             PROJ DES
    ENTER          "1" IF GMP )) ((                             PROJ FILE     VISI-CALC EDITION
**********************************************************************
    ENTER   FOREIGN CURRENCY AMOUNT ))   1.44 EQUALS $    1.00 ((
    ENTER   FOREIGN CURRENCY NAME ))))      STERLING           ((
                                     COST         FEE    PARTICI-
                                   (FOREIGN     COST RATE PATION
                                   CURRENCY)    ( $ ) (%) RATE (%)      FEE
                                   ======== ======== ======== ======== ========
    ENTER      NEW CONSTRUCTION COST))  1440000  1000000  10.00  100.00  100000
    ENTER   REMODEL CONSTRUCTION COST))  730000   500000  16.00  100.00   80000
    ENTER            INTERIORS COST))    730000   500000  12.00  100.00   60000
    ENTER            FURNITURE COST))    730000   500000  12.00  100.00   60000
    ENTER            EQUIPMENT COST))         0                  100.00       0

GROSS ARCHITECTURAL & ENGINEERING FEE:                          $  300000
=========================================================================
LESS CONSULTANT'S FEES:   CONSULTNT    FEE
                          ENTER "1"    BASIS
    MECH/ELEC ENGR 45/75      1      A/E FEE   300000   35.00   75.00   78750
    STRUCT ENGR    10/15      1      CONS COST 1500000  10.00   15.00   22500
    EQUIP CONSULTNT 1/100            A/E FEE   300000    1.00   100.00       0
    KITCH CONSULTNT 2.4/100   1      A/E FEE   300000    2.40   100.00    7200
    LAUNDRY CONSULT .5/100           A/E FEE   300000    0.50   100.00       0
    SITE CONSULTANT 1/100            A/E FEE   300000    1.00   100.00       0
                                                                          0
-------------------------------------------------------------------------
TOTAL CONSULTANT'S FEE:                          36.15 %     $  108450
-------------------------------------------------------------------------
NET ARCHITECTURAL FEE:                           63.85 %     $  191550
=========================================================================
RESERVE FOR PROFIT          ARCH FEE    0.68    20.00   100.00   38310
RESERVE FOR CONTINGENCY     ARCH FEE    0.17     5.00   100.00    9578
DIRECT SALARIES   INDEX 100 ARCH FEE    1.00    29.41   100.00   56338
SALARY BENEFITS   INDEX 35  ARCH FEE    0.35    10.29   100.00   19718
OVERHEAD          INDEX 120 ARCH FEE    1.20    35.29   100.00   67606
EQUIVALENT DPE                          2.52
=========================================================================
SALARY BUDGET     STANDARD  STD %  GMP %   GMP    PHASE   BUDGET  BUDGET
BY PHASE OF WORK  % ALLOC  W/EQUIP  DIST W/EQUIP RATE(%)  SALARY  HOURS
================  =======  ======= ======= ======= ======= ======= =======
AVE SALARIES/HOUR    25      25      25      25                    25.00
PROJ MGT-PRE DES      5       5       7       7       5    2817     113
PROGRAMMING           3       3       3       3       3    1690      68
SCHEMATIC DESIGN     11      11      10      10      11    6197     248
DESIGN DEVELOPMENT   15      13      14      12      15    8451     338
GUARNTEED MAX DOCS                   15      15       0       0       0
CONST DOCS/BID ADM   33      32      18      18      33   18592     744
EQUIPMENT                    4                4       0       0       0
CONSTRUCTION ADMIN   33      32      33      31      33   18592     744
-------------------------------------------------------------------------
TOTAL BUDGET        100     100     100     100     100   56338    2255
=========================================================================
```

11.1 *Fee projections can be calculated with a personal computer, but if integrated with CAD and accounting records, they can be automated. By entering a few basic parameters, total fees, profit, and hourly budget allotments can be extracted. Modifying any parameter adjusts the balance.*

11.2 *Cost tracking of project performance is essential for the profitable office. This analysis compares performance-to-date with budgeted performance, calculates the trend, and projects future performance, which is reflected in the Index (100 = on budget, less than 100 = greater profit).*

```
===========================================================================================
P R O J E C T   F E E   P E R F O R M A N C E                        KENNEDY DESIGN ASSOCIATES

              ENTER DATA BELOW & BETWEEN ")>...((                    COPIES:ELK
    PROJECT NAME >>   SAMPLE              ((                                  MS
  ACCOUNT NUMBER >>     124               ((                                  YS
 AS OF THIS DATE >>    121283             ((
       PRINCIPAL >>    ELK                ((                         PROJ MGR
 PROJECT MANAGER >>     MS                ((                         PROJ DES
   PROJ DESIGNER >>    BSK                ((                         PROJ FILE
-------------------------------------------------------------------------------------------
/PP"^H1D^CIK^CI120N^ECR M132                                         VISI-CALC EDITION    0
===========================================================================================
```

PROJECT PHASE	BUDGET (FROM PROJECT FEE & STAFF BUDGET)				PROGRESS		PERFORMANCE		CUMULATIVE TREND	
					ENTER HOURS SPENT TO DATE EACH PHASE >>	ENTER HOURS REQUIRED TO FINISH EACH PHASE	SUM HOURS SPENT & NEEDED TO FIN EACH	CUM PERCENT OF COMPLET-ION	PROGRESS (HOURS) AHEAD OF SCHED(-) OR BEHIND SCHED(+)	ON SCHED =100 AHEAD OF (100 AHEAD OF BEHIND)100
	PHASE RATE (%)	CUM PHASE RATE (%)	BUDGETED SALARY	BUDGETED HOURS >>		(( ))	((PHASE			
================	=======	=======	=======	=======	=======	=======	=======	=======	=======	=======
AVERAGE SALARY/HR: 25.00										
PROJ MGT-PRE DES	5	5	2817	113	100	0	100	5	-13	89
PROGRAMMING	3	8	1690	68	40	0	40	3	-28	77
SCHEMATIC DESIGN	11	19	6197	248	200	20	220	10	-28	84
DESIGN DEVELOPMENT	15	34	8451	338	100	200	300	5	-38	84
GUARNTEED MAX DOCS	0	34	0	0	0	0	0	0	0	86
CONST DOCS/BID ADM	33	67	18592	744	0	640	640	0	-104	84
MEDICAL EQUIPMENT	0	67	0	0	0	0	0	0	0	86
CONSTRUCTION ADMIN	33	100	18592	744	0	640	640	0	-104	84

```
==============================  ======== ======== ------------------------------------------
BUDGETED SALARIES & HOURS                  56338    2255
-------------------------------------------------------------------------------------------
PROGRESS TO DATE:
    HOURS WORKED:                                            440
    PERCENT COMPLETED:                                                        23
-------------------------------------------------------------------------------------------
PROJECTIONS:
    HOURS REQUIRED TO COMPLETE PROJECT:              1941              1941
    HOURS BELOW (-), OR ABOVE (+) BUDGET:            -314              -314
    CUMULATIVE PROJECT TREND INDEX: (100=AHEAD        86                          86
    PROJECTED SALARIES:                     48524
-------------------------------------------------------------------------------------------
GAIN (+) OR LOSS (-) ON SALARIES         $    7814
    ADD BENEFITS & OVERHEAD FACTOR =  1.55   12112
    TOTAL GAIN ON SALARIES X OVERHEAD       19924
    ADD RESERVE FOR PROFIT/CONTINGENCY  $   47888
ESTIMATED PROFIT:                        $   67814
    PROFIT AS PERCENT OF FEE:               35.40 %
===========================================================================================
```

sheet. In order to work on your computer, you log in to a specific project, thereby starting the time clock. When you've finished, you log off. In this way, the computer keeps a time sheet for you, providing an up-to-date record of the time spent on each drawing and each person's time devoted to a specific project. Depending on your equipment, you can print the file at the close of the work cycle or pass the information directly to the accounting computer. Try to install a time-recording procedure as early as possible so that you can build a database of production costs for future reference.

Project Performance

Every project manager monitors job progress (often as frequently as once a week), preferably with up-to-date information that compares the degree of completion with a previously established time-and-staff budget (and therefore, fee budget). Time spent can be compared to time allocated, providing a means to evaluate performance and progress toward completion.

Profit-and-loss tracking

Collecting all this data is of little use unless it can be distilled into succinct information that is useful for decision making. Many project management tracking systems are offshoots of batch-processed payroll services (the data is collected in the design office, sent to someone who processes the batch, and returns it, usually too late to be useful). Since batch-processed results are often not known for three to four weeks, the information is useless in many cases. If the project manager can call up the data when he wants it, he can run the project analysis program without waiting for the close of the next pay period. He can measure performance when he needs it, and he can make intelligent, timely decisions about a project. He can analyze progress as of the close of yesterday's workday and compare performance against standards or with other, similar projects.

Manpower allocation

If all projects are tracked concurrently, manpower scheduling becomes a natural by-product. As with fee and manpower allocations, the work can also be completed on a standalone microcomputer.

Now let's turn to system management, one area not to be overlooked if you plan to run a profitable CAD system.

12
System Management

Would you allow your design department to try to manage itself without a chief designer? Or your engineering department to operate without a chief engineer? Probably not. Likewise, your CAD system needs to be managed; it won't magically manage itself. In this chapter, you'll learn what is necessary to manage a CAD system and the responsibilities of the system manager.

SYSTEM MANAGER
Even if you have only one computer, someone will need to be the system manager. Don't invest one penny or one minute in a computer system, CAD included, unless you have someone to manage the system, someone who understands its intricacies and who is responsible for maintaining it. I won't categorically guarantee that your computer system will fail without a system manager, but I have yet to see a system succeed without one. Having a system manager is simply a fundamental part of operating a successful CAD system. If you have only one terminal, you won't need a full-time manager, but you should recognize that your one user must devote time for system management.

If you're a professional design firm, a computer is probably your most expensive capital investment. Because computer technology advances so rapidly, you should plan to reach the break-even point on your investment within two to three years. While equipment leases and depreciation may be spread out over five years, you should be operating profitably long before that so that you can trade up to more advanced equipment. Computers do require physical care, but the system manager's principal duty is financial management of your new asset.

What qualities should the system manager possess? Let's look at some of the skills the system manager should have in addition to your particular personnel standards.

The best candidate for an architectural, engineering, or design application blends professional expertise with technical computer competency and management skills. The ideal candidate is a licensed design professional with extensive experience in computer graphics, computer operations, and asset management. Since this person manages your most expensive physical asset, he or she will be the most effective if a principal or senior associate in the firm. On the other hand, don't saddle an unsuspecting individual with the duties unless he/she is already knowledgeable about computers. Almost anyone can learn to draw with CAD in an hour, but it takes a couple of years to become an effective system manager.

If you are unable to find a candidate with all these qualities, then select someone with a strong programming background and place the individual directly under the principal. A programmer, while not versed in the particular application, understands computer operations, always appreciates its intricacies, and loves solving computer application problems. Otherwise, select a design professional from the office who has demonstrated an interest in computers and give him or her all the support you can.

The best time to hire a system manager is before you select your CAD system. You should not make an initial purchase without having selected a system manager. The manager can help you analyze your needs and assist in selecting and purchasing the most appropriate system for your office.

System Manager's Duties

Seymour L. Fish, AIA, the partner responsible for managing the computer systems at Haines Lundberg Waehler, Architects, Engineers, and Planners in New York City, outlines the duties for the ideal CAD manager:

The CAD manager's duties include the implementation, maintenance, and overall responsibility for managing the system successfully. His duties are unique in that he must direct three distinct . . . phases [:] . . . (1) system selection, (2) system startup, and (3) system operation. Each phase places a different set of equally important demands on the CAD manager. Although the first two phases may occur only once, each is vital in establishing a profitable and successful system.

System selection

The CAD manager's goal is to bring together the right CAD system with the firm's management goals and methods of operation. The quality of the manager's leadership during this phase is directly proportional to his or her knowledge of CAD, computers, and the design discipline. The uninitiated manager needs to be prepared to spend a lot of time researching, and selecting your CAD system. A good system manager can help you negotiate your purchase and buy exactly what's necessary—and not more.

Between purchase and delivery of a new CAD system, the manager should take the initial users to the manufacturer for any necessary training and supervise the preparation of the office for the computer.

System start-up

Besides hooking everything together so that it operates properly, start-up involves a lot of critical planning. You'll want to establish standards for graphics, project control, performance reports, and procedures for archiving. In addition, you'll set maintenance schedules, decide who will have access to which files, develop criteria for selecting early projects for CAD, coordinate CAD billing with accounting, and schedule multiple shifts. All of these tasks will be embodied in a set of operating procedures, which should be documented, however briefly.

This phase concludes with system delivery, acceptance trials, and the initial start-up with a pilot project. For this project, select a small but comprehensive project that is typical of your practice. If in doubt, select an "easy" project for the initiation.

System operation

Managing a system requires more than the traditional understanding of the operating system (the housekeeping part of the computer). And system management requires more than facile programming skills. The manager monitors the performance of the system, providing management information on the productivity of users and, consequently, the financial break-even point, that point at which the cost of manual drawing exceeds the cost of CAD drawing. Standards, too, will be closely monitored, including procedures developed during the start-up phase for back-up to prevent the loss of current work (both daily back-ups and weekly archiving). Periodic maintenance visits will also be scheduled.

Training never stops

New people require initial training, and skilled users must maintain proficiency through enrollment in advanced classes. Back-up people must be trained in order to fill in during the absence or loss of your regular CAD staff. There will be software revisions and new applications that require training. You will find that the cost of sending a trainee to the CAD vendor's training class is usually less than that of in-house training because the latter ties up a terminal and an instructor, both of which could otherwise be generating revenue.

Most professionals have some understanding of CAD, but not a full appreciation of its potential. Emphasis will continue to be placed on training in and mastery of the basic skills until the profession at large knows how to use a CAD system.

Among the many other duties of a system manager are identifying software development requirements and deciding which software will be developed in-house and which should be developed by outsiders. You'll also want a system manager to develop demonstrations and promote CAD use in the office.

12.1 *A CAD workstation should be a graphics work place with space for drawings and computer components. Here's one idea using a standard drafting table.*

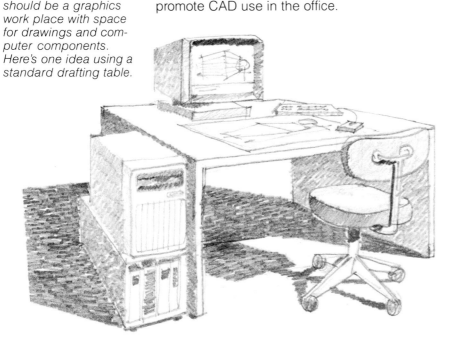

CAD WORKSTATION DESIGN
A CAD workstation needs three basic components: a static-free location, glare-free CRT, and lay space for drawings.

Static-free carpet is best for the floor, but it's not essential. The real trick is to arrange the terminals in such a way as to eliminate any glare on the face of the CRT, which means that the main light source should be in back of the CRT or to one side, but not behind the user's chair. I prefer a room with windows off to one side, for sitting in a dark room staring at a tube all day is unsatisfactory for me. Light the wall behind the CRT with wallwashers on light-colored paint. The ambient light will reduce room contrast and eyestrain. Place the terminal on a drawing board or at the side of a lay table. Most CAD terminals have insufficient reference space—a lot have none. If your system uses a keyboard extensively, place the keyboard at standard keyboard height of 26½ inches instead of at table height (30 inches) or cabinet height (36 inches), both of which are too high.

MAINTAINING A CAD SYSTEM
There's more to operating a computer than just turning it on. Unlike your home stereo or even a microcomputer, CAD and larger computer systems are often maintained through a maintenance contract—not dissimilar to maintenance contracts on other office equipment. Let's look at several requirements for keeping your system running.

Hardware Replacement
You'll probably outgrow most of the computer components long before the hardware physically wears out or fails. To maintain the best-quality hardware and remain on the cutting edge of technological progress, you'll have to replace (**upgrade**) some or all of the components periodically, which generally means replacement before the equipment is completely depreciated.

Software Updates

Software is constantly being revised and upgraded with special features. New releases of software are announced as often as four times a year. The enhancements come from two sources. Planned enhancements are scheduled by the software manufacturer and reflect ongoing revisions or revisions initiated as a result of more sophisticated hardware, hardware operating systems, or third-party software. Other enhancements are the result of corrections to eliminate programming **bugs** (the parts of the software that don't work correctly) or are responses to customer requests. In either case, follow instructions carefully when loading new software.

Conversions

As you probably know, computer data is not necessarily **compatible** among different computer systems. For example, the data necessary to draw a rectangle might be represented on one CAD system in six fields: item number, level, pen, rectangle, coordinate 1, and coordinate 2. On another system, only four fields may describe it: coordinate 1, coordinate 2, level (and consequently, line type and pen weight), and rectangle. If you create a drawing on one computer and want to transfer the data to a second computer, you must convert the data in the first file to a **format** that is compatible with the second computer in order to display or work on this drawing on the second computer. Fortunately, conversions are becoming available between more computer systems.

When software revisions are extensive, the new software may not accept the old files, in which case the old drawings will have to be **reformatted** (converted) to be compatible (usable) with the new software. During conversion, the data from the old drawing is read into RAM, modified into the new format, and rewritten to a new, upgraded sister file. Typical of this type of conversion is a transition from 16-bit to 32-bit technology.

While all computers perform tasks using logic that is almost identical, the data or format may vary significantly between systems. The example of the rectangle is typical.

For some time now, efforts have been made to establish a universal format for exchanging graphics data between computers, although users seem to have been more interested in achieving this interchange than vendors. The National Bureau of Standards has developed a standard called Initial Graphics Exchange Specification (IGES) that specifies a neutral format for exchanging drawing information between different CAD systems. As of this writing, the IGES standard adequately covers the transfer of graphics data, but not, in all cases, the transfer of intelligent data. More work is required to give the standard complete transferability between all systems.

Another means of transfer is through graphic plot files. In order to plot a drawing on a pen plotter, the graphics information has to be converted from the host computer's format to a format compatible with the plotter. Since CAD manufacturers support multiple-pen plotters, an auxiliary method exists to transfer files between different computers.

Maintenance

The purchase of a CAD computer provides hardware and software maintenance. Hardware maintenance covers repair and replacement of the computer itself and computer peripherals, while software maintenance covers upgrading software as it becomes available. You contract for monthly maintenance or buy maintenance as required—that judgment is left to you. Full hardware and software maintenance can be budgeted at about 1–3% of the equipment cost per month. The cost usually represents an excellent value. Vendors pride themselves on giving fast maintenance service and usually live up to their claims. If your computer quits in the middle of a charrette, you need it up and running quickly. Whether you have a maintenance contract or not, you'll probably have a field engineer at your door within several hours, unless your office is far from the engineer's home base.

One feature worth investigating is telemaintenance. Your computer can be connected to a diagnostic terminal in the maintenance office via a modem. A modem allows you to transmit computer data over the telephone network to another computer (also connected to the telephone line with its modem). When a problem develops, you call the maintenance office and, using the telemaintenance modem, "connect" your computer to the maintenance engineer's computer. He performs various tests from his terminal via the modem to isolate the fault on your computer. He may be across town or across the country, but he can, in most cases, diagnose the problem with your computer over the telephone line, and bring the correct parts with him if necessary, speeding repair and reducing downtime.

Static

For most CAD terminals and users, static can be more than a nuisance; it can be a real problem. When you touch one of the components, static discharges into the computer, and on the average you can expect a computer to cease working properly about 50% of the time. Your present work can be rendered useless. (Did you remember to save frequently?) Ground yourself before touching the keyboard or any other component. On cold, dry days, don't even get close to the computer if the disk drive is spinning; you could destroy a file with one zap. That zap need change the data in only one place to render the entire file or disk unusable—so don't risk the loss. Losing a program disk could put your computer out of business until the disk is replaced.

Antistatic carpet seems to work well. Floor and keyboard mats that are wired to positive grounding are very effective, as are sprays. Any other means you can devise that discharges static before you touch the computer may also be used.

Fire Protection

Do not overlook ordinary fireproofing precautions. If your computer is contained in an atmospherically controlled room, you can install a fire safety system that uses a gas called haylon; it will extinguish a fire with minimum damage to a computer's electronics. However, since most CAD systems today no longer require a separate computer room, you should keep a haylon or Class C (CO_2 or dry chemical) fire extinguisher nearby for electrical fires. Do *not* use water or a Class A fire extinguisher (that's for wood or paper fires) to put out a computer fire.

MANAGING HARD-DISK MEMORY SPACE

Your software and drawings can be stored on a hard disk. The software requires a fixed amount of space, leaving the remainder of the disk available for drawings, figure libraries, and other data. But the computer memory space is just like a file cabinet: Empty space gets filled. One of the system manager's perpetual duties is to manage the use of memory on the system: deleting redundant files, copying files from the work-in-progress directory to the approved-drawings directory, and archiving files frequently. Maintaining free space in memory will be an ongoing task. As disk memory capacity increases, there is a tendency to keep more data and drawings on the disk for ready access, rather than archiving them. Let's look at some of the ways that a system manager can maintain sufficient space in memory.

Copy to Disk

The easiest way to free up space on a disk is to copy some of your files and drawings to floppy disks, cartridge, or tape. You will "copy to floppy" primarily when a phase of a job is finished. Directories have a way of filling up with all sorts of files: good, big, rubbish, duplicates, and unknowns. Cleaning up these files soon becomes a chore, tempting you to save the entire directory rather than remove unneeded files. Working on the same project day after day can make remembering correct file names a difficult task. Appending the date and/or the revision number to the newly saved file certainly helps.

If your system automatically stores the date as one of the file name attributes, you may be able to save all the files created on or after a given date and time by specifying a wild-card file name coupled with a date option that identifies all files created after a certain date and time. You could then restore those files in the same directory the following day by specifying that all the files on your floppy disk be merged with the files on the hard disk. You can either replace duplicate files on the hard disk with those on the floppy or maintain hard-disk files with duplicate file names. Both are handy techniques.

Multiple Terminals in a Network
If your system is connected to a network (that is, linked with other CAD terminals in a communications network), you might place the software on one node, work-in-progress on another, and approved drawings on yet another. In order to find a particular file or directory on another computer in the network, you create a reference entry on your node that points to (tells the computer where to look for) the actual directory on the correct node. In this way, you can store an item on your hard disk just once, without duplicating it on each node, thereby preserving hard-disk storage space.

Eliminating Utility Programs
Talk to your CAD vendor's technical staff and determine which of the utility files can be deleted from your active hard disk. Rarely used utility programs, alternative utilities for similar hardware configurations, or test programs are often included when the computer is delivered, and they can be deleted from the hard disk, as long as you have the original disk. Other rarely used programs might be saved as a group on a working disk, a handy means for loading the files should you need them.

Hidden Files
When you run the computer, the system sometimes saves certain files automatically. Log files, backup histories, and other reference files are examples. These files are generally small temporary files that should be deleted frequently.

Some systems create temporary **plot files** of graphics and **print files** of text. These files are usually queued in the plotter or printer buffer called a *spooler*, plotted or printed, and then automatically deleted. If, on the other hand, your computer does not delete these files, free space can diminish dramatically. In addition to storing an active graphics file on the system, you may also be storing the companion plot file, which may, in fact, be larger than the original graphics file. So keep an eye on these directories when you're cleaning up your disk.

PROPER CARE
Like any fine electronic instrument, a computer requires proper care and attention to maintain it in top shape.

The one resource your computer consumes is electricity, and reliable operation depends upon an uninterrupted flow of it. You will remember that when the power stops, all the data entered into RAM is instantly lost. Follow the manufacturer's recommendations about power connections. Don't try to cut corners. While many computers will run on an ordinary household outlet (a 110-volt, 15-amp circuit), you should not run other electrical devices off the same circuit. An isolated ground is recommended.

Keep your hands out of the computer's insides. An accidental discharge of static electricity from your touch could damage the electronics. Dust can be harmful to disk drives, so it's best to use dust covers. The recording (read/write) head is particularly sensitive: One spot of dust in the wrong place—namely, between the read/write head and your disk—need change only one 0 to a 1 to corrupt your data. Which data? You may never know, and finding it is next to impossible. What's the moral? *Keep the computer as dust-free as possible.*

Vibration of the disk drive when it is running can physically damage the disk. Hard disks spin at high speeds and are sensitive to vibration. If you shake the disk drive at the wrong time, you can permanently damage the head and/or the disk (called a **head crash**). Before moving a hard disk, even across the room, lock the disk. Floppy disks are not so sensitive as hard disks, but they should be handled with the same care as when handling a stereo phonograph record or cassette.

Floppy disks are permanently sealed within a soft, lined jacket. As the disk turns, the jacket wipes dust from the disk surface. *Never* touch the surface of a disk—*never*. Use a felt-tip pen when writing on labels; *never* use a ballpoint, avoid heat, don't fold or bend, and keep the disks away from anything magnetic, particularly graphics tablets.

Keyboards take a lot of punishment and stand up remarkably well, but there are limits to their endurance. So treat them as you would any electronic typewriter.

An occasional cleaning with window cleaner will spruce up the cabinet, the keyboard (which gets very dirty), and the CRT display, which tends to collect a thin black coating of dust (probably attracted by the magnetic field within the display tube). By the way, CRT faces remain clean the same way drawings stay clean, by keeping your fingers off the surface, an etiquette long known to design professionals. A portable vacuum cleaner also comes in handy.

CONTROLLING ACCESS TO FILES AND TERMINALS

The question that often arises is whether Smith can work on the same drawing that Brook is working on, or can Brook change the drawing Smith is working on. Fortunately two people cannot work on the same drawing at the same time, but Smith might be able to use Brook's drawing for reference. On some CAD systems, corrections are automatically updated in the database so that anyone accessing the drawing sees the corrections as they happen (actually, when the view is refreshed).

On other systems, you work on a copy of the drawing, leaving the original drawing intact, until you save your updated copy in place of the original. Depending on the system, your colleague may not be able to view the copy while you're at work on the original.

Drawing Access

Not everyone in the office should have unlimited **access** to the CAD terminals, the software, or the drawings. While you may need to maintain confidentiality of a drawing, most likely you will want to control access in order to limit who can originate and change (write) or review (read) drawings. You don't want the architect changing ductwork or the mechanical engineer moving walls. Access control also prevents accidental (or intentional) removal of important data.

The system manager is responsible for controlling access and assigning appropriate access rights. There are two levels of rights: read-and-write access, which gives full drawing rights, and read-only, or view only access.

Read-and-write access should be reserved for the system manager on all projects and for the principal-in-charge and the project manager for their projects. An individual who creates a drawing should have read-and-write privileges while creating drawings. But once the drawing is approved and transferred to the approved-drawing directory, then only the principal-in-charge and the project manager should have read-and-write privileges. The project manager thereby controls corrections and other changes, insuring that work is not altered without approval. Otherwise, read-only access should be available to anyone on the project team and to the project consultants.

Log-In to a Computer

To gain access to a computer, you must log in and give your **password**, a short code word that grants you access and keeps unauthorized people from using the computer. Passwords take many forms, usually a combination of letters, numbers, or other characters. More sophisticated systems use a tiered system, such as name, organization, and project. This allows one individual to log in and work on one project, but not on another.

Work-in-Progress

Brook might be assigned to draw the third-floor plan—say, drawing A203. He would be assigned full read-and-write access rights to drawing A203. While work proceeds, the drawing is stored in a **work-in-progress directory**.

Approved Drawings

Once drawing A203 is completed and approved, the project manager moves the drawing to an **approved-drawings directory**. Any other team member can then look at (read) the drawing but not change it. Thus, Su starts the ceiling plan by loading a copy of Brook's approved floor plan, which can now be used as a template. Su can make alterations to the ceiling, but not to the floor plan, for which Su only has read access. When Su completes the ceiling plan and the project manager approves the work, the ceiling plan is moved into the approved drawing file.

Is Access Control Necessary?

Not always. Only compelling circumstances should require access control: either the complexity of the job, confidentiality, or the size of the workforce. What you gain by adding access control must be weighed against the operational overhead and complexity it creates.

Now that you have mastered software applications, we turn to the last part of the book: three chapters on computers. I have left this until last because understanding CAD makes understanding the intricacies of computers much more meaningful.

Part V

COMPUTERS

Not everyone who needs to learn about CAD will need to master basic information about computers. If you are the kind of person who likes to know how something works, Part V will satisfy your curiosity. If you read this part closely, it will give you a strong foundation in computers. The three chapters introduce the fundamentals of how computers work, explain how you communicate with the computer in its own language, and give an introduction to computer programming. If you want to explore these subjects more deeply, you can find many excellent books at a computer bookstore, in the computer section of any good-sized general bookstore, or in a public or college library.

13

Computer Logic

When you're working with computers, it often helps to understand some principles of how computers work. In this chapter, you will take a conceptual look at what computers do: how they execute instructions, how you "talk" to one, and how it talks to you.

THE CONCEPTUAL VIEW

There is a poetic simplicity in the way computers work: The heart of the computer is the switch—in fact, many thousands of switches. The electrical switch can be turned on or off.

On-Off Switches as Yes-No Logic

It is the logic assigned to the on-off switch that is significant. "On-off" is converted into "yes-no." Pretend that all questions could be answered either *yes* or *no*. For example, for the question "Is the brick red?" there are really only two basic answers, "yes" and all the others: "No," "I don't know," "I can't tell," "I don't care," "I'm color blind." If the answer is *yes*, then go to the next step. If the answer is anything else, ask "Is your answer now no?" If the response is "No," then ask "Is it that you don't know?" You continue the questions one pair at a time until the question matches the response. While it may take several minutes for you to read through these sequences, a computer will process these questions in a fraction of a second.

Let's move to the next step. Suppose you decide that *yes* equals the number 1 and *no* the number 0. Then assume that if a current of electricity is applied, the number 1 is activated, and if no current is applied, the number 0 remains. When you activate *yes*, the computer registers the number 1 and consequently "turns on" the switch. You have stored the answer *yes*.

Reversing the process, you can retrieve the answer *yes* by looking at the value of the number stored in that particular switch or set of switches. Since each switch is numbered beginning at zero, you can examine the contents of any switch by looking at the value in a known numeric location, called an **address**. When the switch is "on," the answer reads 1 and means *yes*.

Binary Numbers

The following table shows a dozen selected decimal numbers and their binary and hexidecimal (used primarily by programmers) equivalents.

Decimal	Binary	Hexidecimal
0	00000000	00
1	00000001	01
2	00000010	02
3	00000011	03
4	00000100	04
8	00001000	08
10	00001010	0A
12	00001100	0C
13	00001101	0D
15	00001111	0F
16	00010000	10
1986	11111000010	7C2

Whereas the decimal numbering system consists of the ten numbers 0 through 9, the binary system consists of only two numbers, 0 and 1. As with other numbering systems, the two binary numbers are combined to represent larger numbers. The first number, or switch, may be either 0 or 1 (off or on), representing, respectively, the numbers 0 and 1. When a second switch is added, four number combinations are possible: 00, 01, 10, and 11, representing the numbers 0, 1, 2, and 3.

If all the computer's switches represent numbers, how does it accommodate letters, as in the word *architect*? Let's back up a little. Eight switches can be arranged in many different combinations. In fact, 2^8 combinations, or 256 decimal numbers, can be represented by eight switches. A group of eight switches is universally recognized as the smallest working unit in a computer; it is called a byte. Eight switches are capable of more than enough combinations of on-off positions to represent all the letters, numbers, punctuation marks, and other symbols in Western alphanumeric systems. There is, in fact, a standard called ASCII (American Standard Code for Information Interchange) that assigns a unique number for each letter, number, punctuation mark, and symbol. In it, the capital letter *A*, for example, is assigned the decimal number 65 (hexidecimal number 41), quotation marks are assigned the decimal number 34 (hexidecimal 22), and so on.

There are also special words that you use to instruct the computer to perform specific tasks. These special words are called computer **commands**; when they are grouped together, they constitute a **programming language**. Each word is also assigned a number, or **token**, and when interpreted by the computer, it executes a basic programming function, such as the command PRINT. Typically, a command like PRINT (hexidecimal number 78 in BASIC language) is the first word in a discrete set of instructions, and it is followed by the

appropriate specific value, or **parameter**. Hence, the computer interprets the following command and parameters:

78	22	65	82	67	72	73	84	69	67	84	22
print	"	A	R	C	H	I	T	E	C	T	"

(For more about language and programming, see Chapters 14 and 15, respectively.)

Sequential Flow
Fundamentally, a software program is nothing more than a set of instructions to activate selected electronic switches in a specific sequence. The process is much like the reading of this book: You start at the beginning and progress to the conclusion; your course may alter—bypassing a section of computer code (skipping a chapter), branching to a subroutine (jumping to another section in the book), or looping (rereading a chapter)—but fundamentally a program or a book is linear, like the flow of electricity that activates the program.

As programs become increasingly powerful, they grow in both size and complexity. Ultimately, the measure of a good software program is not only the raw power of the programming language or of the programmer's expertise in using the language, but the programmer's organization.

RIGHT OR WRONG INPUT
Some people worry that computers will replace people. But until computers learn to think for themselves, you can be reassured that computers do only what they are instructed to do. Computers are very precise, and they are wholly dependent on our instructions.

There's a rather appropriate computer aphorism: Garbage in, garbage out. Crude, but absolutely true. If you are asked to enter the file name of your current work, you must enter the name exactly as it appears in the directory (or catalog). You can't add an extra space here or leave one out there. In some cases, you may not be able to substitute lowercase letters for capitals, or vice versa. And you *certainly* can't substitute the letter l for the number 1. Some systems may not allow spaces between words and use underlining or dashes to improve readability.

Such precision can work to your advantage, however. A computer query that accepts only *yes* or *no* as a response will repeat the request if you attempt any other response. More importantly, this also means that you will obtain the correct results time and time again, as long as the data is entered accurately.

HOW COMPUTERS STORE INSTRUCTIONS

Computers calculate, compare, and sort data. How do they perform these tasks? By using programmed instructions that read and interpret your instructions, computers execute their tasks sequentially. But you may alter the sequence. When you select an alternative, you change the sequence and redirect the flow of the program. If you are asked to select *doors* or *windows*, your selection will determine which subroutine of the program is performed next.

To understand how this works, let's explore how instructions are stored. CAD systems vary in the manner in which software is stored within the computer and rendered accessible. Each system, however, strives to balance its internal memory utilization with the computer's expected application. First, let's examine a computer's permanent—read-only—memory: ROM.

Read-Only Memory

ROM contains all of the permanently coded instructions placed there by the manufacturer to perform the most basic commands. These tasks include housekeeping information and can also include language, interpreter, or operating-system software. ROM instructions start the computer, define all the letters and other characters in ASCII code, and cause the computer to beep at you when you make certain types of mistakes. In smaller CAD systems, ROM contains drawing **primitives** (built-in software that draws lines, circles, rectangles, and so on). This information can only be read (and then only by an experienced user) and cannot be changed. Typically, as the size of a CAD system grows, ROM becomes less specific, allowing more flexibility in determining basic commands and memory use. In any case, turning off the power has no effect on the information stored in ROM—the data is permanent.

Random-Access Memory

RAM is frequently confused with ROM because of the similarity of the acronyms and the fact that both can be found on chips inside the computer. However, they are fundamentally different.

While the computational work takes place in a special chip called the **microprocessor**, all data is shuttled to and fro in random-access memory (RAM) sometimes called simply memory. This is the temporary storage place where data is processed. As you edit, data is changed, and when you're finished, you copy (save) the contents of RAM for further use. Here live the 128K (128,000 bytes) or 512K you see advertised for personal computers. In CAD systems, RAM ranges from .5MB to 10MB (one half to 10 million bytes).

Programs are executed in RAM. If a program is transferred from disk memory to RAM, it executes more quickly than a program whose every instruction must be read from the disk before execution. When a program is loaded into RAM, it is **mapped** to specific memory locations: One area stores the program, another stores variables, and other areas accommodate additional needs as required. If the program is too large to fit into RAM, segments are selectively loaded into RAM as they are needed.

Random-access memory is the measure of "horsepower" in microcomputers: 1Mb is the equivalent of a supercharger. Graphics programs that will fit within RAM will run faster than programs that must remain on the hard disk. Unfortunately, it is harder to find RAM space than it is to find data to which you would like to have ready access.

You change the contents of RAM by altering the flow of electrical current. Removing the current turns off a switch; applying current turns on a switch. Just as you can control the contents of RAM by altering the flow, you can lose the contents of memory if the power fails.

When you turn a computer off, all the data in RAM is altered, in effect resetting all the switches to 0. If the electric power fails—or even drops below a certain voltage level—any file you are working on at the time is lost. That's why it is important to protect the electrical circuits, avoid static electricity, and save your drawing periodically.

Firmware
A board, or interface card, containing auxiliary ROM can be plugged into a special slot in the computer. It contains any program used regularly, such as a graphics display processor. ROM chips are used. Other typical examples include printer interface boards and math coprocessors that speed mathematical calculations.

Ram Boards
Your computer comes with built-in random-access memory, but you can increase the total RAM by simply plugging a RAM board into one of the computer peripheral slots. In fact, most of the memory in a CAD system can be found on the RAM boards. Systems differ tremendously in

their use and management of RAM, but in general, additional RAM lets you load larger drawings or manipulate your present drawings faster.

Software Programs
A program is a set of instructions. As with your calculator, some standard instructions, such as those that add and multiply, are stored in ROM, but when you ask the computer to solve a problem for you, the program and data are stored in RAM. You might enter a simple program like PRINT "Architect," a one-line instruction. Your CAD program, however, contains many lines of instruction (or code), far too many lines to be entered each time you run the program. Consequently, the lines of instruction are saved on a disk as a software program. To use a program, you copy the data from your program disk into RAM (you load your program), duplicating each character in the same sequence as saved earlier. When you run the program, the computer reads and executes each instruction in sequence.

Figure 13.1 shows a sample program printout. This program is written in the programming language BASIC and uses line numbers for identification. If you examine the program, some of the instructions will be understandable, even if you have little or no programming experience.

Disk Storage
Finally, there is the hard disk, which on larger systems contains all the software. As needed, the software, all or parts of it, is transferred to RAM to be executed. You can load the software once and forget it. With the aid of a local area network, you have access to all disks on the system, which in effect increases your disk capacity to that of all the hard disks combined.

As you work on a drawing on some CAD systems, revisions are automatically updated in the database as they occur. These CAD systems manage graphics database dynamically, updating the mainframe database continually and making revisions immediately available across the system. In other systems, you work on a copy of the drawing, keeping the original on hard disk. When you save the corrected drawing, it replaces the earlier drawing. Some CAD systems delete the earlier copy, while others amend the original by renaming it with a suffix like .BAK to indicate that it is now the backup file.

```
10   TEXT : HOME : HGR : POKE  - 16302,0: PRINT  CHR$ (4);"BLOAD LOGO.A$300
     ": POKE 232,0: POKE 233,3:C = 3
20   HCOLOR= C: ROT= 0: IF C = 0 THEN I = 67: GOTO 40
30   FOR I = 1 TO 67: SCALE= I: DRAW 1 AT 140,96: IF I < 67 THEN  XDRAW 1 AT
     140,96: NEXT : IF C = 3 THEN C = 0: GOTO 20
40   FOR J = 0 TO 63: ROT= J: DRAW 1 AT 140,96: NEXT : IF C = 3 THEN C = 0:
     GOTO 20
50   TEXT : HOME : VTAB 12: HTAB 21: INVERSE : PRINT "THE ARCHITECT": VTAB
     14: HTAB 21: PRINT "APPLE ]"; CHR$ (91);" MICRO-CAD" NORMAL : VTAB 1
     8: HTAB 21: PRINT "PROTOTYPE"
60   FOR T = 20 TO 23: HTAB 21: VTAB T: READ T$: PRINT T$:: NEXT
70   DATA  COPYRIGHT 1982,KENNEDY,DESIGN,ASSOCIATES
80   VTAB 24: SPEED= 188:T$ = ")STANDBY": FOR T = 1 TO (40 -  LEN (T$)): HTAB
     T: PRINT T$:: NEXT : SPEED= 255
90   HOME : PRINT "SELECT MICRO-CAD OPTION": FOR T = 1 TO 9: VTAB (T + 4): PRINT

     T;")  ":: READ T$: PRINT T$: NEXT : PRINT
95   FOR I = 250 TO 0 STEP  - 1: IF  PEEK ( - 16384) = < 127 THEN  VTAB 15
     : HTAB 5: PRINT I:: CALL  - 868: NEXT :T2$ = "8":T% = 8: GOTO 120
100  GET T2$:T% =  ASC (T2$): IF T% < 49 OR T% > 57 THEN  VTAB 23: INVERSE
     : PRINT "OOPS...PLEASE REENTER": NORMAL : GOTO 100
110  DATA     THE DRAFTSMAN,THE DRAFTSMAN 2,DRAFTING TAPE 2,AUTOPRINTER T
     EXT FILE,AUTOPRINTER,ARCHITECTS TEMPLATE,LETTERING TEMPLATE,MICROCAD,
     QUIT
120  RESTORE : FOR T = 1 TO 12: READ T$: IF  VAL (T2$) = (T - 4) THEN  HTAB
     5: PRINT "LOADING "T$: PRINT  CHR$ (4);"RUN "T$
130  NEXT
```

13.1 *A software program tells the computer what to do. This example loads a graphic shape, animates it, presents a menu, and asks the user to make a selection.*

14

Computer Languages

Programming languages, like spoken languages, are the means by which you communicate with the computer, and a given computer may be able to "speak" one or several languages. BASIC, FORTRAN, C, Lisp, and Pascal are well-known examples of programming languages.

At the core of a computer, however, is a language unique to that particular type of computer. It's called **machine language**, and it reads a little like "ug wug zup da thum" to the uninitiated. Machine language can be compared to your native tongue: It's the most efficient language for a computer to perform its operations.

Programming in machine language, however, is complex and difficult. As a result, programs are written in languages (like BASIC) that are easily understood by you and me but not by the computer. To bridge the gap, the computer translates the programming language into machine language, which the computer understands.

Just as it is hard to discuss natural languages without considering grammar, any discussion of computer languages overlaps with programming. In this chapter, you'll focus on the concept of how languages work for you; and in the following chapter, you'll learn the basics of computer programming.

USING LANGUAGES TO INSTRUCT A COMPUTER

In Chapter 13, you learned how the number 78 could be used to represent the command PRINT, one of many commands in the popular language called BASIC.

All languages follow certain rules of grammar, and programming languages are no exception.

In fact, the grammatical rules of a programming language are very precise, and computer **syntax** is far more rigid than that taught in any English class. Syntax has to be exact because computers don't read between the lines.

Unlike a spoken language, a computer language contains relatively few words in its vocabulary. The number of commands ranges from as few as 50 to perhaps as many as 200. The BASIC lexicon comprises about 120 commands—with variations, roughly 200.

Since a computer will attempt to execute a command when it encounters a word like PRINT, LOAD, or SAVE, you must avoid using these **reserved words** except in their intended contexts. If you attempt to load a program called SAVE, for example, you will experience what computer people euphemistically call unpredictable results. To overcome this inconvenience, many languages now use short look-alike mnemonic words for commands. If you experience unpredictable results, or the computer barks an unfamiliar **error message** like BAD SUBSCRIPT or UNDEFINED STATEMENT, you may be trying to use a command word outside a command context. Unless you are programming, the chance of this happening is rare, but if you do experience trouble, contact your CAD technical representative. He will be happy to provide you with a list of the reserved command words.

HOW LANGUAGES INSTRUCT COMPUTERS

To understand how a computer language works, assume that you'd like your computer to execute a very simple instruction: to display the uppercase letter *N* on the screen. Most programming languages use this syntax: command followed by a parameter—written in the generic form COMMAND (parameter). The command is entered exactly as shown, followed by a parameter of your choosing. You may think of the instruction as a sentence composed of three elements: the implied noun *computer*, a verb, and a direct object, as in COMPUTER PRINT "N".

Using the BASIC command PRINT, enter your sample program using the syntax PRINT "any string". That's easy. Your program would therefore be PRINT "N".

The computer doesn't really understand what PRINT means, though. Consequently, the computer substitutes a number for each command (about 120 numbers in BASIC). Let's use the number 78 (called a token) to represent the command PRINT. When the computer program encounters the number 78, it will activate a task that prints your request.

In fact, your program, PRINT "N", is first translated (interpreted) from BASIC into machine language, becoming only four numbers, 78 22 78 22, which are stored in RAM. Later, when you save your program onto a floppy disk, the same set of numbers will be magnetically copied as your file.

When you run the program, the computer first reads and deciphers each computer statement, separating (**parsing**) it into segments that the computer will then process sequentially. The initial word (or rather, number) in a statement is expected to be the command token (if not, you get an error message). The computer identifies the first 78 as the valid command PRINT and points to an instruction that initiates a specific operation stored in ROM. In this example, the instruction will display the character(s) within the quotation marks on the screen.

Next, the PRINT command examines the balance of the line—22 78 22—for the number 22, indicating quotation marks. After 22, the computer encounters the number 78, which in this case represents the character *N*. The interpretation of 78 depends on the context in

which it is used: When 78 is the first number (token), it's interpreted as the command PRINT; otherwise, it is interpreted as an upper-case *N*. When the computer encounters the final 22, it knows that only the character *N* will be displayed. Finally, the computer reads a carriage return (or some other character) as the signal to terminate the command line. In a split second, the uppercase *N* appears on the screen.

PROGRAMMING LANGUAGES

In the early days of computing machines, people didn't communicate with computers using languages. Because the computers had been built as a box full of switches, they were programmed by literally flipping switches or rearranging a maze of plugs to reroute the electrical current. (The process is reminiscent of telephone operators who connect parties with a pair of plugs.)

When several switches needed to be activated in order to execute a command, they were grouped together in one location. This group is called a subroutine, and the command is activated by directing the flow of current to the first switch in the subroutine. You'll learn more about subroutines in the next chapter. Now look at the backbone of computer languages.

Machine Language

Each on-off switch is located by a number, or its address. A call to that address activates the subroutine, in our example, the PRINT command. An assemblage of these numbers came to be called machine language, known as a **low-level programming language**. When you wanted to print something, you entered the command 20 DB3D—effective for the computer, but not easily recognizable by you or me, and certainly easy to enter incorrectly.

This language executes its instructions faster than any other language, but it requires great skill to write. Very few programmers write programs in pure machine language.

Assembly Language

In time, some functional words were substituted for numbers. The command 20 DB3D became JSR: DB 3D, or "jump to the subroutine at memory location DB3D" (the location of the PRINT subroutine). *JSR*, which describes what the computer should do, is known as a **mnemonic** word. A compilation of these mnemonic words constitutes **assembly language**, the haute programming language, and the first step "up" from machine language. Programming in assembly language can be compared to baking a soufflé: It's a task best left in the hands of experts. Today, languages are written to describe the desired result, rather than the desired computer action. These languages are known as high-level languages.

High-Level Languages

Opposite the low-level mnemonic languages are languages that describe expected results in more or less understandable English. Examples of high-level languages are BASIC and LOGO, which contain commands that resemble English sentences: PRINT X + Y; IF X IS EQUAL TO 27, THEN PRINT "OK"; or SORT NAMELAST, SORT NAMEFIRST, PRINT. Even if you've never had any programming experience, you have a reasonable idea of what the language is describing and what the program expects.

The sample program PRINT "N" described earlier in the chapter is written in a high-level language. In between BASIC and assembly language lie languages like FORTRAN, Pascal, and C. These are fast, elegant, and powerful languages, although none are as easy to use or understand as BASIC.

Translated Languages

Although writing programs in BASIC is easier than in assembly language, there is a price: High-level languages execute more slowly than their low-level companions. In fact, ease of writing seems destined to always vary inversely to speed of execution.

Ultimately, every program is executed by the computer in its native machine language, and there are two routes to that goal: write in machine language; or write in a language that is easy for you, and let the computer translate your program into machine language. Since writing in machine language is impractical, all programming is written in some form of a high-level language and then translated. Translation is achieved in three different, though related, means: interpretation, assembly, or compilation.

Interpreted languages

With this method, each line of high-level language is translated into machine language as the program is being executed, one line at a time. In our example, the computer reads the BASIC command PRINT and interprets the instruction as the number 78, which the computer's machine language understands as an instruction to execute the PRINT program stored in ROM. The interpretation continues for each element of each line of the program. Because the translation occurs line by line while the program is being executed, processing time increases. While the easiest to write, interpreted programs are the slowest of any language to execute. BASIC is an example of an interpreted language.

Assembled and compiled languages

In the second method of translation, every line of a program is assembled or compiled into machine language before the program is executed.

It is a technical point, but assembly language is assembled and high-level languages are compiled. Both are achieved with the same technique. You run a program that converts (assembles or compiles, as appropriate) the **source code** (that's what you wrote) into binary **object code**, or machine language. This method achieves the best of both worlds by combining ease of writing with speed of execution.

In the simple example above (PRINT "N"),

save the program with the name MYFIRST. When you compile (run the compiler program), the computer reads every BASIC statement and translates it into a complete line of machine-language code, namely 78 22 78 22. Compilation continues until the complete program has been translated into machine language, whereupon the computer then automatically saves the binary version with an identifying suffix (.BIN) as MYFIRST .BIN. The binary version will execute exactly as the nonbinary version, except notably faster.

Now that you have a fundamental understanding of how to communicate with the computer through a language, let's look at the fundamentals of programming.

15
Computer Programming

As you become more proficient in drawing on your computer, you'll want to customize some parts of one program, add to others, or modify your menus. Sooner or later, you'll want to write special software for your own use.

When you reach that level, you will begin to discover the real power of the computer. When you begin writing instructions for your computer, you'll be joining the world of computer programming. Programming is a natural outgrowth of computer use and marks your graduation to advanced standing. Whereas programming skills once belonged to a select few, today many computer users have well-developed programming expertise.

GETTING STARTED
Programming frightens many people, but learning how to write your own macros is the very minimum you must achieve if you wish to master CAD. You will become an active partner with the computer rather than a passive user of it. Programming skills will give you the tools to use a computer creatively in solving problems.

Programming in all languages (including macrolanguages) is fundamentally the same. There are variations of usage or syntax, but the basic structure and logic are the same on all computers. You can learn BASIC on a computer costing less than $100 and gain fundamental computer literacy. And if that $100 computer you hook into your television set will let you draw lines and circles, a little practice will give you insight into graphics programming. Furthermore, if you understood the database examples earlier in this book, then you have the foundation for understanding how any database program works. All advanced graphics software relies on database technology. Even using a

spreadsheet, while not meant to teach programming, will subliminally instruct you about the principles of computer programming.

ELEMENTS OF A COMPUTER PROGRAM
In this chapter, you'll learn about the six primary elements of programming:

1. **Input:** entering information
2. **Output:** retrieving information
3. **Variables:** substituting different data
4. **Processing:** performing a task
5. **Loops:** performing the same task again
6. **Branches:** changing tasks

Input
Very few, if any, programs run entirely by themselves, without any input from the person using the program. If you were unable to enter information, the results of the program would always be the same. It would make little sense to continue using a program that always gives you the same answer.

When a computer asks for a file name, or for the scale, or "How many risers in the stair?" or says "Press 'Yes' to continue," it is asking you for input. When the range of possible answers is known, you can structure the program in such a way that the computer is prevented from accepting other answers.

No matter what the input is or how it is entered, it is stored in a unique memory location set aside for specific input, in much the same way that mail is stored in a unique box set aside for a specific addressee. This input is called the **argument** of a variable. (Variables are covered later in this chapter.)

How do you communicate with your computer? In Chapter 1, you learned that data can be entered using a keyboard, cursor, digitizer, or menu device. Your principal form of data entry will be graphic points, entered primarily with a graphics device like a pen, mouse, or graphics tablet or entered directly from the keyboard.

Beginners push buttons

Beginners like to push menu buttons; so do a lot of experienced users. The menu, with a picture or diagram (called an icon) of the function, is fast, easily recognizable, and, most important, easy to use. Most new users have one principal concern: ease of learning and use (making the computer **user-friendly**).

If one fact has encouraged designers to accept CAD, it is the development and use of the graphics tablet menu and the onscreen menu. Each is activated by pressing the stylus or moving the crosshairs over the desired item. Outside of writers, secretaries, or Teletype operators, few people born before 1960 have had to use a keyboard consistently. For people who resist using a keyboard, learning CAD with the aid of a graphics menu provides an excellent transition from manual to CAD drawing because the keyboard is rarely used. In fact, some CAD systems use menus so effectively that the keyboard can be unplugged.

Menu-driven programs

Software programs that produce very specific results are often structured with highly defined pathways from start to finish, that is, the flow of instructions is highly sequential. Programs for architecture, interiors, engineering, space planning, and facilities management are excellent examples.

Menus are the ideal vehicle for executing instructions in these programs. You are presented with a list of options on a menu, and you press a corresponding code key. Then the program either presents another menu or executes that portion of the program. A principal (main) menu controls your course through each of the subsidiary menus along the hierarchical tree. Pressing a function key will return you directly to the main menu. Because you are given options (prompted) at each step, menu-driven programs are easier to run for the novice than command-language programs.

Command-driven programs

Programs that allow you to enter any one of many options, each with many alternatives, are open-ended. Because the range of options can be extensive, menus are impractical, except for commonly used functions. General drawing programs are typically command-driven, as are most PC-based database software programs.

You execute instructions to these programs by entering a pseudo-programming command (collectively, they are called a command language). For example, you might enter the command-language instruction DP, p1 p2 (where p1 and p2 are opposite points of a display window) to display a new CRT window. Other commands include CC for circle and R for rectangle. Some systems support multiple command entry, such as the following: MVE ITM FEN XTX P1 P2 DISP LIN P3 P4, INIT FR P5 TO RELX 8, which translates as "move all items defined by the fence of points 1 and 2, except text but including the lines near points 3 and 4, from point 5 to a point 8 inches in the X direction." Although a powerful command, it is so complicated that it is little wonder that command languages have never been popular.

A command language often looks and behaves enough like a full programming language to be mistaken for one, but a command language contains an incomplete set of key programming elements. More about this topic will be covered later, in the section entitled Macro programming.

Advanced users find the elegant way

Just as rolling your pencil along the edge of a parallel bar produces an exquisitely straight line, the advanced CAD user invariably seeks the fastest or most elegant means to execute any CAD operation. He or she uses the best means available to enter data. As your skills advance, you will learn to mix menu entries with keyboard entries. When entering a command, it is usually easier to respond to menu prompts, but it is often faster to enter the command from the keyboard, even with multiple parameters, once you've familiarized yourself with all the commands.

Output

The data you enter (input) is processed by the computer program, and the result is displayed as output. If you enter the length of a line, the computer draws the line to that length and displays the result on the graphics CRT. Other output may be displayed on the command prompt line, on the CRT graphics status lines, or on a separate alphanumeric terminal. Alternatively, you may reroute data from the graphics terminal to the printer or plotter.

Variables

Computers would not be of much use if you were unable to enter different values and retrieve different answers. You do, of course, make changes to drawings, and these changes are stored in variables. The programmer establishes which data should be entered as a variable. There are two principal variable types: One stores numbers, and the other stores literal character entries like "N," "Su," or "November 12, 1934."

Numeric variables may be whole numbers like 4 or 1024, called **integer variables**, or real numbers like 3.14157 or -47.53, called **real variables**. Integer variables use less memory space and can be processed far more quickly than real variables. In the equation $X = A + 5$, X is the variable and A is the argument. Changing the value of the argument changes the value of the variable. So if $A = 7$, then $X = 12$.

A word or phrase is identified as a *literal* by enclosing it in quotation marks, whereupon it is called a character string. Words like *the* and *architects* cannot be manipulated in the mathematical sense, but you can "add" several strings together by joining them sequentially: "The " (note the addition of the blank space) and "architects" becomes "The architects." Joining strings together is called concatenation (frequently shortened to catenation).

String variables can also be combined by using math-like equations. For example, the "equation" $X\$ = A\$ + "5" + B\$$, is interpreted to mean that the string variable $X\$$ (pronounced X-string) is the concatenated sum of the two subordinate string variables $A\$$ and $B\$$ and the character "5". If $A\$ = $ "The ", and $B\$ = $ "architects", then $X\$$ would equal "The 5 architects".

As you can see, numbers are manipulated mathematically if treated as numeric variables, but they are treated like any other character when assigned to a string variable. And no, you can't mix numeric and string variables in the same equation: The computer will beep and print a rather stern message like "DATA MISMATCH."

If, on the other hand, your program prompts "Enter name of profession" and assigns your input to the string variable $B\$$, you may change the value of $B\$$ each time you are asked "Enter name of profession." You might enter "engineers." Then, a request to display $X\$$ will yield the output "The 5 engineers."

EXECUTING COMPUTER TASKS

In the previous section, you learned how to enter and retrieve data. Here you'll see how the computer processes the data.

Processing Data: Do a Task

A computer program performs some task. Unless diverted, a program runs sequentially—in one direction only—from beginning to end. Data items entered at the beginning are used to calculate other data, which is subsequently used to calculate still other data until the final answer appears. Zoning-envelope calculations are typical: You enter the site area and then the yard and easement requirements, which determine the net buildable area; then you enter the floor area ratio, and the program generates a theoretical maximum building volume, expressed as the number of floors allowed. Throughout, there is a logical progression, with each succeeding entry modifying the balance.

While many software programs run in a single long progression, graphics programs do not. You are brought to the main menu quickly, and at the conclusion of each graphics task (each of which is a short sequence), you are returned to the main menu.

Repeat a Task: The Computer Loop

Loops and branches are the fundamental variations in the straightforward processing performed by the computer. Performing a task repeatedly is called a loop. As you will soon realize, loops and branches give programming its richness.

Yet, a program loop that repeatedly draws columns, for example, is of little use if the repetition continues unchecked. You must be able to tell the computer when to stop. It's a simple but essential concept: The computer stops a loop by comparing two values, and when a match occurs, the computer moves on to the next task.

You instruct the computer to repeat a task a specific number of times. A simple loop might insert six columns, equally spaced. FOR X = 1 TO 6: DRAW "WF 12X12": STEP 30'-0": NEXT is a simple BASIC instruction that inserts columns at 30'-0" centers repeatedly along the X axis until the counter reaches 6.

When the loop starts, the value 6 is placed in a special variable called a **counter**. As each segment of the loop is executed, a second variable is **incremented** by a value of 1. The value of the second variable is compared with the counter. If the values are unequal, the loop draws another column. When the numbers match, the loop ends, and the computer continues to the next instruction. You can start counting at any number, skipping some numbers if you wish, and finish at a higher or lower number than where you started. For example, you can insert the columns, in order, on the sixth, fourth, and second grid lines. You can ask the computer to repeat the same loop—to loop a loop, so to speak. A loop performed within another loop is called a nested loop, and it is one of the most powerful computer tools. It's architectural equivalent is sometimes called a matrix or array.

To draw a grid of 18 columns, three up and six over, the computer would repeat the loop described above three times. A nested loop looks like this: FOR Y = 1 TO 3: FOR X = 1 TO 6: DRAW "WF 12X12": STEP 30'-0": NEXT: STEP 25'-0": NEXT. When the program runs, six columns are placed along the X axis at 30'-0" centers in what is called the inner loop. Then the second row is entered. The outer loop steps 25'-0" up along the Y axis and repeats the inner loop, inserting the second row of six columns. The program continues until 18 columns are drawn. A second variable and counter are added to accommodate the Y axis.

The loop insert sets CAD apart from the drawing board and allows you to draw repetitive items accurately and quickly without tedium. The next time you see columns or light fixtures zipping onto a drawing, you'll understand how they are drawn. If you think column inserts are great, wait until you start the reflected-ceiling plan.

Select Another Task: Unconditional Branch

You learned previously that a computer program is sequential. In reality, a program consists of any number of smaller subprograms (subroutines) within the body of the program. The **unconditional branch** irrevocably diverts the flow of a program to another location in the program. The command GOTO, common to both BASIC and FORTRAN, causes the program to branch unconditionally. (You will recognize the famous line "Go to jail; do not pass Go; do not collect $200," but did you know that this line is a classic example of the unconditional branch?) When you finish a task using a graphics menu, the program will return to –GOTO–) the menu.

Select an Alternative Task: Conditional Branch

But suppose you want a choice: to branch if certain conditions are met. The **conditional branch** allows you to do just that. You may recognize it in the command IF . . . THEN . . . ELSE, that is, IF a condition is met, THEN do this or ELSE do that.

Here's a classic example of a conditional branch. When you instruct the computer to delete a file, the computer usually responds with the question "Are you sure? Enter 'Yes' or 'No.' " The computer is asking for input. The next line of computer code will say something like "IF answer = 'Yes,' THEN delete file, ELSE abort and continue to next task." If you enter "No" or an irrelevant response like "Su huh," then the conditions for deleting the file have not been met and the program will continue to the next task.

CAD uses the branch in menus. After completing an instruction, the computer waits for you to press the next menu button. When you press the button to set the scale, for example, the computer goes to the section of the program containing the relevant subroutine and prompts you to enter a value for scale. Once completed, the program waits for you to press the next menu button. This process continues until you press the Quit button.

A loop is a special form of the conditional branch, repeating a task until a condition is met: "If the counter is less than 6, THEN draw another column, ELSE quit."

GRAPHICS SOFTWARE AND PROGRAMMING

Graphics may be created using drawing software created either for general or specific graphics applications. For example, consider how you might draw a wall. One way is to draw individual lines mixed with rectangles and double lines—an example of *general* drawing techniques.

Or you might specify an 8-inch concrete block wall with ¾-inch furring on one side and faced with ⅝-inch gypsum board. A CAD system capable of drawing the required four lines appropriately spaced is a *specific* drawing application. Both approaches have their advantages and disadvantages.

General Graphics Software

General drawing software concentrates on providing a generic set of highly flexible and powerful computer graphics primitives for drawing, dimensioning, editing, text insertion, creation of intelligent graphics, three-dimensional capability, and presentation graphics. Specific tasks for specialized applications are executed with the help of macro commands.

You get versatile software in general systems, rich in drawing capabilities and growth potential, but frequently the software lacks sufficient depth in a specific discipline to be considered of professional quality. Many of these programs are command-driven, making them difficult to learn. If you have to customize the software with macros to accommodate your professional needs, you may find that the rewards of future richness fall short of your software requirements now.

Specific Graphics Software

By contrast, specific drawing languages are designed to execute a particular set of instructions in the most efficient manner possible. Characteristically, this software is highly specialized, focuses upon a specific discipline, is carefully planned and designed, and can be executed with grace and finesse—much like the qualities of fine architecture. It is easier to learn, easier to use, and faster to run—but it's so specific that you won't be able, for example, to calculate duct sizes with architectural software, only with HVAC software. It's also easy to recognize inferior software that is masquerading as professional-quality software: The shortcomings and omissions are embarrassingly obvious to the professional.

Macroprogramming

Macroprogramming is something of a misnomer because it is not a language and, originally, not programming. Rather, it is a term that describes the procedure for saving a string of **command language** keyboard entries in a log file (a record of every keystroke). You "run" the macro file by "replaying" the log. The computer automatically reenters the command string internally, obviating the need for you to keyboard (enter) the same string each time you need it. If you look at the command string described earlier in this chapter, you will readily understand why macros developed a popular following. Macros offer the user and the programmer a means of expanding and customizing software. Some macro capabilities have been expanded well beyond keystroke entry logs to full programming capability. This makes it possible for the user to create special software to augment that furnished by the vendor. Although complex to use, command languages are extremely powerful. The very nature of a command-language statement makes it a particularly useful and potent tool because the command is written to execute a very specific instruction, such as dimensioning or drawing walls.

All that's needed to upgrade a macro to a language is the addition of some auxiliary commands to perform arithmetic logic and some others to control the flow of data. These additional commands allow you to enter and retrieve data and to perform mathematical calculations and logic operations, which compare items for similarity. Such comparisons permit conditional (IF-THEN) and unconditional branching (GOTO and GOSUB), all of which are essential for programming.

Consult your CAD manufacturer for details on macroprogramming. You can read any elementary book on programming to understand the fundamentals. And if you concentrate on the following 15 BASIC commands, you will understand the fundamentals of programming: FOR-NEXT, IF-THEN-ELSE, GOTO, GOSUB, SAVE, LOAD, RUN, INPUT, PRINT, COLOR, LINE, NEW, LET, STOP, and END.

Index